VERY DIFFERENT, BUT MUCH THE SAME

Very Different, But Much the Same

The Evolution of English Society Since 1714

W. G. RUNCIMAN

OXFORD
UNIVERSITY PRESS

OXFORD
UNIVERSITY PRESS

Great Clarendon Street, Oxford, OX2 6DP,
United Kingdom

Oxford University Press is a department of the University of Oxford.
It furthers the University's objective of excellence in research, scholarship,
and education by publishing worldwide. Oxford is a registered trade mark of
Oxford University Press in the UK and in certain other countries

First Edition published in 2015

Impression: 1

Published in the United States of America by Oxford University Press
198 Madison Avenue, New York, NY 10016, United States of America

British Library Cataloguing in Publication Data
Data available

Library of Congress Control Number: 2014937974

ISBN 978–0–19–871242–8

Printed and bound by
CPI Group (UK) Ltd, Croydon, CR0 4YY

Preface

There are no original findings presented in any of the chapters to follow. As with volume 3, published in 1997, of my *Treatise on Social Theory*, which explored some of the same themes in relation to twentieth-century England, the evidence on which their conclusions are based is drawn entirely from secondary sources which I believe to be sufficiently authoritative and reliable for my purpose. From the perspective of evolutionary sociology, what is puzzling about the structure of English society over the past three centuries is how little has changed in the nature and distribution of power between its constituent roles despite all the changes in the experiences, attitudes, manners, and beliefs of its people which have been abundantly documented by its historians. How is this disjunction to be explained?

Readers unfamiliar with the concepts and methods of current evolutionary theory will, I hope, find the Introduction sufficient to dispel any preconceptions they may have that it has anything to do with either the outdated teleological presuppositions of Spencer or Marx or the discredited fallacies of so-called 'Social Darwinism'. In the United States, a neo-Darwinian approach to the evolution of human societies is widely taken for granted.[1] But the advances in the study of social behaviour that have been made over recent decades by evolutionary ecologists, anthropologists, psychologists, and game theorists are still largely ignored by the majority of British sociologists as well as historians. I doubt whether many of either are likely to agree that 'Recourse to the wide panoply of behavioural sciences constitutes the most important advance in the discipline of history since its first contact with demography and anthropology in the 1950s and 1960s.'[2] But it is no longer a question of whether, but only of how, that panoply can best be deployed in the study of cultural and social change. I have not footnoted more than a handful of references to some of the relevant literature. But a summary of the current state of evolutionary sociology can be found in my chapter in the forthcoming *Handbook of Evolution and Society: Towards an Evolutionary Social Science* edited by Jonathan Turner, Alexandra Maryanski, and Richard Machalek to be published by Paradigm Publishers in 2015.

It is likely also that some readers will take against the two neologisms that will be deployed without further comment from now on: 'meme' and 'systact'. Both, however, are terms of convenience without which there would be no alternative to cumbrous and unnecessary periphrases. 'Meme', coined by Richard Dawkins, stands for any and all units of information affecting behaviour transmitted by imitation or learning from mind to mind. 'Systact', coined by myself, stands for any

---

[1] E.g. Stephen K. Sanderson, *Human Nature and the Evolution of Society* (Boulder, CO, 2014).
[2] Gregory Hanlon, 'The decline of violence in the West: from cultural to post-cultural history', *English Historical Review* 128 (2013), p. 400.

and all sets or clusters of roles located above or below one another in social space. The principal advantage of 'systact' is that it covers, as a leading historian has put it, 'all types of social division, into classes, orders, castes, strata, interest-groups and so on, without having to claim that any one of these is analytically prior'.[3] It thereby circumvents, if nothing else, some of the seemingly interminable debates by which sociologists, and not only sociologists, are divided over the meaning and uses of 'class'. 'Class' cannot be dispensed with in any discussion of how power is distributed within English society. But it does need as far as possible to be divested of any pre-emptive implication that social evolution is driven by one rather than another of the selective forces which in combination make societies of different kinds into the kinds of society that they are.

My thanks are due to Robert Faber, and the anonymous referees selected by him, for useful criticism of an earlier draft; to Ross McKibbin and Anthony Heath for their comments on Chapters 2 and 5; to my long-serving secretary and assistant Hilary Edwards for her help in seeing yet another book through to publication; and to the Council of my College for continuing research support.

W.G.R.

Trinity College,
Cambridge,
June 2014

---

[3] Chris Wickham, 'Systactic structures: social theory for historians', *Past & Present* 132 (1991), p. 192.

Contents

Introduction

I

The aim of this book is to bring to bear on the political, ideological, and economic institutions of English (and to a more limited extent British) society over the past three centuries the neo-Darwinian theory of evolution within which collective human behaviour patterns are analysed as the acting out of information encoded and transmitted at the three separate but interacting levels of the biological, the cultural, and the social. It is therefore a work both of sociology and of history. But it is not history of an orthodox kind. It touches on such topics as population, technology, war, trade, religion, medicine, art, science, entertainment, and sport only if or where these are relevant to the explanation of the variation and selection of the practices defining the social roles by which English society's institutions have been constituted. The distribution of power between these roles is then analysed in terms of a tripartite distinction between modes of coercion, persuasion, and production—coercion, because political institutions are underwritten by the capacity of the rulers to bring physical force to bear on the ruled; persuasion, because ideological institutions are underwritten by the capacity of the higher ranked to discriminate against the lower; and production, because economic institutions are underwritten by the capacity of the owners or controllers of property to allocate or deny material resources to those with less or none.

Individual men and women are the protagonists in this story only as carriers of the practices that define their social roles and of the shared beliefs and attitudes that have either accelerated or retarded the practices' diffusion and reproduction. This focus on practices as the objects of selection rather than on the individuals whose practices they are is central to everything that follows: in social-evolutionary theory, practices and the roles defined by them are what societies are made of. But that does not imply that human beings are merely the passive instruments of impersonal forces. On the contrary, they are active agents whose individual choices can, and often do, divert what would otherwise have been their society's evolutionary trajectory. Behind the long and ongoing sequence of heritable variation and competitive selection of information affecting social behaviour are countless purposes, plans, and projects which have led successive generations of self-conscious decision-makers in their various political, ideological, and economic roles both to act as they have and to refrain from acting as they might. But although their decisions are not random in the technical sense unless deliberately made so—you can, if you wish, decide what to do by tossing a coin—their psychological causes do not and cannot explain their sociological effects.

The extension of evolutionary theory from the analysis of natural to that of cultural and social selection is sometimes dismissed by sceptical opponents as 'merely metaphorical'. It may, therefore, be as well to emphasize from the outset that information is not a metaphorical concept. It is not, that is to say, standing in for anything else. Biological, cultural, and social evolution alike come about through a common underlying process of information transmission which determines the different kinds of species, cultures, and societies in the world in which we—human beings, that is—find ourselves. The difference between the three levels of selection is in the mechanisms by which the information affecting behaviour is transmitted. In biological evolution, it is transmitted from organism to organism by genetic inheritance; in cultural evolution, it is transmitted from mind to mind by imitation or social (as opposed to individual trial-and-error) learning; and in social evolution, it is transmitted from role to role through rules encoded in the practices by which the roles are defined. Hence the fundamental distinction between *evoked* behaviour at the biological level, *acquired* behaviour at the cultural level, and *imposed* behaviour at the social level. The sociologist's objective at each level is the same: to identify and trace the information whose diffusion explains the collective behaviour of the population chosen for study within a path-dependent but open-ended sequence of change.

Some readers will no doubt regard the assertion that psychological causes cannot explain sociological effects as a statement of the obvious. But in others, it may provoke the response that it is precisely the causal antecedents of the individual actions which did set off what did turn out to be significant political, ideological, or economic changes about which they wish to learn. Those, however, are questions of a different kind. There is no contradiction between either the aims or the methods of narrative history and evolutionary sociology. Their contrasting approaches emerge particularly clearly in evolutionary game theory, where the differential replication of one rather than another strategy over a long-run series of encounters between players is analysed by reference to the instructions encoded in the strategies, not to the players' individual reasons for adopting the strategies that they have: the players themselves 'recede from view'.[1] Evolutionary sociologists want to explain the reproduction and diffusion of the practices that have made different human societies into what they are, whatever was going on in the minds of whoever were the men and women whose actions initiated the sequences of events that have had that effect. The motives that impelled King James II to behave as he did in 1688, and King William III to behave as he did then and thereafter, are among the multitude of antecedent causes of the unique events whose punctuation (in the idiom of evolutionary theory) of a pre-existing institutional equilibrium furnishes

---

[1] Bryan Skyrms, *Evolution of the Social Contract* (Cambridge, 1996), p. 10.

this book with its agenda. But their motives no more account for the subsequent effects of those events than the motives of whoever introduced rabbits into Australia account for the subsequent evolution of its ecology.

The long resistance to neo-Darwinian theory within as well as outside the biological sciences is not difficult to understand. It was not until the mid-twentieth century that population genetics and molecular biology made possible the definitive solution to questions about natural selection which Darwin himself had been unable to answer and it could be seen precisely why the misuses of his ideas in the name of 'Social Darwinism' were not only morally reprehensible to their opponents but scientifically untenable. But controversy was reignited in the last quarter of the century following the publication of E. O. Wilson's *Sociobiology* in 1975. The vehemence of the disputes that it provoked was such as to call for sociological explanation in itself.[2] But by the early years of the twenty-first century it had come to be generally recognized that Darwin's model of what he called 'descent with modification' does not turn sociology into applied biology. Cultural evolution is now seen as continuous with, but not reducible to, biological evolution.[3] In consequence, the naturally selected mental capacity of humans and some other species for imitation and social learning leads to a co-evolution of genes and memes,[4] in which memes are not only separately diffused and reproduced under pressure from their environment but can alter the course of natural selection itself.[5] Whatever the misgivings of cultural anthropologists and historians, neither behavioural ecology nor evolutionary psychology has, or will, put them out of business.

At the same time, recent advances in palaeoanthropology and archaeology have shed increasing light on the transition from cultural to social evolution[6]—that is, from the pre-institutional world of our hunting and foraging ancestors to the world of markets, armies, churches, bureaucracies, and courts (in both senses) where individuals succeed one another in social roles not of their making and 'social mobility' becomes one of the standard topics on the sociological agenda. The evolution of social out of cultural evolution, like that of cultural out of biological evolution, was both gradual and patchy. But thereafter, gene-meme co-evolution is supplemented by meme-practice co-evolution.[7] Sociologists then have to assess the relative contribution of cultural and social selection to collective development in the same way that psychologists have to assess the relative contribution of natural and cultural selection to individual development. It is a pity that some researchers working within the neo-Darwinian paradigm draw only a single distinction

[2] Ullica Segerstråle, *Defenders of the Truth: The Sociobiology Debate* (Oxford, 2000).

[3] Andrew Whiten et al., eds., 'Culture evolves', *Philosophical Transactions of the Royal Society B* 366 (2011), pp. 935–1187.

[4] Stephen Shennan, *Genes, Memes, and Human History: Darwinian Archaeology and Cultural Evolution* (London, 2002).

[5] William H. Durham, *Coevolution: Genes, Culture, and Human Diversity* (Stanford, 1991).

[6] Kent Flannery and Joyce Marcus, *The Creation of Inequality: How Our Prehistoric Ancestors Set the Stage for Monarchy, Slavery, and Empire* (Harvard University Press, 2012).

[7] W. G. Runciman, *The Theory of Cultural and Social Selection* (Cambridge, 2009).

between biological and 'sociocultural' evolution.[8] But if the mechanisms of social selection were no different from those of cultural selection—which they very obviously are—the 'socio' would be redundant. It can hardly be questioned that there is a difference of kind between spontaneous conformity to a collective behaviour pattern whose rules are acquired by imitation and learning, and conformity to a pattern imposed by rules underwritten by institutional sanctions irrespective of the beliefs and attitudes that the individuals performing their social roles are carrying in their heads.

Natural selection, ever present as it is, works too slowly for there to be any large-scale biological differences between the populations of early eighteenth- and early twenty-first-century England other than those consequential on immigration from alien gene pools; and even then, its effects are of little or no sociological significance independently of cultural and social selection. Behaviour genetics, despite the many things it reveals about intra-population differences, is of little help in accounting for population-level changes in collective behaviour patterns across as few generations as, in a human population, three centuries contain. The relevance of biological theory to evolutionary sociology is rather that capacities, dispositions, and susceptibilities, which are innate in all physiologically normal members of the human species, are among the reasons for which the members of any and all human populations behave as they do in their different environments. The history of English society, as of every other society in the world, would have been very different if the naturally selected universals of sexuality, sociality, parental care, language learning, reciprocal exchange of favours, and the combination of intra-group cooperation with inter-group aggression were other than they are.[9]

The different forces driving biological, cultural, and social evolution are always and everywhere in interaction with one another, and many collective behaviour patterns are, at the same time, evoked, acquired, and imposed. (The obvious example is warfare.) But it is principally in the relationship between cultural and social selection that there lies the explanation of the evolution of England's political, ideological, and economic institutions between the early eighteenth century and the early twenty-first. It is a difficult relationship to analyse, not simply because the memetic composition of the culturally transmitted 'skills, beliefs, values, and attitudes' of the English population has a long and complex history of its own.[10] It is difficult also because so much of the information passing by imitation and learning from mind to mind has less causal impact on the evolution of the practices that define their interacting carriers' roles, and thereby determine the form of their society's political, ideological, and economic institutions, than the carriers

---

[8] E.g. Marion Blute, *Darwinian Sociocultural Evolution: Solutions to Dilemmas in Cultural and Social Theory* (Cambridge, 2010).

[9] Samuel Bowles and Herbert Gintis, *A Cooperative Species: Human Reciprocity and its Evolution* (Princeton, 2011).

[10] Peter J. Richerson and Robert Boyd, *Not By Genes Alone: How Culture Transformed Human Evolution* (Chicago, 2005), p. 62.

themselves suppose. The evolutionary sociologist's problem is to sift out both the arguments at the cultural level which should be discounted as 'noise' and the activities at the social level which should be discounted as 'clutter'. Both the noise and the clutter are of intrinsic interest to historians whose aim is to recover the lived experience of past generations and preserve from it as much as they can of what posterity will wish to recall. But they are at best an irrelevance, and at worst a distraction, to sociologists concerned with the variation and selection of the units or bundles of information that generate distinctive collective behaviour patterns and thus the outcomes at the institutional level which call to be explained.

In social selection, the information whose diffusion and reproduction sustains a distinctive behaviour pattern is often easier to trace than it is in cultural selection, since the formal instructions which the incumbents of social roles must follow have to be sufficiently explicit for them to know that they are following them. It is a truism of sociology that structure cannot be separated from meaning. You cannot be a government minister or a university professor or a company director without understanding what you have to do to be one. This does not mean that law-codes, contracts, statutory regulations, and so forth are all to be taken at face value. But the redundant component is if anything easier to detect and discount when the relationships between the incumbents of interacting social roles are formally imposed and underwritten by institutional sanctions than it is when conformity to culturally acquired conventions is sanctioned informally by friends, associates, or members of a peer group. When, to take an example to which Chapter 2 will return, the effects of the policies that gradually extended the power of the British state over its citizens during the course of the nineteenth century are examined in detail, it is not difficult to identify the mutant practices that redefined the roles of rulers and ruled. But these mutations took place within a culture permeated by both religious and secular attitudes and beliefs which influenced their selection, diffusion, and reproduction in ways that need to be separately analysed, even—or especially—when their carriers themselves invoke them in their own accounts of what they did and why they did it. Running through all of the chapters to follow are similar contrasts between successive generations' awareness of the cumulative cultural changes through which they were living and their lack of awareness of the forces of social selection which were reproducing much the same structural distribution of power between their society's political, ideological, and economic roles.

It is for these several reasons no easier for sociologists to measure the relative strengths of the forces of cultural and social selection than it is for psychologists to measure the relative strengths of the forces of biological and cultural selection. Sociologists have long discarded both the one-sided model in which the history of human societies was seen as the working-out of the self-realization of the human spirit and the equally one-sided model in which it was seen as the working-out of the effects of a material base on an ideal superstructure. But within any chosen evolutionary sequence, the right account of how the outcome was arrived at will be a story in which sometimes cultural and sometimes social selection is the stronger force. Sociologists and historians are as familiar as each other with the difficulty of assessing the influence of ideas on behaviour dictated by either individual or collective interests. How much did the doctrines of Islam contribute to the success of the Arab conquests? Did the teachings of Luther and/or Calvin lead Protestant entrepreneurs to conduct their businesses differently from their Catholic counterparts? Did the so-called Enlightenment undermine the legitimacy of the French monarchy to the point that it was a contributory cause of the French Revolution? Max Weber used the metaphor of ideas as 'switchmen' who direct material interests down one railway track rather than another. But it's not the right one: there are no laid-down tracks to be followed in social evolution, and no termini at the end of the line.

Critical to the understanding of the evolutionary process at all three levels is the concept of adaptation. The information affecting behaviour, at whichever of the three it is transmitted, is 'adaptive' to the extent that its probability of diffusion and reproduction is enhanced by selective environmental pressures; and it is an 'adaptation' to the extent that its history is one of selection for a particular function.[11] But selective pressure comes to bear not directly on the information itself but on its behavioural effects. These may be either distinctive behavioural traits such as aggression or cooperation, or such extended phenotypic effects as birds' nests in natural selection, artworks in cultural selection, or forms of government in social selection.[12] Not all mutations are adaptive. There are not only 'exaptations', where a behaviour pattern persists for reasons other than those which initially favoured its diffusion and reproduction, but also 'maladaptations', where mutations turn out to function in ways which will impair their own reproductive success. Nor is adaptation, as in functionalist theories, a mechanism of self-equilibration which brings a system back to its prior state. Local equilibria may evolve where mutually adaptive mutations sustain the diffusion and reproduction of one another. But there is always a trade-off in competitive advantage. At the biological level, the gestation period of the human infant is a trade-off between an anatomy favouring bipedalism and an increase in brain size at birth. At the cultural level, rituals that reinforce intra-group consensus are a trade-off between ease of performance and emotional arousal. At the social level, bureaucracy is a trade-off between consistency of role-performance and constraint on innovation. Adaptation does not lead to a best of all possible worlds, whatever (on earth) that might mean.

At all three levels of selection, the line of demarcation of the relevant population is at the researcher's discretion. Neither societies nor cultures nor species are natural kinds. Cultures extend across social boundaries, just as societies extend across geographical ones. 'English' society has at various times included soldiers, administrators, and officials as far away as Australia and New Zealand, missionaries of one

---

[11] Kevin N. Laland and Gillian R. Brown, *Sense and Nonsense: Evolutionary Perspectives on Human Behaviour* (Oxford, 2002), ch. 4.
[12] Richard Dawkins, *The Extended Phenotype* (Oxford, 1982).

or another Christian denomination carrying the gospel into some of the least accessible regions of Africa and Asia, and merchants, traders, and entrepreneurs operating wherever in the world they see a prospect of profitable business to be done. No history covering the eighteenth, nineteenth, and twentieth centuries can fail to include some account not only of England's relations with other independent societies but also of its acquisition and loss of an empire whose size at its fullest extent was out of all proportion to its own. It is an extraordinary story of victories and defeats, overreach and withdrawal, triumphalism and hesitancy, exploitation and amelioration, and an eventual recognition of the impossibility of continuing to keep the subordinated populations in Lord Halsbury's 'convenient state between annexation and mere alliance'.[13] It affected the careers, outlooks, lifestyles, and fortunes of countless men and women from all systactic origins and in all walks of life. But the story was played out within a domestic distribution of power which it neither brought initially into being nor subsequently transformed. As the drama of Kipling's 'Recessional' drew to its close, and the pomp of yesterday became one with Nineveh and Tyre, the metropolitan society's role structure continued to be reproduced much as before. The radical change in Britain's place in the wider world over the past three hundred years, however it is to be accounted for, gives more, not less, point to the question why its own political, ideological, and economic institutions have themselves remained as impervious to radical change as they have.

There is, however, a related problem familiar to sociologists and historians alike which has to be confronted at the outset: the relation of 'English' to 'Scottish' society. In 1707, the Act of Union formally transferred 'ultimate responsibility for the proper observation of law and order' under an already united monarchy from Edinburgh to London,[14] and at the same time dismantled at a stroke the institutional barriers between the Scottish and English economies. But it permitted the legal, ecclesiastical, and educational institutions of Scotland to be reproduced unchanged, and the Scots continued to see themselves, as well as to be seen by the English, as a separate nation with its own customs, codes, and cultural traditions. It accordingly calls for, and has often (as Ireland has) been accorded, a historiography of its own which is of a different order from the parochial histories of the English regions and counties whose distinctive characteristics evolved within a much more closely integrated institutional catchment area. But the relative autonomy enjoyed by the Scots fell far short of de facto, let alone *de jure*, independence— which is precisely what fuelled the periodic resurgence of Scottish (like Welsh[15]) nationalism, which is in itself conclusive testimony to the persistent domination of English over Scottish institutions. Even after the devolution of powers to a Scottish parliament in 1999, when 'the Scottish nation undeniably embarked on another

---

[13] W. G. Runciman, 'Empire as a topic in comparative sociology', in Peter Fibiger Bang and C. A. Bayly, eds., *Tributary Empires in Global History* (Cambridge, 2011), p. 99.
[14] J. C. Smout, *A History of the Scottish People 1560–1830* (Glasgow, 1969), p. 206.
[15] Kenneth O. Morgan, *Rebirth of a Nation: Wales 1880 to 1980* (Oxford, 1981).

exciting stage in its long history',[16] it was not—or at any rate, not yet—a separate society. This book's title, therefore, is both a recognition that Scotland has a history of its own to which the book makes no attempt to give more than incidental coverage, and a reaffirmation that, whatever may happen next, the institutional relationship between England and Scotland (unlike Ireland) is at the time of writing much the same as it was in 1707.

II

There will always be scope for disagreement in the study of any society over an extended period about what does or doesn't count as 'major' as opposed to 'minor' change. 'Modal' changes are by definition changes of kind, and the word 'mode' is familiar to both sociologists and historians from the modes of production which in Marxist theory evolve along a predetermined sequence out of feudalism through capitalism into socialism. But once power is recognized as being of three mutually irreducible kinds, modes of coercion and persuasion must both be conceded their autonomy. It is theoretically possible for power to be so distributed between a society's constituent roles that they could all be ranked along a single vertical scale. But there are always discrepancies. In the ideal type of a pure political system, the distribution of both ideological and economic power is determined by the exclusive control of the means of coercion in the hands of an autocratic elite; in the ideal type of a pure ideological system, the distribution of both political and economic power is determined by the exclusive control of the means of persuasion in the hands of a hierocratic elite; and in the ideal type of a pure economic system, the distribution of ideological and political power is determined by the exclusive control of the means of production in the hands of a plutocratic elite. But no society conforming to any one of the three has ever existed or ever will.

There are, moreover, subdivisions within modes which themselves mark differences of kind.[17] Political power can attach to either military or administrative roles; ideological power can attach to either sacred or secular roles; and economic power can attach to industrial, financial, or property-holding roles. Different combinations will be adaptive in different local environments. Marxist sociologists will be disposed to emphasize economic relationships, whereas Weberians will be more likely to emphasize political relationships of *Herrschaft*, and Durkheimians the ideological relationships dictated by the society's *conscience collective*. But there are no lawlike empirical generalizations. Both within and between societies, the ongoing variation and selection of practices will sometimes favour one and sometimes another. Incipient change in one direction or another is always liable to be

---

[16] T. M. Devine, *The Scottish Nation 1700–2000* (London, 1999), p. 617.

[17] Michael Mann, *The Sources of Social Power*, vol. 1: *A History of Power from the Beginning to AD 1760* (Cambridge, 1986).

retarded or advanced by actions or events which, although not random in the technical sense, might as well have been.

The explanation of modal changes (or their absence) is, regrettably, made more difficult still by sociology's continuing lack of a coherent Linnaean taxonomy underwritten by a consistent Darwinian rationale. (Darwin: 'All true classification is genealogical.') I shall take it for granted from now on that English society from the early eighteenth to the early twenty-first century can be characterized as democratic, liberal, and capitalist. But all three of these terms, quite apart from the value judgements they may provoke in different readers, are used by different writers in conflicting ways with conflicting overtones. I mean by them no more (if no less) than a mode of coercion grounded in parliamentary sovereignty and a rule of law, a mode of persuasion grounded in open dissemination of ideas and competition for social prestige, and a mode of production grounded in market exchange and private property. But I cannot bind you or anyone else to do the same.

To make matters worse, it is not only words like 'democracy', 'liberalism', and 'capitalism' that have no precise and universally accepted meanings. Nor even does 'rule of law', of which it has aptly been said that 'everyone is for it, but have contrasting convictions about what it is'.[18] Both sociologists and historians are constantly using words like 'militant', 'deferential', 'reactionary', 'egalitarian', 'sub-versive', and many other such without any attempt to define them. Of all too many there could be said, as has been said of 'Puritan' by a leading cultural historian of Britain, that they are 'capable, at any given moment, of accommodating wildly discrepant meanings'.[19] What is more, they are often used not to report or explain an observed pattern or sequence of social behaviour so much as either to describe what it felt like for the people whose behaviour it was or to pass a moral or political value judgement on it. If such terms are to be put to effective use in accounting for large-scale change (or its absence), the information affecting behaviour denoted by them should as far as practicable be identified as such. Only then can causal hypotheses be unambiguously framed which will link the successive institutional states of a society as they were at one time to what they evolved into being at a later one. The reader is entitled in every case to ask the writer to answer two questions: first, 'Just what memes and practices are you talking about?'; and second, 'Are you telling me what was happening, or why, or what "they" felt about it at the time, or whether it was a good thing or a bad one?'.

Whatever the answers, one fundamental distinction follows from the distinction between cultural and social selection which needs to be taken into account in any report, explanation, description, or evaluation of any item or sequence of social behaviour. It is the distinction between an 'association', which is a collectivity of persons held together by acquired conventions of interpersonal conduct, and an

---

[18] Brian Tamanaha, *On the Rule of Law* (Cambridge, 2004), p. 3.
[19] Raphael Samuel, *Island Stories: Unravelling Britain* (London, 1998), p. 276.

'institution', which is a collectivity of persons held together by the imposition of binding rules by which social roles are defined. The distinction is not a hard-and-fast one: Weber even called it '*natürlich absolut flüssig*'.[20] (The obvious example is kinship relations.) Associations can, and often do, evolve into institutions. But the interpersonal threats and inducements that hold a rioting mob together are different in kind from the formal regulations and disciplinary powers that hold an army together; the influence that leaders of fashion exercise over their imitators is different in kind from the power exercised over the listening, reading, and viewing public by the controllers of the institutional means of persuasion; and the conventional understandings that prescribe the terms of interpersonal gift-exchange are different in kind from legally enforceable agreements in a market for commodities and labour.

There is no disagreement among historians about the 'associational voluntarism' long characteristic of English society.[21] In and after what one of them has called 'the landslide of associational activity in the eighteenth century',[22] England has been full of comings-together of people in pursuit of collective aims, from the Over Norton Association for the Prosecution of Felons in Oxfordshire to the Manchester and Salford Sanitary Association, from the Breeches-Makers Benefit Society to the Christian Excavators Union, from the National Association for Promoting the Political and Social Improvement of the People to the British Association for the Advancement of Science, from the Church Rate Abolition Society to the National Council for Civil Liberty, from the London Society for Promoting Christianity among the Jews to the Social Purity League, from the British Legion to the National Council of Women, from the Charity Organization Society to the Child Poverty Action Group, and from the National Anti-Vivisection Society to the Gay Liberation Front. There are Freemasons and Oddfellows, Pioneers and Rechabites, the Oxford Movement and the Salvation Army. They can have large memberships or small ones, long lives or short ones, and they may make more or less difference, or none whatever, to the evolution of the modes of coercion, persuasion, or production within which they are embedded. They have their own subcultural histories, their own organizational forms, their own memetic innovations and traditions, and their own more and less adaptive customs and rituals. Their lives and deaths follow standard Darwinian sequences of emergence and extinction. In the mid-nineteenth century, many (but not all) of the longest-lasting were those funded by monetary subscription, so that resources were available to their leaders with which to engage in ongoing campaigning subject to the tacit consent of the subscribers. In the course of the twentieth century, they came under pressure from an environment of increasingly bureaucratized welfare and

---

[20] Max Weber, *Wirtschaft und Gesellschaft*[3] (Tübingen, 1956), vol. 1, p. 28.

[21] Helen McCarthy, 'Associational voluntarism in inter-war Britain', in Matthew Hilton and James McKay, eds., *The Age of Voluntarism: How We Got to the Big Society* (Oxford, 2011), pp. 47–68.

[22] Peter Clark, *British Clubs and Societies 1500–1800: The Origins of an Associational World* (Oxford, 2000), p. 470.

increasingly privatized leisure. But they were an integral part of England's cultural and social history, and still are.

When associations evolve into institutions, the transition sometimes comes from below, as for example with the Royal Society for the Prevention of Cruelty to Animals whose inspectors, having successfully lobbied for legislation in 1822 and again in 1855, became statutorily empowered to act against offenders detected in breach of it (which did not, to be sure, include the foxhunting gentry some of whom were among its subscribers). But it can equally come from above when like-minded individuals are subjected to institutional sanctions which impose on them a role defined by the state. Thus, the estimated 4 per cent of Anglican clergy who declined to take the oath of allegiance to William and Mary were initially united simply by a shared sense of continuing allegiance to James II as their legitimate sovereign. But this caused them to be not merely culturally marginalized but socially penalized as defectors from the political settlement governing the institution of the Anglican Church, with the result that they could be deprived of their benefices. Like the 'conscientious objectors' of the time of the First World War, the 'non-jurors' were then confronted on the one side by informal rejection by their associates if they gave way, and on the other by formal penalties imposed by the agents of the state if they did not. In between, both chronologically and sociologically, were the Catholic parliamentarians whose emancipation from civil disabilities in 1829 required them to promise not to 'disturb or weaken' the Protestant religion or Protestant government—a promise which some were not prepared to give (or not unless given specific leave to do so by the Vatican) but most honoured with 'scrupulous care'.[23]

It is, however, as true of institutions as of associations that they depend on a minimum degree of voluntary acquiescence. The roles occupied by the members of English society at any stage of its evolution are defined by practices which few of them are attempting to abolish even if they might like to if they could. It is not, admittedly, impossible for intransigent individuals to opt out of their social roles: they can simply decline, at whatever personal cost in the sanctions they thereby bring on themselves, to conform to the practices that define them. They can refuse to obey the commands of the state, flout the established hierarchy of social prestige, and drop out of the market in commodities and labour. But the overwhelming majority accept the institutions of their society as they are and perform the roles constitutive of them in a routinely consistent manner. English society brings out as well as any other the force of what has come to be called Gellner's Paradox: 'How can a species genetically granted by Nature such remarkable freedom and licence, nevertheless observe such restraint, such naturally defined limits, in its actual conduct?'[24] Were it not for that restraint, sociology would not be possible at all.

---

[23] Owen Chadwick, *The Victorian Church* (London, 1966), vol. 1, p. 24.

[24] Ernest Gellner, 'Culture, constraint and community: semantic and coercive compensations for the genetic under-determination of *Homo sapiens sapiens*', in Paul Mellars and Chris Stringer, eds., *The Human Revolution* (Edinburgh, 1989), p. 516.

III

Current social-evolutionary theory offers no more scope for master narratives of inter-systactic struggle leading inevitably to successive revolutionary transfers of power than it does for master narratives of inter-systactic collaboration leading inevitably to peace and harmony. The history of English society between the early eighteenth and early twenty-first centuries is full of enmity and discord as rival individuals and groups contend with each other for power and privilege. It is also full of agreement and joint endeavour as advances are made in the acquisition and application of useful knowledge. Marx wasn't mistaken in pointing to the extent to which the interests of wage-labourers were opposed to those of their employers, any more than Macaulay was mistaken in pointing to the extent to which the nation's prosperity had been enhanced since the reign of Queen Anne. Their mistake was to construct their chosen narratives by too exclusive a concentration on those parts of the evidence which could be deployed best to accord with evaluative presuppositions of their own.

No historians or sociologists of the period covered by this book, whatever their personal opinions and values, will seek to deny that during it English society underwent continuous cultural and social change. But to call it, as many do, a process of 'modernization' does nothing in itself to explain either what did change or what didn't, however illuminating the inter-societal comparisons and contrasts that the word can be used to bring to light.[25] All periods of a society's history are 'modern' in their time, only to become 'ancient' in their turn. At the beginning of the twentieth century, 'modernity' was, so to speak, all the rage: the phrase 'we moderns' was, as one historian has remarked, 'widely used as a self-explanatory expression not just by artists and critics (the self-conscious protagonists of aesthetic modernism) but by economists, lawyers, anthropologists, and practical men and women of affairs'.[26] But their Victorian predecessors could equally well have said the same about their Hanoverian ones. Indeed, it has been argued that 'The idea that the early nineteenth century was the moment of modernity, the turning point from the "old" world to the "new" . . . was an invention of the early Victorian intelligentsia.'[27] Or if, as has also been argued, the English at the beginning of the eighteenth century were already 'obsessed with modernity',[28] that is merely to say that they were aware of living through a period of change which was making their society very different, by their standards, from what it had been earlier. We are all,

---

[25] S. N. Eisenstadt, *Comparative Civilizations and Multiple Modernities*. 2 vols. (Leiden, 2003).

[26] José Harris, *Private Lives, Public Spirit: A Social History of Britain 1870–1914* (Oxford, 1993), p. 32.

[27] Richard Price, *British Society 1680–1880: Dynamism, Containment, and Change* (Cambridge, 1999), p. 4.

[28] Alan Houston and Steven Pincus, 'Introduction: modernity and later seventeenth-century England', in Alan Houston and Steven Pincus, eds., *A Nation Transformed: England after the Restoration* (Cambridge, 2001), p. 1.

in our various ways, as modern as we think of ourselves as being, and a self-conscious ambition to break away from traditional forms may well lie behind a cultural or social mutation which turns out to be adaptive. But when applied to political, ideological, or economic institutions, the word is either explanatorily vacuous or surreptitiously teleological, however descriptively apt in conveying to the reader what 'their' experience was like for 'them'.

It is true that in some contexts 'failure to modernize' can be advanced as an explanation of why one society loses out in competition with another, not least in war. But that is only to say that the one has, but the other has not, adopted the strategy, technology, or form of organization on which it can be seen in retrospect that success depended in the local environment at the relevant time. Sometimes, this is sufficiently obvious to make the apparatus of evolutionary (or any other) theory otiose. When (to borrow now from Hilaire Belloc) 'The reason is that we have got the Gatling Gun and they have not', there may be no need to look further for the explanation of who won the battle in question and who lost it. But few 'what-if?' counterfactuals in military (or any other) history are as unproblematic as that one. However much either researchers or policymakers might wish it otherwise, sociology is not and never will be a predictive science. Only by what evolutionary biologists call 'reverse engineering' is it possible to specify in hindsight the features of institutional design which turned out to have a critical advantage over their competitors.

There are, however, occasional institutional comparisons to be drawn from the historical record which lend themselves to limited quasi- or semi-deductive sociological inferences. To go no further afield, both historians and sociologists have often pointed to differences between England's, France's, and Germany's legal and governmental, educational and religious, and financial and industrial institutions which help to explain the adaptiveness both of the political, ideological, and economic practices unique to each and of those selected by convergent evolution rather than lateral diffusion in response to environmental pressures common to them all. Inter-societal comparisons can not only identify the trade-offs that enabled the more successful practices to outcompete their rivals but also demonstrate how a trade-off that is optimal in one environment can be suboptimal in another. In the Conclusion, I shall briefly suggest why it was as improbable as it was that twentieth-century Britain would evolve into either a socialist or an authoritarian mode. But all through the eighteenth, nineteenth, and twentieth centuries there were pertinent inter-societal contrasts to be drawn, and both domestic and foreign observers from Montesquieu onwards often drew them. English commentators were likely to do so either to reinforce an insular self-satisfaction about the superiority of England's institutions over those of others or to deplore their fellow countrymen's inability to profit by others' example. But however partisan their arguments or simplistic their judgements, they were correct in their assumption that under some possible alternative combinations of selective pressures arising out of some possible alternative sequences of contingent events England's political, ideological, and economic institutions could have evolved in such a way as to have been either more or less different from those of other societies than they were.

IV

The practices whose variation and selection determine the course of social evolution are not, as their carriers are, open to attribution of praise or blame, any more than memes or genes are. You can, if you wish, say that a gene that increases the probability that its carriers will suffer from mental illness is a 'bad' gene, that a meme that increases the probability that its carriers will foment religious persecution is a 'bad' meme, and that a practice that increases the probability that its carriers will impoverish instead of enriching the society of which they are members is a 'bad' practice. But the genes, memes, and practices cannot themselves be claimed to be either wicked or virtuous. They can only be shown to be more or less successful in having a higher or lower probability of reproduction and diffusion than their competitors within the relevant population. No doubt both sociologists and historians have and cannot help having views of their own about whether one state of a society is to be preferred to another. Some of the best-known historians of England have had no inhibitions whatever about seeking to persuade their readers to share their personal value judgements, and there is nothing that prevents them from so doing. No reader of E. P. Thompson can be in doubt that Thompson wants his readers to agree with him that the industrial capitalism of eighteenth- and nineteenth-century Britain was an evil system of social organization to which its victims ought never to have been subjected. No reader of Corelli Barnett can be in doubt that Barnett wants his readers to agree with him that Britain's twentieth-century welfare state was a misguided attempt to create a better world which encouraged a deplorable dependence on tax-funded handouts among an undeserving proletariat. But from the perspective of evolutionary theory, their mutually irreconcilable convictions are as irrelevant as each other. Their readers can accept or reject their respective (and not always incompatible) explanations of how Britain became a capitalist industrial society and a welfare state whether or not they are disposed to agree that it was a bad thing. The right 'how come?' story is right (if it is) however much different historians or sociologists (or their readers) may welcome or deplore the outcome.

It does not, however, follow that the story of a society's political, ideological, and economic evolution either should or could be told in a value-neutral language. The carriers of the genes, memes, and practices whose effects on behaviour are being reported and (it is hoped) explained are human agents, and it is intrinsic to the concept of human agency that agents can behave either well or badly by criteria presumptively shared between author and reader—they can be brave or cowardly, generous or mean, kind or cruel, wise or foolish, industrious or lazy, and so on. What is more, such concepts can be, and often are, deployed in explanation of agents' actions: it is not meaningless, even if it may be mistaken, to say that it is because they were brave or cowardly, generous or mean, etc. that the incumbents of whatever were their social roles behaved in them as they did. The chapters to follow, which relate how mutant practices have resisted or displaced or lost out to their competitors, have not been purged of what analytical philosophers call 'thick' concepts in which fact and value are fused. There feature in them, even if not individually identified, more and less corrupt politicians, callous employers, diligent administrators, competent craftsmen, ill-disciplined policemen, complacent clerics, dishonest shopkeepers, generous philanthropists, even-handed magistrates, and so on.

Agreement may even be easier to reach in practice, if not in theory, about what was the 'bad' behaviour of the corrupt politicians or callous employers which triggered a mutation of existing practices than about what were the selective pressures which subsequently favoured the reproduction and diffusion of the mutants. It is, for example, easier for historians to agree how far Lloyd George was personally dishonest in his financial dealings than how far his legislative measures determined the future constitution of the 'welfare state'. But it makes no difference how much some commentators do, but others don't, disapprove of the behaviour in question. If, for whatever reason of your own, you wish to argue that the 'corrupt' politician or 'callous' employer is undeserving of disapproval, or the 'courageous' rebel or 'generous' philanthropist undeserving of approval, that will neither strengthen nor weaken whatever is your proffered explanation of its consequences. For sociologists' as opposed to philosophers' purposes, value judgements implicit in attributions of motive can be neutralized by the traditional rhetorical device, as familiar to Cicero as to Hobbes,[29] or to any twenty-first-century spin doctor or to the wag who first coined the joke 'I am a traveller, you are a tourist, they are trippers', of paradiastole—that is, 'deliberate redescription for the perlocutionary purpose of changing an interlocutor's point of view'.[30] So long as the evidence is such that we can agree what the behaviour is—which is to say, what is the information being acted out in it—it doesn't matter for the purpose of explaining its consequences that what you call 'cowardice' I call 'prudence', or what you call 'compassion' I call 'sentimentality', or what you call 'paying good wages' I call 'feather-bedding'. Even if, in presenting our rival 'how come?' stories to our readers, we have to make whatever disclaimers our use of thick concepts requires, our postulated connections between causes and effects are right (if they are) however many thick concepts they contain.

That, as I expect to be reminded, is by no means the end of the matter. Even if the 'how come?' question is answered by a story consisting entirely of accurately

[29] Quentin Skinner, *Rhetoric and Reason in the Philosophy of Hobbes* (Cambridge, 1996), pp. 139–53.
[30] W. G. Runciman, 'Cultural selection, axiological reasoning, and paradiastole', *Archives Européennes de Sociologie* 47 (2007), p. 185.

reported observations of behaviour and validated (or so far unfalsified) causal connections between them, readers with mutually incompatible moral and political convictions will not be dissuaded from protesting at what they regard as misleading emphases, biased omissions, or neglect of counterfactual conditionals which would, they think, lend support to their apportionment of praise or blame. (I have already cited both Marx and Macaulay as examples.) Readers are also likely to have strongly held views about the wider significance and value of the reports and explanations presented to them. Although Barnett explicitly agrees with Thompson that the alienation of the British working class was 'a consequence of *laissez-faire* unbridled by government yet coupled with state repression',[31] the two of them could no more agree the text of a jointly authored history of England (or Britain) over the period in question than (to borrow again from Weber) could a Jesuit and a Freemason agree the text of a jointly authored history of the Papacy. But the answers to the 'how come?' questions which are the stock-in-trade of evolutionary theory are no more discretionary in sociology than they are in biology. They may not be possible to answer with anything approaching an indefeasible sequence of hypothesis, inference, and test. But they are questions to which the answers are not up to you or me in the same way or to the same degree as are and always will be the questions of how far industrial capitalism, the welfare state, or the Papacy are 'good' things or 'bad'.

[31] Corelli Barnett, *The Audit of War: The Illusion and Reality of Britain as a Great Nation* (London, 1986), pp. 189–90.

1

What Changed, and What Didn't?

I

Although there is no such person as an ideal observer by whom a society's evolution can be definitively reported to the exclusion of alternative versions, there is one prolific commentator on early eighteenth-century English society whose interests cover many of the same topics that this book does: Daniel Defoe. Traveller, novelist, tradesman, pamphleteer, bankrupt, and one-time secret agent, his curiosity about England's politics, religion, and economy and the various roles and ranks of its people makes of his impressions an almost ready-made starting point. It is true that those impressions reflect, to a sometimes obsessional degree, both his personal likes and dislikes and his self-consciousness about his own social position. He is, for example, as hostile to stockjobbers as he is to gentleman tradesmen, and he happily voices the contradictory complaints that high wages make workmen idle and that they motivate them to emulate the habits of consumption of their superiors. His *Tour thro' the Whole Island of Great Britain*, published between 1724 and 1726, contains both exaggeration and hearsay, and he is not above dissimulation and even invention throughout his numerous writings. But suppose that he could be brought back to life at the beginning of the twenty-first century and taken to revisit the places in England and Wales that the *Tour* describes. By what differences, and what resemblances, would he be most forcibly struck?

Among the resemblances, he would surely be struck by the continued presence of a hereditary monarch and the continued existence of a bicameral Parliament in which one House is elected and the other not. He would not fail to notice a similarly large difference between the homes and possessions of the rich and of the poor, and the extent to which the wealth of the seriously rich exceeds that of the lesser rentiers, manufacturers, merchants, and professionals, just as theirs in turn exceeds that of the handicraftsmen, labourers, mechanics, and those whom he calls 'tradesmen of lower degree'. He would find the bankers, brokers, promoters, and underwriters of the City (already so called in his day) as committed to the pursuit of gain as they ever were. He would notice successful lawyers, financiers, and businessmen continuing to buy country estates. He would see currently fashionable consumer goods being displayed in shops and promoted by advertisers in an active provincial as well as metropolitan market. He could mingle with similar patrons in inns and coffee houses, and take part in similar discussions of the affairs of the day as reported in the newspapers. He would find public provision of welfare still being supplemented by private philanthropists and charitable foundations. He could attend similar race meetings at Epsom or Newmarket in the company of a similar cross-section of the populace. He could go to the theatre and see some of the same plays still being performed. He could visit hospitals where he would find surgeons carrying out operations like the one he himself underwent in 1725 for bladder stones. He could be taken to the site of what in his day was Newgate Prison and watch criminal trials still being conducted by bewigged judges before twelve-person juries charged with deciding the guilt or innocence of the accused. He would find the same gradations of rank in the army, the navy, and the Church. He would detect similar differences in spoken English according to region and status. He would hear similar complaints about the burden of taxation, and similar disagreements about the entitlements or otherwise of the deserving and undeserving poor. Witnessing the hostility directed against immigrants, he might be reminded of the protests aroused in 1709 against the admission of some 12,000 Palatines which was denounced as a scheme for depriving English-born workers of jobs. In the provinces, he would find in agricultural districts a similar mixture of large landowners, tenant farmers, landless labourers, and smallholders, and in the towns similar local elites of professionals, businessmen, and rentiers. He would see successive Lord Lieutenants still being appointed by the Crown. If he revisited 'that antient and truly famous Town and University of *Cambridge*',[1] he would find, as at Oxford, colleges that he remembered standing unchanged. Across the country, he would detect the same minorities of thieves, beggars, prostitutes, hooligans, drunkards, and ne'er-do-wells. He would readily equate the social problems caused by heroin and cocaine with those caused in his day by gin. He would be as conscious as ever of the predominance in both size and influence of London over the provinces. And he would be just as concerned as he had been when giving an Englishman's account of Scotland that he should neither 'flatter' the Scots nor 'deceive' them.[2]

Whatever else, on the other hand, he might be more or less struck by, neither Defoe nor any of his contemporaries could fail to be astonished by the ease and speed of travel itself, by road, rail, and (still more amazingly) air, or by the invention and use of cameras, telephones, electric lighting, radio, television, and computers. The total size of the population might equally surprise him, as might the degree of its concentration in cities or 'conurbations' vastly larger than the manufacturing, harbour, market, and cathedral towns he had known. He would not expect so high a proportion of the working population outside of the army and navy to be employed by the state. He would notice that responsibility for the maintenance of public order lies with the police rather than the army or militia, that the government raises revenue more by taxation than by excise, that all adults are entitled to

---

[1] Daniel Defoe, *A Tour Thro' the Whole Island of Great Britain, Divided into Circuits or Journies* (London, 1727) vol. 1, p. 78.
[2] Defoe, *Tour*, vol. 2, p. 690.

vote in both local and parliamentary elections, that some (although far from all) working people combine in trade unions which negotiate their wages and conditions with their employers (including the state), and that anyone past working age is entitled as of right to a pension. He would wonder what had become of all the resident domestic servants. He would appreciate by how much the severity of the criminal law and the punishment of convicted offenders has been moderated, how different are the methods of recruitment into the army and navy, and how much less significant a part is played by religion in both public and private life. He would be startled by the degree of toleration accorded to homosexuality and to births out of wedlock. He would sense that social relationships in general have become less tightly bound up with personal and familial ties. And perhaps he would be struck more than anything else by women occupying and performing roles from which in his day an unchallenged cultural stereotype had excluded them and by their children being no longer at work from an early age—from four, as he claims to have seen in several parts of the country—but in universal, state-funded schooling into their teens.

Furthermore, there would be no disagreement between Defoe and ourselves about the changes in the quality of life brought about by advances in sanitation and medicine (including not least anaesthesia), improved housing, higher real incomes, less arduous working conditions, healthier diet, reduced infant mortality, longer life expectancy, better education, a wider range of leisure activities with an increasing amount of free time in which to enjoy them, and a decline in both public and private violence of the kind that he and his contemporaries took for granted. He would soon be aware that public executions, the flogging (sometimes to death) of soldiers and sailors, the killings of demonstrators by militiamen, excisemen by smugglers, and gamekeepers by poachers, duels, physical assault (sometimes to the point of murder) in industrial disputes, death sentences passed on rioters as well as thieves and highwaymen, regular beatings of children by fathers and schoolteachers, stocks, man-traps, bare-knuckle prizefights, street brawls, and broken heads on the cobbles to which no one paid any attention whatever had come to be viewed as barbaric symptoms of the norms of a bygone age. Add to that the spread of literacy, a decline in superstition and bigotry, and a broadening of social horizons through travel and tourism, and it becomes little exaggeration, if any, to talk of a transformation in the lived experience of the British people, whatever the perspective from which it is viewed.

Yet all the differences in manners, mores, and styles and standards of living came about within a set of practices and the power attaching to the roles defined by them which Defoe would find not merely recognizable but thoroughly familiar. He would recognize a mode of coercion grounded in parliamentary sovereignty and the rule of law, a mode of persuasion grounded in open dissemination of ideas and competition for social prestige, and a mode of production grounded in market exchange and private property. He would see that no more than in his day could England be labelled a feudal society or a theocratic society or a caste society or a despotic society, or in twentieth-century terms a fascist or a communist one. He would appreciate that the authority of the government had not at any point since his lifetime been subverted by usurpers, invaders, or separatists, that the military remained subordinate to the civilian power, and that its public offices were neither bought and sold en masse as in pre-revolutionary France nor attached to a service nobility as in Petrine Russia or assigned to slaves of the monarch as in Ottoman Turkey, neither filled by election as in the United States of America nor in the gift of a single ruling party as in Soviet Russia or the People's Republic of China. As he looked round the world as it had become, he would have as much reason as ever to remark on the distinctiveness of his own society's political, ideological, and economic institutions.

II

As soon, however, as we envisage a detailed and thoroughgoing discussion with Defoe about just what has and hasn't changed in those institutions between his time and ours, we come up against the question as to whether his sociological vocabulary could be reconciled with ours. As a veteran propagandist, he would not need to be reminded that what you are understood to be saying about the world in which you live depends on how you have chosen to say it, and that the terms in which one person talks about his or her place in society can be very different from the terms in which another does so. He would be fully alert to the need to get behind the clutter of superficial appearances and noise of disingenuous rhetoric, and to the risk that a seemingly disinterested report of an observed behaviour pattern might be concealing not only ignorance but also prejudice on the observer's part. It would not take him long to extend his sociological vocabulary of 'sorts', 'ranks', and 'degrees' to include ours of 'class', 'ethnicity', and 'gender'. But agreement might not be as easy to reach when we moved to discussing changes (or the absence of them) in the location in social space of higher- and lower-ranked roles and the distribution of the population between them.

There would be no difficulty where a new word has been substituted for an old one designating a role whose defining practices are unchanged. Defoe would, for example, grasp readily enough that when we refer to a person who robs strangers of their watches when they are walking in the street as a 'mugger' we are talking about someone he would call a 'footpad'. Neither would there be any difficulty when we told him about roles that didn't exist in his day, like 'air traffic controller', or about roles that have ceased to exist, like 'witch'. He might be particularly interested to hear about witches, since he himself, having in 1711 affirmed a belief in them as confirmed by both holy scripture and common experience, appears to have decided by 1726, when he published *A System of Magick*, that they are no longer to be taken seriously. But he would understand very well what had gone on when we told him that following the repeal of the witchcraft statutes in 1736, the idea of a witch, although lingering on in country districts and finding expression in occasional local acts of violence against women, had steadily faded to the point of surviving only in fairy stories, children's dressing-up games, and mock-serious rituals performed by dabblers in the occult. Our talk would, however, take a more problematic turn if we were to start discussing what has and hasn't changed since Gregory King's celebrated Table in which the incomes of the 'Families of England' in 1688 were distributed among twenty-six 'ranks, degrees, titles, and qualifications'. Defoe would be as aware as ourselves that King's was only one among other possible ways of categorizing the population as it was in that year by one among other possible criteria of differentiation. Indeed, he might agree that it was already beginning to be out of date by the time he was writing *Robinson Crusoe*. He would grasp well enough what we could tell him about the criticisms to which it and others were subjected and about the very different categories later used by Registrars General compiling the national census, academic sociologists construct-ing scales of occupational 'class' or 'status', and marketing agencies assigning letters of the alphabet to groups of prospective consumers in a descending order of rank. But could he and we arrive at an agreed classification of roles and their defining practices that would provide a common basis for comparing the structure of English society in his day with ours?

Implicit in that question is the suspicion that there is an inherent irreconcilability between the different pictures of a society that its different members carry in their heads, and that this irreconcilability derives not so much from the differences they observe in how people behave towards one another as from the different idioms in which they conceptualize their observations. The vocabulary of social differenti-ation is a long-standing topic in cultural history, with a rich and extensive literature of its own. The different words that different people with their different perspec-tives use to designate what they regard as significant distinctions between them vary not only within the population as constituted at any one time but between one generation (or even less than one) and the next. Although 'working class' is not found before 1789, the language of 'class' was already displacing that of 'rank' by the middle decades of the eighteenth century.[3] This partly reflects an increasing emphasis on wealth, particularly if acquired within a single generation, rather than inherited status. But 'rank' wasn't driven to cultural extinction, and 'class' con-tinued to be used, as it still—confusingly—is, for differences in manners, lifestyle, and patterns of endogamy and commensalism alongside or instead of relation to the mode of production: critics of 'the English class system' are usually attacking the distribution of social prestige more than that of income and wealth.

There was, moreover, always a difference between the usage of commentators who sought to capture the niceties of what some sociologists were to see as a smooth continuum of 'socio-economic status' and commentators who were more attracted

---

[3] Penelope J. Corfield, 'Class by name and number in eighteenth-century Britain', in Penelope J. Corfield, ed., *Language, History and Class* (Oxford, 1991), p. 123.

to what other sociologists were to call a 'dichotomous image of society'. But the terms in which a two-tier model was imposed on the continuum were themselves highly diverse, from the top-down version of 'elite' and 'mass' to the bottom-up version of 'us' and 'them'. Some were variations on the ever-resonant theme of the 'two nations' of rich and poor (or the 'haves' versus the 'have-nots'). But some were based on a political distinction between government and people; some were based on an ideological distinction between the lettered, genteel, and civilized and the uneducated, undisciplined, and unwashed; and some were based on an economic distinction between the productive 'toilers' and the unproductive 'spoilers'. All were based on oversimplifications which a tour much briefer than Defoe's would disconfirm in a matter of days. But the influence of these distinctions—including not least the influence of the one between 'proletariat' and 'bourgeoisie'—has been such as to make it tempting to conclude that in their observation of social relationships people see only what, for whatever reasons of their own, they want to.

But that conclusion would be another oversimplification in its turn. The differences in the power attaching to a society's constituent political, ideological, and economic roles are not fictions devised by ignorant and prejudiced bystanders, or unscrupulous and self-serving politicians, or remote and doctrinaire academics. It is true that fictions, whatever has inspired them, can and sometimes do affect behaviour to an extent that demands separate explanation. But in Defoe's day unequal social relationships between rulers and subjects, landowners and tenants, officers and soldiers, magistrates and defendants, teachers and pupils, or employers and wage-workers, were no more artefacts of the language in which they were reported, explained, described, and evaluated by either observers or participants than they have been since. There doesn't need to be a single universally recognized measure of a person's, family's, or household's political influence or social standing or material resources for there to be general agreement about whose roles are more powerful than whose. There are bound to be arguments about the nature and degree of the inequalities between them. But such arguments will be resolved not by further semantic debate but only by detailed examination of the practices that define the reported roles and thereby locate them above and below one another in social space.

Although, accordingly, no two observers can be expected to report the role structure of English society as it was in the early eighteenth century, or at any time since, in identical terms, they cannot refuse to acknowledge, whatever the words they use for it, a fourfold distinction between an elite (to Defoe, the 'rich and great'), an intermediate category of what Defoe and his contemporaries called the 'middling sort', a 'working class' (as it would come to be called) made up of those who to him were 'labouring people', and what would still later come to be called an 'underclass' of those whom he characterized as the 'really miserable'. Defoe does not say who exactly he has in mind as the really miserable or how many of them he thinks there are or what proportion of them he assumes to be so for the whole of their adult lives. But he would not be surprised to hear about a supposed 'submerged tenth' or thereabouts, or about the 11.4 per cent which 'can reasonably be treated as a minimum figure for the average incidence of dependence on the parishes in 1803',[4] or about Rowntree's calculation that a third of the 28 per cent of poor families in York in the 1890s were in what he called 'primary' poverty, or about the 'nearly 5 million people depending on social assistance' when the Supplementary Benefits Commission was closed down in 1980.[5] Nor would he be surprised to be told that the 'rich and great' never amounted to more than one in perhaps fifty of the population, depending on how exclusive a definition is adopted, and that among them the very rich and very great have never ceased to be much richer and greater than the rest.

It is, however, about the social space in between the 'rich and great' and the 'really miserable' that rival observers are likeliest to disagree. Early in *Robinson Crusoe*, Defoe puts into the mouth of Crusoe's father the passing remark that the 'middle state, or what might be called the upper station of low life' is 'the best state in the world'. Whatever is meant by 'best', Defoe evidently shared the view of twentieth-century sociologists of what many were then calling the 'manual/non-manual distinction', since he explicitly distinguishes his 'labouring people' by the fact that they 'depend upon their hands' from shopkeepers who 'do not actually work upon, make, or manufacture the goods they sell'. Then, as since, the 'manual/non-manual' distinction has to be qualified by the sculptors and surgeons who work with their hands and the low-paid routine service workers who don't, and by the second decade of the twenty-first century it was being increasingly dismissed by sociologists as outdated and misleading. But Crusoe's father's remark is characteristic of a discourse in which social self-differentiation is bound up with a culturally acquired sense of self-regard. For many of those who think of themselves as belonging in the middle, it was then, and has been since, seen not only, or not so much, as an economic or occupational category as a repository of responsibility, self-restraint, and good sense as distinct from the selfishness and arrogance of those above it and the fecklessness and intransigence of those below. At the same time, it has often been seen from both above and below (and sometimes from within) as the repository of tight-fistedness, narrow-mindedness, self-righteousness, and snobbery.

There has always been scope for paradiastole in the choice of thick concepts to be applied to the presumptively characteristic behaviour patterns of the people whom G. K. Chesterton described as no more likely to drop an aitch than to pick up a title. Just as some respondents whom twentieth-century sociologists would instruct interviewers to code as 'manual' would nonetheless describe themselves as 'middle class', so others to be coded as 'non-manual' would describe themselves as 'working class'. It became apparent from in-depth interviews conducted in the late twentieth

[4] Lynn Hollen Lees, *The Solidarities of Strangers: The English Poor Laws and the People, 1700–1948* (Cambridge, 1998), p. 45.
[5] David Donnison, *The Politics of Poverty* (Oxford, 1982), p. 14.

century that respondents could acknowledge the meaningfulness of that distinction while disputing its relevance to their own 'sense of self-identity',[6] much as in the eighteenth century an army sergeant might style himself 'gentleman' in a deposition to a church court even if well aware that he would not be so styled by the officers of his regiment.[7] A perennial disagreement of a different kind was between commentators who hoped or feared that in the event of overt political conflict the middling would side with those above them, and those who argued that they would, on the contrary, side with those below: between the outbreak of the French Revolution in 1789 and the killing of peaceful protesters at St Peter's Fields, Manchester ('Peterloo') in 1819, newspapers, periodicals, and pamphlets were filled with conflicting representations of the 'middle classes' (or 'orders' or 'ranks') as either the friends or the enemies of the 'labouring classes' (or 'lower orders') in the struggle for 'reform'. But all the arguments depended on a consensus that wherever exactly the dividing lines were drawn, there could be distinguished by any and all observers *a* 'middle' located below the elite but above the rest.

At the same time, closer examination of the practices defining middling and labouring roles reveals variations persistently reproduced within both of them which in each case amount to a further subdivision into three ranked categories of roles. After the language of 'rank' was superseded by the language of 'class', contemporary commentators were as likely to refer to both the 'middle' and the 'working' class(es) in the plural as in the singular. Before as well as after the French Revolution and its Napoleonic aftermath had infused the language of 'middle class' with newly charged political overtones, it was not difficult to see that in political authority and social standing as well as income and wealth a 'middle-middle' category of businessmen, lesser professionals, rentiers, shopkeepers, schoolteachers, journalists, farmers, and managers was outranked by the financiers, merchants, judges, senior civil servants, higher professionals, senior army and navy officers, and county gentry above it, at the same time that it outranked the clerks, technical and sales workers, petty traders, and rural smallholders below, and that women, whether independent or taking 'secondary' rank from a family or household head, could be as readily assigned to one or other of the three as men.

Within the 'working class' it was equally easy to differentiate a semi-skilled category of operatives below the craftsmen and artisans but above the labourers below them, with the kind of 'stout fellow' who assured Defoe that he preferred 'going-a-begging' to labouring assigned to the underclass even if he was successful enough at begging (or thieving) not to be among Defoe's 'really miserable' (or those whom Charles Booth at the close of the nineteenth century classified as 'always in want'). The readiest indicator of social location was always the gainful occupation

---

[6] Mike Savage, Gaynor Bagnall, and Brian Longhurst, 'Ordinary, ambivalent and defensive: class identities in the Northwest of England', *Sociology* 35 (2001), p. 882.

[7] Peter Earle, 'The middling sort in London', in Jonathan Barry and Christopher Brooks, eds., *The Middling Sort of People: Culture, Society and Politics in England, 1550–1800* (London, 1994), p. 149.

or ownership of property of a presumptively breadwinning household head. 'Skill' was and is one of those words that can lend itself to being used to construct a role that wouldn't otherwise exist. It can have as much to do with reward for long service, imputed trustworthiness, or connection to managerial or proprietorial authority as with the complexity of the task performed, and it sometimes denotes work culturally defined as unsuitable for women or juveniles and socially imposed in accordance with that definition. But there were always manual and low-grade service occupations for which the necessary training and experience could be acquired 'on the job', as opposed to both those above them requiring lengthy apprenticeship and those below them requiring nothing more than what any 'stout [or not so stout] fellow' could bring to the farmyard, the dockside, the warehouse, the building site or the domestic or commercial premises. No doubt Defoe would be initially baffled by the minutiae of the Classification of Occupations into which twentieth-century registrars divided the employed population for the purpose of compiling the census. But it would not take him long to see that *a* meaningful tripartite subdivision among the 'labouring people' could be drawn in accordance with criteria within which, however contestable the dividing lines and however different our vocabulary from his, he would feel at home. Nor would he be other than fully aware of the enduring sociological significance, however he might choose to phrase it, of the difference between the working-class 'job' and the middle-class 'career'—that is, between an occupational role to which there attaches, and one to which there does not, an inherent prospect of upward mobility in social space in the course of the incumbent's adult life.

III

Defoe could not, however, fail to notice that wherever exactly the dividing lines were drawn, the relative proportions of the population to be assigned to the middling and the labouring were far from the same three centuries after his time. It is no more possible to specify a percentage which makes such a change a qualitative and not merely a quantitative one than it is to fix precisely the boundaries by reference to which the percentage is to be calculated. But to give an example familiar to comparative sociologists, although nobody can say at exactly what point a 'society with slaves' becomes a 'slave society', a society in which there are a handful of imported domestic slaves in the houses of the rich is not in the same category as one in which the productive labour force is predominantly servile, or one in which, although the productive labour force is formally free, its military and administrative institutions are largely staffed by slaves. Defoe would see that the labouring, although ceasing to be so overwhelming a majority of the population, long continued to outnumber the middling. But he would also see that the middling had expanded far beyond what they had been in his day, and he would be fully alive to the implications that this had for the chances for labouring families' children to rise out of their systact of origin.

During the nineteenth century, it was commonplace to picture a society such as England's as a hill with a few highly privileged roles close to the top and a steadily increasing number of diminishingly privileged roles at each level below, much as Saint-Simon in France took it for granted that '*la classe la plus nombreuse*' was '*la plus pauvre*'. The statistician R. Dudley Baxter, when looking at mid-nineteenth-century England, likened it to the Island of Tenerife 'with its long low base of labouring population, with its uplands of the middle classes, and with the towering peaks and summits of those with princely incomes'.[8] But such images, although much more accurate than the simplistic dichotomies, fail to reflect the relative size of both the middling and the miserable, which makes a pear a more appropriate shape than either a triangle or a diamond. Defoe would not expect to see so large an expansion in the number of lower-middle occupational roles and the number of women as well as men occupying them. Unprepared as he would be to be told that in the census of 1891 there were half a million men in England and Wales in what came to be called 'white-collar' as opposed to 'blue-collar' occupations, he would be still less prepared to find them supplemented by two hundred thousand 'white-blouse' women. He might not be surprised by the late nineteenth- and early twentieth-century increase in demand for clerks, bookkeepers, technicians, shop assistants, and lower-grade administrators generated by the growth in size and complexity of the national economy. But he would surely find surprising the scale of the increase in demand for non-manual workers in the employment of central and local government. And he would not fail to notice how many of them were the sons or daughters of 'labouring' people.

The rise and fall of individuals within the role structure was as much a topic of interest, not to say fascination, to Defoe and his contemporaries as to any twentieth-century sociologist. Whether social mobility was ever a cause, or only a symptom, of changes in the overall role structure is a question to be addressed in Chapter 5. But the possibility of ascent from humble origins to high position was a staple of biography, rhetoric, and fiction. Although it was an arithmetical impossibility for more than a handful of the lucky and determined few to match the achievements of the exemplary nineteenth-century subjects of Samuel Smiles's best-selling *Self-Help* and *Lives of the Engineers*, it was a matter of institutional fact that there were no legal restrictions blocking the way to the top. Equally fascinating to contemporaries were the spectacular falls from the heights to the depths, whether through political failure, social disgrace, or financial ruin. Defoe himself had at one stage of his career been stood in the pillory, and was in hiding from his creditors at his death. But the collection of statistical data on social mobility lagged well behind the collection of data on health, income, crime, education, and the rate of growth of the population by which nineteenth-century

---

[8] R. Dudley Baxter, *National Income of the United Kingdom* (London, 1868), p. 1.

rulers extended their knowledge of, and thereby control over, the ruled. As early as 1828, one perceptive commentator was inferring from changing housing standards and consumption patterns that 'the middle classes are receiving from the lower in much greater numbers than the latter do from the former'.[9] But such an observer, however astute, could not, any more than Defoe, consult or construct inflow and outflow tables in which the extent of such movement in social space would be revealed.

Defoe would, however, be just as well able to follow such calculations as he would to grasp the twentieth-century sociological vocabulary of 'class', 'ethnicity', and 'gender'. He would readily appreciate the distinction between mobility result-ing from the increase in the number of new roles at a given level available to be filled, and mobility resulting from the replacement of the downwardly mobile by the upwardly mobile. He would not need to be told that if the labouring people are having on average many more children surviving into adulthood than the middling sort, despite higher mortality rates, the relative opportunities their children will have for upward mobility will be diminished in consequence, or that they will be influenced also by rates of immigration and emigration. However struck he might be by the number of middling roles being filled during the twentieth century by children from labouring families, he would be unsurprised by the finding that in the 1970s, despite the increased numbers of the middling, the probability was higher than three out of four that a male manual worker in England and Wales aged between twenty and sixty-four would be the son of a father employed in some form of manual work or as a foreman or lower-grade technician.[10] He would expect middling parents to continue to do what they could to protect their children from leaving their location of origin and to have the cultural as well as material resources with which to assist them, just as he would expect to find a relative lack of parental encouragement and individual ambition among the families of labouring people by comparison with those of the middling sort.

Nor could he fail to notice that despite the general rise in living standards, the difference in lifestyles between top and bottom was much the same as ever. He might be intrigued to be taken back up to Northumberland to revisit Alnwick Castle, in his day 'still in tolerable repair',[11] but at the end of the twentieth century, after a costly mid-Victorian renovation, a much-frequented tourist attraction as well as the seat of a duke who, although not as rich as the Duke of Westminster, was still one of the richest landowners in England. He could also, if he asked to see the living conditions of the 'really miserable', be taken to a run-down, boarded-up, weed-ridden, graffiti-covered housing estate in a major city. In between these

---

[9] W. Jacob, quoted by M. Dorothy George, *London Life in the XVIIIth Century*[2] (London, 1930), p. 402 (n134).
[10] John H. Goldthorpe (with Catriona Llewellyn), 'Class mobility in Britain: three themes examined', in John H. Goldthorpe, ed. (in collaboration with Catriona Llewellyn and Clive Payne), *Social Mobility and Class Structure in Modern Britain*[2] (Oxford, 1987), p. 47.
[11] Defoe, *Tour*, vol. 2, p. 662.

extremes, he would be bound to notice the extent to which even the poor have come to regard as necessities possessions and amenities which were once luxuries even for the rich. But he would not find that any of the distinctions we had been drawing in our discussions with him, whether in his terminology or ours, had lost their significance. He would be in no doubt that the aspiration of the Chartist leader Bronterre O'Brien was still a long way from fulfilment—the aspiration, as O'Brien put it in 1833, that the 'working class' should be 'at the top rather than the bottom of society—or rather that there should be no top or bottom at all'.[12]

IV

Anyone of Defoe's generation who grew up among reminiscences of regicide, protectorate, and restoration, and then lived on through Monmouth's Rebellion of 1685, the overthrow of the Stuart monarchy in 1688, the 'rage of party' under Queen Anne, and the Old Pretender's attempt to win back the throne in 1715 would have been unlikely to predict for England a future of internal peace, stability, and order. Defoe was a vigorous defender of the settlement of 1688. But he would not have been surprised that its interpretation should long continue to be contested by Whigs, Tories, and Radicals who drew widely different implications from it for widely different purposes of their own. He could no more have foreseen how the discourse of politics might be recast by events in America and France than how political practices elsewhere might also be affected by them. But if he had, he might have been still more inclined to predict that the upheavals of the seventeenth century would not be the last of their kind. Treasonable conspiracies, popular uprisings, magnate feuds, and civil wars were all part and parcel of England's history. What reason was there to suppose that later centuries would not witness one or more similarly disruptive episodes whose sociological effects would be of similar magnitude?

Discussion of that question is inevitably bedevilled by differences of view about what does or doesn't amount to a 'revolution'. The meaning given by contemporaries to the word—as, likewise, to the word 'reform'—has a cultural-evolutionary trajectory of its own. In nineteenth-century England it was bound to carry implicit reference to events in France after 1789, just as in twentieth-century England it was bound to carry implicit reference to events in Russia after 1917. In the eighteenth century it was bound to carry implicit reference to the 'Glorious Revolution' of 1688, even though to some that event had been revolutionary but not glorious, while to others it had been glorious but not revolutionary. But if, following the *Oxford English Dictionary*, a revolution involves 'a complete overthrow of the established government in any society or state by those who were previously subject

---

[12] Quoted by Asa Briggs, 'The language of "class" in early nineteenth-century England', in Asa Briggs and John Saville, eds., *Essays in Labour History* (London, 1960), p. 69.

to it', there can be no disagreement that there was a revolution in 1688—the reigning monarch was driven into exile by force—and that in England, at any rate, it was never followed by another. English society's subsequent evolutionary trajectory was one of gradual variation and selection of practices and roles without an authentically revolutionary punctuation of the kind familiar both from its own past and from the experience of other societies in Europe and elsewhere during the eighteenth, nineteenth, and twentieth centuries.

Agreement is made still more difficult than it would otherwise be by the propensity of historians to label 'revolutionary' any unforeseen social change whose importance to their chosen theme they wish to stress, even though it has come about only through the diffusion and reproduction of mutant practices over an extended period of years. The 'Industrial Revolution', despite the initial capital letters conventionally accorded to it, was only intermittently and patchily industrial and very far from amounting to a 'complete overthrow'. The 'agricultural revolution', which enabled England to absorb the results of its 'demographic revolution' without widespread starvation, was a lengthy process of adaptation which included the application of previously developed techniques, long drawn-out modification of patterns of tenure through enclosure and engrossment, successive injections of fresh capital, and a regionally variable rise in the acreage devoted to arable cultivation. The 'consumer revolution', which was under way in Defoe's day, took over a century to lead to a 'retailing revolution' in which practices pioneered by the co-operative societies were diffused and reproduced among multiple and department stores and extended from the sale of food, drink, shoes, clothes, and in due course household appliances to what one historian has called the 'Kellogg effect, or cornflakes revolution'.[13] The 'democratic revolution', which was accompanied by a 'revolution in government', was a sequence of events in which a fitful extension of the parliamentary franchise gradually evolved in approximate parallel with a fitful increase in the power of the state. At a more general level still, what one historian has called 'the social revolution itself, which consisted in a rise in the scale of human organization, not only in industry, transport and commerce, but in almost every other social activity, from religion to government',[14] was no more (if no less) than a cumulative concentration of increasing numbers of people brought together in their various roles in larger collectivities by a diversity of selective environmental pressures over many decades.

To guard against inappropriate use of the word 'revolution' is not to deny that there is a sense in which social change is as 'revolutionary' as the people who live through it feel it to be and therefore describe it as being. Irrelevant to the explanation of the change as their feelings may be, when a historian of eighteenth-century England says that the 'polite and commercial' people of the 1780s

---

[13] F. M. L. Thompson, *The Rise of Respectable Society: A Social History of Victorian Britain 1830–1900* (London, 1988), p. 42.

[14] Harold Perkin, *The Origins of Modern English Society 1780–1880* (London, 1969), p. 107.

'did not, in any fundamental sense, inhabit the same society' as in the 1730s,[15] he is saying something that may very well convey an authentic sense of what the difference felt like to *them*. Similarly, the self-improving Victorian working-class autodidacts, whose 'frequently expressed belief was that in the course of the century they had lived through monumental and unparalleled change',[16] *had*, by virtue of that belief, lived through monumental and unparalleled change. The same was true of many of those born in the early years of the twentieth century who lived through its two unprecedently disruptive world wars and their aftermaths. People are themselves the best authorities for the impact of the disturbance of accustomed ways of life and hitherto unquestioned assumptions which they have experienced directly, even if they are disposed to exaggerate it in their own descriptions. But from the perspective of comparative sociology, their testimony brings out all the more forcibly the disjunction between contemporaries' sense of change and the reproductive fitness of the practices which continued to contain the evolution of their society's mode of coercion within parliamentary sovereignty and the rule of law, of its mode of persuasion within open dissemination of ideas and competition for social prestige, and of its mode of production within market exchange and private property.

The commentators in Defoe's day and since who either hoped for or feared revolutionary change are not to be dismissed as either stupid or ignorant. Defoe had good reason to take seriously the Jacobite threat to the Hanoverian succession, and although he didn't live to witness the Young Pretender's attempt in 1745 to achieve what the Old Pretender had failed to do in 1715, he would not have been surprised by the panic it caused on the Stock Exchange when the news reached London that the Jacobite army was at Derby. However improbable the sequence of events that turned a *révolte nobiliaire* into the French Revolution, it was not palpably foolish of the government of the day to take precautions against the eventuality that something of what took place in France between 1789 and 1794 might take place in England. It was not impossible that in the second quarter of the nineteenth century the Chartist movement might turn into a popular rising sufficiently widespread and coordinated for the army and militia to be unable to suppress it, or that after the First World War a general strike and campaign of civil disobedience might paralyse the national economy so effectively as to threaten the authority of Parliament. But how is it that, despite all the differences between the world in which Defoe wrote *Robinson Crusoe* and the world in which this book has been written, they came about within what he would recognize, however he chose to phrase it, as institutional modes of coercion, persuasion, and production not—or at any rate, not yet—different in kind?

---

[15] Paul Langford, *A Polite and Commercial People: England 1727–1783* (Oxford, 1989), p. 725.
[16] Patrick Joyce, *Visions of the People: Industrial England and the Question of Class, 1848–1914* (Cambridge, 1991), p. 175.

2

Politics and the Power of the State

I

To the question 'To whose roles did political power attach in the social structure of Defoe's England?', the uncontroversial answer is a ruling elite whose members had an effective monopoly of the means of coercion through Parliament, the army, the militia, the courts, and their own retainers (including not least their gamekeepers). It was, moreover, as clear to their fellow-citizens as to themselves that their rulership was buttressed by both an ideological domination based on birth, upbringing, and lifestyle and a near-exclusive ownership or control of the principal sources of wealth. But Walpole was not prime minister of a one-party state; the City of London, the lesser gentry, and the middling sort could all mobilize political influence of which ministers had to take account; ratepaying parish vestrymen could only be overruled, if at all, by local magistrates; elections to the House of Commons, for all the anachronisms and inconsistencies of the system of constituency representation, were not decided exclusively by magnate influence; and despite the severity of the punishments inflicted on lawbreakers, their impact was both limited and arbitrary. Examples exposing the weakness of the rulers included the Excise Bill of 1733 and the Jew Bill of 1753. Historians who agree about the stability—which is not to be equated with peacefulness—of eighteenth-century English society have presented it to their readers very differently. Where some have portrayed a closed patrician class defending its monopoly of power by draconian legislation, others have portrayed a gradation of ranks cross-cut by alliances of interest within which outbreaks of inter-systactic hostility were tempered by a common concern to protect the liberty of the citizen against the encroachment of an overmighty executive. But wherever the emphasis is placed by observers of different persuasions, the roles constitutive of the political institutions of eighteenth-century England were defined by a distinctive mixture of adversarial and collaborative practices whose relative adaptiveness was a function of the trade-offs between them.

Those historians who have stressed the more collaborative practices have sometimes attributed them to 'paternalism'—that is, to a culturally transmitted acknowledgement by the elite of a quasi-familial obligation to have regard to the well-being of dependants who in return acknowledge and accept their authority. But, as pointed out by a twentieth-century sociologist in a detailed study of East Anglian farmworkers, it is a 'fallacious inference' from what is seen to be 'largely quiescent social and political behaviour' to adherence to a 'deferential image of society':[1] it was, after all, from Norfolk that Joseph Arch, the 'Moses of the agricultural labourers', was elected to Parliament in 1885. In a still predominantly rural environment where effective economic sanctions attached to the roles of land-owners and tenant farmers, large-scale movement off the land into towns and cities was only beginning, and the incumbents of dominant and subordinate roles were likely to be personally known to one another, a tacitly negotiated trade-off, by which favourable treatment was negotiated for loyal service, was a strategy adaptive on both sides. But if physical violence against landowners, employers, and magis-trates was unusual, defiance of authority was not. No historian of the period disputes that the practices of poaching, smuggling, and theft were endemic. Rioting was a standard form of protest against not only increases in food prices but turnpikes, encroachments on common land, and reorganizations of the militia. Nor were riots always confined within narrow local limits: 'The rioting crowd was prepared to travel, often prodigious distances, to impose their will.'[2] Both foreign and domestic observers, echoed by later historians, viewed the English common people as turbulent, disorderly, and insubordinate. A society in which 'mobs' had to be suppressed by military force on perhaps as many as a hundred occasions in the 1760s alone is difficult to characterize as 'deferential', however many of its citizens conformed for however much of the time to culturally transmitted norms of conduct and address in their routine encounters with members of the elite.

It may therefore seem to pose a social-evolutionary conundrum that the Han-overian state was not weakened by internal disorder more severely than it was, given its lack of the practices and roles of a strong central government with a large standing army and a reliable corps of local agents, clients, officials, and informants at its disposal. But however much the controllers of the means of coercion left the 'people' to their own devices, the means of coercion that they controlled were adequate to uphold the defence of the realm and restore public order if or when under serious threat. The state's vulnerability was glaringly exposed by the Gordon Riots of 1780, which continued in the capital city for over a week before the troops were called in and order forcibly restored. But the rioters were not carriers of practices of the kind that define the roles of followers of magnate frondeurs or clan chieftains or local caciques. Whatever the grievances or resentments that had provoked them, and however violent the behaviour in which they were given expression, they were not going to disempower the elite or overturn the existing role structure. When the country was at war, as it frequently was in the eighteenth century, the state raised the money, recruited the soldiers (including foreign mercenaries), and built the ships that protected the overseas trade routes. The

---

[1] Howard Newby, *The Deferential Worker: A Study of Farm Workers in East Anglia* (Harmondsworth, 1977), p. 144.

[2] Adrian Randall, *Riotous Assemblies: Popular Protest in Hanoverian England* (Oxford, 2006), p. 310.

press gangs were empowered to kidnap the trained seamen needed to man the fleet in open violation of statutory guarantees, and some 4,000 excisemen were deployed by an office which had not only a 'complex system of measurement and bookkeeping' and a 'rigorous hierarchy based on experience and ability' but also 'strict discipline from its central office'.[3] It may not have been as 'strong' a state as some of the rulers, then as thereafter, would have liked it to be. But if it had been a 'weak' one, the ongoing reproduction of the practices defining its constituent roles would be puzzling to the point of inexplicability.

The explanation of its stability is that the critical practices were not only military but financial. Enough of the population contributed enough money, in their roles as fundholders and taxpayers, to sustain the level of expenditure required. There is no way of measuring accurately the trade-off in economic growth between lower civilian investment and the indirect gains from the reallocation of surplus resources to the army and navy. But that question would not arise at all without the ongoing reproduction of financial practices which did not face the environment that they had faced in seventeenth-century England (and continued to face in eighteenth-century France). The individual contenders for incumbency of the roles to which there attached control of the political institutions of eighteenth-century England competed not only strenuously but unscrupulously with one another. But their factional quarrels, shifting alliances, and personal successes or failures did nothing to change the practices defining the roles that gave them control of the state, any more than did those of their nineteenth- and twentieth-century successors.

But what exactly was 'the state'? To some commentators, it was the Crown and its servants. To others, it was Parliament and the courts. To yet others, it was the embodiment of the national will (as one influential civil servant explicitly phrased it in 1847[4]) or, as Matthew Arnold stated in Chapter II of *Culture and Anarchy*, the 'organ of our collective best self, of our national right reason'.[5] Whereas to Cobbett and the many early nineteenth-century radicals who agreed with him, it was 'Old Corruption' or 'The Thing', by 1924 it had become for the statistician Sir Josiah Stamp 'nurse, doctor, chemist, benefactor, guide, philosopher, and friend'.[6] You do not have to be a Hegelian idealist to agree that the state is more than the individuals who make up the ruling elite at any one time and that the behaviour of both rulers and ruled can be influenced by their culturally acquired conceptions of it. But the Conservative conception of it as coterminous with the nation is as one-sided a construction as the Liberal conception of it as a neutral referee between competing interests or the socialist conception of it as the executive committee of the

---

[3] John Brewer, *The Sinews of Power: War, Money and the English State, 1688–1783* (London, 1989), p. 68.

[4] Kay-Shuttleworth as quoted by Peter Mandler, *Aristocratic Government in the Age of Reform: Whigs and Liberals, 1830–1852* (Oxford, 2006), p. 247.

[5] Matthew Arnold, *Culture & Anarchy*, ed. J. Dover Wilson (Cambridge, 1960), p. 97.

[6] Quoted by José Harris, 'Society and the state in twentieth-century Britain', in F. M. L. Thompson, ed., *The Cambridge Social History of Britain 1750–1950*, vol. 3: *Social Agencies and Institutions* (Cambridge, 1990), p. 81.

bourgeoisie. Sociologically, the state is the totality of practices defining the roles to which there attaches institutional power underwritten by coercive sanctions, and it is the variation and selection of those practices that determine its functions. The disagreements among and between England's rulers and ruled about what the state ought or ought not to be doing were partly about how much power should attach to those roles, partly about which roles it should attach to, and partly about where and how it should be applied to monitor, direct, or restrain the behaviour of the ruled.

Neither rulers nor ruled could predict the form into which the state would evolve or how far its reach would extend either at home or abroad. But both could see for themselves that even when governments were most concerned to keep the cost as well as the scope of the state's domestic activities to a minimum, the practices defining the roles of the investigators, inspectors, commissioners, assessors, surveyors, registrars, auditors, receivers, visitors, supervisors, administrators, guardians, and enforcers charged with the implementation of decisions taken by the holders of political office were being both widely diffused and consistently reproduced. However much historians of the period are divided over the measurement of government growth, or alternatively 'shrinkage',[7] during it, no observer of the twentieth-century state could dispute that it became involved in the oversight and control of the ruled to an extent that would have startled the mid-nineteenth-century leader-writers for *The Times* and *The Economist* no less than it would Defoe. But it all came about within a set of political institutions that remained much the same throughout.

The practices whose reproduction and diffusion most obviously enhanced the power of the state were those conventionally subsumed under the heading of 'bureaucracy'. In the Weberian theory of progressive rationalization, the chosen policies, whatever they happen to be, of whoever are the decision-makers in office become easier to implement as the working routines of those hired to implement them approach the ideal type of 'precision, dispatch, clarity, familiarity with the documents, continuity, discretion, uniformity, rigid subordination, savings in friction and in material and personal costs'[8]—an evolutionary trajectory punctuated only by the random appearance of charismatic leaders who fuse the source and agency of political power in their own persons. But that is not a 'how come?' story that can comfortably be fitted to the English case.

At first, although the efficiency of the Excise was explicitly acknowledged by the Commissioners for Examining the Public Accounts appointed by Lord North in the aftermath of defeat in the American War of Independence, its practices were no more widely diffused than the Salt and Leather Offices. The slowly expanding civil service was extensively bureaucratized only under selective pressure from what the

---

[7] Joanna Innes, 'Forms of "government growth", 1780–1830', in David Feldman and Jon Laurence, eds., *Structures and Transformations in Modern British History* (Cambridge, 2011), p. 85.

[8] Max Weber, 'The development of bureaucracy and its relation to law', in W. G. Runciman, ed., *Weber: Selections in Translation* (Cambridge, 1978), p. 350.

Northcote–Trevelyan Report of 1853 was to call the 'great and continuing accumulation of public business'—an accumulation still very modest by the standards of the mid-twentieth century, by which time it could be measured by the miles of shelving annually required to store the departmental files to be preserved in the Public Record Office. By then, what Carlyle had—characteristically—called 'the Continental nuisance called Bureaucracy' had expanded the number of permanent officials in both central and local government far beyond anything envisaged by Northcote or Trevelyan. But the British civil service evolved no more nearly to becoming the quasi-military arm of an authoritarian state on the Prussian model than to becoming the administrative arm of a socialist state on the Fabian one. Bureaucratic practices were successfully resisted by critics of 'officialism', 'functionarism', or, worse still, 'despotism', not all of whose writings and speeches can be discounted as noise. Their diffusion was retarded not simply by ministerial parsimony, parochial self-interest, and popular hostility but by sustained competition from the persistently self-replicating practice of patronage. It would be as much of a mistake to claim that England was governed entirely through bureaucratic practices in the twentieth century as that it had been governed entirely without them in the eighteenth.

By the nineteenth century, contemporary observers were all aware that the patronage formerly exercised by the Crown itself had 'waned' to the point of 'destruction' under the pressures of parliamentary opposition, a perceived need for retrenchment, and hostile comment in the press.[9] But networks of patronage continued to extend outwards and downwards in government, the army, the navy, the Church, the judiciary, and the magistracy from the ruling elite through gatekeepers to so-called 'friends'. The difference was not that patronage was being socially driven to extinction, but that it had now to be made culturally acceptable. The change from the time of Walpole to the time of Gladstone was the outcome of a co-evolutionary sequence in which a combination of mutant religious and secular memes prescribed standards of conduct which brought selective pressure to bear on the practice of patronage in the forms that Walpole and his contemporaries had taken for granted.

Much has been written in this context about the impact of the Evangelical and Utilitarian movements. The extent to which their individual adherents effectively initiated, implemented, or modified specific measures enacted by Parliament has not proved easy to demonstrate to the satisfaction of rival historians. But the historians are agreed that the culturally transmitted influence of both extended far outside the catchment area of theological or philosophical disputation. From the perspective of the sociology of religion, the Evangelicals are a classic example of a sect whose doctrines were an adaptive response to an environment similar to environments which at many other times and places have favoured the diffusion

[9] A. S. Foord, 'The waning of the "influence of the Crown"', *English Historical Review* 62 (1947), p. 506.

of a belief that earthly misfortunes are a punishment which only a regeneration of both private and public virtue can expiate. To the Evangelicals, therefore, those who rejected their injunctions were sinful, whereas to the Utilitarians those who rejected theirs were merely foolish. But by both, as by Dissenters more generally and by the more liberal-minded Anglicans, a role within the state came to be culturally defined less as a personal perquisite than as a public trust.

The incumbents of ministerial roles who more or less ostentatiously distanced themselves from the now questionable practices of which their predecessors had been the carriers were no doubt acting from a variety of motives, and the publicists who inveighed against the morals (or lack of them) of the politicians no doubt had ambitions of their own. Individual Evangelicals might be more preoccupied with eradicating vice than rewarding virtue, Utilitarians more with making government efficient than directing it to the satisfaction of unmet needs, Dissenters more with their lack of social prestige than the misdemeanours of the elite, and liberal Anglicans more with keeping the working classes quiescent than persuading governments to enhance their welfare. Pitt's success in bequeathing an image of probity contrasted, in the eyes of his critics, with much of his actual behaviour, despite his having ostentatiously waived his right to the lucrative sinecure of Clerkship of the Pells. But as always, personal motives, however interesting in themselves, do not explain the reproductive fitness of the mutant memes which generated, in contrast to the standard sociological model, a trickle-*up* effect as beliefs and attitudes in the heads of middle-class carriers, by now '*born* into Dissent',[10] spread to those of their superiors who were ready to agree (or appear to agree) with Hannah More that 'Reformation must begin with the GREAT, or it will never be effectual' and changed their behaviour in consequence.[11]

It was in this new cultural environment that there evolved a selective affinity between the ideals of personal probity and public frugality. It was particularly evident in the environment of the Indian Civil Service, where self-conscious high-mindedness evolved in opposition to the excesses, as they were now seen as being, of the old East India Company. But a similar trajectory was visible in the home civil service among the 'mandarins', as they came to be called, who believed, in the much-quoted (and much-mocked) words of one of them in the twentieth century, that 'the gentlemen in Whitehall really do know better what is good for the people than the people know for themselves'.[12] Such protestations of disinterested benevolence were easy to make fun of as spurious justification of practices at once self-serving and anti-democratic. But whatever conflicting value judgements it might

[10] John Seed, 'Gentlemen Dissenters: the social and political meanings of rational Dissent in the 1770s and 1780s', *Historical Journal* 28 (1985), p. 315.

[11] Quoted by Philip Harling, *The Waning of 'Old Corruption': The Politics of Economical Reform in Britain, 1779–1846* (Oxford, 1996), p. 40.

[12] Douglas Jay, *The Socialist Case* (London, 1937), p. 317.

provoke, a new code of conduct was being diffused across England's political institutions by the two standard mechanisms of cultural selection—frequency-dependence, where the rate of diffusion is a function of its perceived extent, and indirect bias,[13] where the rate of diffusion is a function of its perceived extent among carriers of high prestige.

Yet despite the strength of the cultural reaction against 'Old Corruption', there evolved in response mutant practices of patronage which adapted successfully to the new environment. Their fitness was discernible not only within the institutions of the state but within the factions that evolved out of Whigs and Tories into the Liberal, Conservative, and in due course Labour parties (and also, in due course, within some trade unions whose officers' roles were filled by local 'dynasties'[14]). Neither the Northcote–Trevelyan Report nor the Order in Council of 1870 which laid down open competition as the principle of appointment to roles in government service drove appointment by patronage to extinction. Although both the Home and the Foreign Office gave way after an initial period of refusal, by the time that competitive examination had become the institutionalized method of recruitment, the effect, as one historian puts it, was that 'patronage was not destroyed but passed to the public schools',[15] and, as another puts it, 'Open competition served to perpetuate a type which had already come to the top'.[16] The Indian Civil Service, no less than the home departments and the Foreign Office, drew extensively on graduates of Oxford and Cambridge through practices that turned out to accord surprisingly closely with Gladstone's stated wish to see a strengthening of the links between what he called the 'highly educated class' and the 'higher parts' of the Civil Service.

In any case, whatever lip service was paid to the practice of open competition, the expanding number of recruits into roles in government service made it impossible to institute competitive examinations for them all. In 1914, after Liberal legislation in such fields as health insurance and labour exchanges had come into effect, the answer to a parliamentary question disclosed that over two thousand out of over five thousand permanent, and over nine thousand out of ten thousand temporary, roles had been filled by entrants who had sat no examination whatever, and the Royal Commission on the Civil Service, in its Fourth Report, accepted that such roles were being filled by patronage whose abuse was, in theory, precluded by the replacement of an individual patron with a board or committee. Nor were the topmost roles within the service ever filled, whether from within or from without, other than by patronage. Outsiders were brought in on the personal choice of ministers under Liberal, Conservative, and Labour governments in peacetime as

---

[13] Robert Boyd and Peter J. Richerson, *Culture and the Evolutionary Process* (Chicago, 1985), p. 10.

[14] H. A. Clegg, *A History of British Trade Unions since 1889*, vol. 2: *1911–1933* (Oxford, 1985), p. 451.

[15] J. M. Bourne, *Patronage and Society in Nineteenth-Century England* (London, 1986), p. 34.

[16] Henry Parris, *Constitutional* Bureaucracy: *The Development of British Central Administration since the Eighteenth Century* (London, 1969), p. 159.

well as during the wartime coalitions headed by Lloyd George and Churchill, and they were often empowered to bypass or override established civil servants. Roles within government-created organizations were filled on the nomination of the ministers in power, and politicians who had complained about them when in opposition continued to rely on them or their functional equivalents in their turn. Within the political parties, selection of candidates for safe seats in the House of Commons was as much in the gift of the party leaders in the days of salaried career MPs as it had been in the gift of aristocratic patrons in the days of 'pocket boroughs'. After 1959, the Life Peerages Act brought into Parliament a growing intake of party-appointed placemen (and women) selected entirely by patronage. The 'pressure groups', as they were now called, seeking to influence ministerial policy used personal connections no differently from their eighteenth-century counterparts who had lobbied backbench members of the House of Commons to introduce bills favourable to the interests of themselves and their local associates.

The boundary separating practices culturally defined as corrupt from practices accepted as a necessary and therefore venial aspect of political life remained both fluid and indistinct. Even in 1725, the Lord Chancellor, Lord Macclesfield, had been impeached for selling places and favours, and his argument that he had acted in a manner sanctioned by custom and law was unanimously rejected by his peers. But it did his career no fatal damage. Over the course of the second half of the eighteenth century, a court decision established that bribing a parliamentary elector was a common law offence, the honorary freedmen of a borough were debarred from voting unless they had been freedmen for six months or more, customs officials and tax collectors were disenfranchised altogether, and county electors were required to have been on the register for at least a month. But money and favours were still channelled to voters as before, and Wilberforce is to be found in 1807 defending sinecures on principle on the grounds that their holders 'should not be allowed to fall from the connections and rank to which they had been accustomed'.[17] The further culturally constructed norms of political conduct transmitted by imitation and learning had evolved from those of the time of Walpole, the more apparent became the fitness of patronage. It included, moreover, the practice of exchanging favours in the gift of the ruling elite for cash. Gladstonian rectitude did not preclude the elevation to the House of Lords of a provincial linoleum manufacturer and a Jewish financier in return for donations to Liberal funds—a transaction negotiated with the Liberal Chief Whip and honoured by Rosebery after he succeeded Gladstone as Prime Minister in 1894.

Conclusive evidence of 'corrupt' practices is for obvious reasons difficult for historians to find. But the references that survive in letters, diaries, and memoirs leave no doubt of it, along with the role of 'honours tout' that it brought into being. Assurances such as that given by the banker Horace Farquhar in 1890 that he would 'of course give what was asked for at the next Elections' were unlikely to go

---

[17] Quoted by Harling, *The Waning of 'Old Corruption'*, p. 109.

unheeded.[18] The expansion of the parliamentary franchise made twentieth-century party managers as eager for cash in hand to fund the costs of campaigning as had been the eighteenth-century candidates and their patrons who used it to buy votes outright. The Corrupt and Illegal Practices Act of 1883 did not make contested elections cheaper, but transferred the costs from the constituencies to the centre. Candidates' election spending declined, and attitudes towards electoral morality changed 'dramatically', but there was a 'concomitant increase in spending between elections, and in expenditure by political organisations both locally and nationally'.[19] Politicians and journalists continued to exchange claims and counterclaims in culturally transmitted idioms which ranged across the spectrum of paradiastolic redescription from censorious outrage to cynical levity. The issue was raised more than once in one or other House of Parliament before the First World War only to be shelved. The furore over the Lloyd George Fund in the 1920s was an embarrassment to the Conservatives as well as to Lloyd George himself, but it did not lead to criminal prosecutions. Underneath the noise and clutter, scrutiny was no more than nominal: the principal effect of the passing of the Honours (Prevention of Abuses) Act of 1925 was to oblige 'hopefuls', as one historian calls them, to 'go through the motions of giving to charity and serving the party in a voluntary capacity'.[20] Writing in 2001 about the sale of honours, a Cambridge economist and one-time civil servant concluded that 'This has recently been as scandalous as it was in Lloyd George's time, except that the money from the sales has not gone into the prime minister's pocket, but into the funds of his or her party.'[21]

The roles of the senior officials of the increasingly bureaucratized civil service were, for the most part, immunized against accusations of malpractice. Indeed, tributes to the integrity of the British civil service were, according to one historian, generated on such a scale that 'citations could be multiplied to a degree that would be tedious'.[22] But some revealing episodes came to light. One in 1916 involving clothing contracts with the War Office prompted Parliament to pass a Prevention of Corruption Act in that year, and in 1974 a Royal Commission on Standards of Conduct in Public Life was set up in response to one involving bribes paid to officials by an architect. The Royal Commission pointed out, and the Law Commission subsequently acknowledged, the difficulty of securing a conviction under the Acts of 1899 to 1916. Commentators suspicious of avowals of conformity to 'best' practice did not fail to remark that the Commission was carefully restricted in its terms of reference, that the witnesses on whose testimony it drew were

---

[18] T. A. Jenkins, 'The funding of the Liberal Unionist Party and the Honours System', *English Historical Review* 105 (1990), p. 924.

[19] Kathryn Rix, 'The elimination of corrupt practices in British elections? Reassessing the impact of the Corrupt Practices Act of 1883', *English Historical Review* 123 (2008), pp. 97, 96.

[20] M. Pinto-Duchinsky, *British Political Finance, 1830–1980* (Washington DC, 1981), p. 112.

[21] Robert Neild, *Public Corruption: The Dark Side of Social Evolution* (London, 2002), p. 195.

[22] Philip Harling, *The Modern British State: An Historical Introduction* (Oxford, 2001), p. 206.

predictably disposed to maintain that corruption was a matter of isolated incidents, and that its report 'stayed largely within existing standards and procedures, and placed a great deal of responsibility back on individuals in the public sector'.[23] Local government continued to attract widespread suspicion, particularly where networks of patronage extended from councillors and officials to representatives of commercial interests with an interest in councillors' decisions. Although the sanctions, both cultural and social, against the practice of improper or illegal patronage were strong enough to give its carriers an obvious incentive to conceal it, there is enough evidence on record to show that they were very far from strong enough to drive it to extinction.

Moreover, it was not only the practice of patronage that continued to compete with the bureaucratic practices that were invading the institutions of the state. So too did the practices defining the roles of the members of what came to be called the 'voluntary sector'. This surprised many commentators who expected the twentieth-century state to dispense with both the need and the opportunity for incumbents of non-governmental roles to perform what were now governmental functions. In the eighteenth-century environment, it was unsurprising that there should emerge a generation of self-appointed social reformers if only because 'there was so much to reform'.[24] In the nineteenth-century environment, it was equally unsurprising that when the state's expenditure was being deliberately restricted, voluntary financial contributions to philanthropic causes should be on a scale such that those for London alone were, as *The Times* commented in 1885, greater than the budgets of many European states. There were always critics sceptical of the efficacy of private philanthropy and scornful of the type of person who engaged in it. Nor were the recipients always as grateful as they were expected to be. But there could be no doubt about the scope afforded in the cultural and social environment of both the eighteenth and the nineteenth centuries for 'voluntary sector' practices to be reproduced and diffused outside the state's institutional catchment area. By the mid-twentieth century, it was as apparent to those who welcomed as to those who deplored it that the churches, through which much charitable giving had previously been channelled, had become redundant as dispensers of alms, and that private donors who had previously contributed to the funding of their local hospitals or schools were ceasing to feel the same obligation to do so that their parents and grandparents had felt. Yet the practices defining the roles of the members of the voluntary agencies, far from being driven to extinction, were reproduced in mutant forms no less adaptive than those of the eighteenth and nineteenth centuries had been.

Their continuing fitness offers a clear illustration of the evolutionary process whereby the success of one set of mutations can enhance opportunities for its

---

[23] Alan Doig, *Corruption and Misconduct in British Politics* (Harmondsworth, 1984), p. 342.
[24] Gertrude Himmelfarb, *The Idea of Poverty* (London 1984), p. 38.

competitors. Voluntary associations of like-minded individuals could be funded by the state and thereby combine in their officers' roles the practices of consultation with ministers and officials within it and of pressure-group politics from outside it. But the trade-off was that the more bureaucratic the state was perceived to be, the more the voluntary associations were perceived as having the independence, the flexibility, and the capacity for innovation which the agencies of the state conspicuously lacked. The 'surge of voluntarism' of the 1960s was one behavioural outcome,[25] as were the increasingly active pressure groups seeking to modify or redirect government policy. The services that the voluntary associations offered their clients included help not only in meeting needs for which the state was failing to provide but in making claims against the state whose failures they were. Their manner of doing so and the beliefs and attitudes acted out in it differed increasingly from those which had given the Charity Organization Society and similar bodies, whether church or lay, their reputation for meddlesomeness and condescension. But their members were carriers of both cultural and social mutations whose homologous descent could be traced back through the Victorian philanthropists to the eighteenth-century humanitarians who had taken up the causes of foundlings, prisoners, seafarers, and the aged poor.

Constrained in these ways though they were, bureaucratic practices did nevertheless extend the power of the state beyond what had been foreseen or, when it happened, welcomed by many of the policymakers of whose predecessors' decisions it was the unintended consequence. But if the question is then asked what difference it made to the distribution of political power between the society's constituent roles, the answer has to be: remarkably little. The distances between them in social space remained much what they had been. The roles of the bureaucrats themselves were triply differentiated in the same way that those of their much less numerous predecessors had been between upper-middle seniors interacting on near-equal terms with members of parliament and local elites, middle-middle intermediates exercising authority delegated from their seniors, and lower-middle juniors performing the same routine tasks of recording, copying, and filing. The circumstances of the 'people', and the scale and nature of the resources devoted to their welfare, were very different in the twentieth century from what they had been in the eighteenth. But a single mother refused supplementary benefit by a local official on the grounds of cohabitation under the regulations in force in the 1970s was in much the same position as she would have been in the 1770s under questioning from the parish overseer. Her personal life might be very much easier than that of her eighteenth-century predecessors, but the roles themselves were much the same.

---

[25] Geoffrey Finlayson, *Citizen, State, and Social Welfare in Britain* (Oxford, 1994), p. 304.

II

Voting is a practice whose impact on the distribution of political power in societies of different kinds down the ages and across the globe can hardly be in doubt. Its diffusion involves by definition a process of 'democratization', since it gives to however many of the ruled are granted it some degree of power, however limited, which the rulers had previously reserved for themselves. But when Proudhon, looking at the nineteenth-century French electorate's endorsement of the rule of Louis Napoleon, called universal suffrage a 'device to make the people lie', he was acknowledging, as many observers of other 'democratic' societies were to do, that the vote can so function as to leave the electorate in their roles as citizens not with more power but with less. In England, a society where the quarter or less of adult males empowered to vote for a chosen representative in Parliament in the early eighteenth century had been exposed to inducements and sanctions brought openly to bear on them evolved into a society in which every registered adult who went to a polling station was entitled to cast a ballot in secret for his or her preferred candidate. But why was the result not the modal change in the nature and distribution of political power that many contemporaries had hoped for and many others had feared?

The story has been told by observers of different persuasions in predictably different ways. There was a Conservative story in which responsible statesmen made a series of prudent accommodations in accordance with long-established English traditions. There was a Liberal story in which those of the people qualified by their own good sense were willingly accorded the privilege of political participation by enlightened parliamentarians. There was a socialist story in which bourgeois politicians made fraudulent concessions to the better-off workers under what Engels called 'theoretical camouflage, even justification, which, naturally, are feasible only by means of sophisms, distortions and, finally, underhand tricks'.[26] But from a social-evolutionary perspective, it is a story of fitful diffusion of the practice of voting for rival candidates to represent local constituents in a national legislature in the course of which each such extension made a further one more probable. The individual manoeuvres and stratagems that led up to the successive reform bills have understandably fascinated generations of political historians. Nobody knows how different the story would have been if Wellington, Peel, Gladstone, Disraeli, Salisbury, Asquith, and Lloyd George had not acted (or declined to act) as and when they did. But once they were enacted, they made further extensions of the franchise more probable, not because they did so much as because they did so little to change the existing distribution of political power.

From the 1820s onwards, the association in public debate of 'middle-class' reformism with extension of the parliamentary franchise led some observers to

---

[26] Karl Marx and Frederick Engels, *On Britain*[2] (Moscow, 1962), p. 529.

conclude that a fundamental transfer of power was taking place. In 1889, Sidney Webb saw the 'great' Reform Bill of 1832 as having brought about the supersession of 'aristocratic rule' with the 'reign of the middle-class'.[27] But that, to the extent that it was not a sociological contradiction in terms, meant only that there had been some narrowing of social distance between 'middle' and 'upper', some increase in individual mobility from the first to the second, and some greater disposition on the part of both Conservative and Liberal governments to have regard to industrial and commercial interests. If middle-class voters ever thought of themselves as a political 'class' acting as such, it was not as a body of electors now empowered to dictate to the makers of public policy what it should be, but one conscious of needing to be safeguarded against policymakers too sympathetic, as it seemed to many of them, to working-class interests and demands. Hence the middle-class 'defence groups' which 'sprang up all over the land' after 1906,[28] and the appearance, after the First World War, of Middle Class Unions and later still, under the then Labour government, of a short-lived Middle Class Association formed in 1974. But these had no impact whatever on government policy or anything else.

Far from following a steady or even discernible trend, the results of the general elections after the 'leap in the dark' of 1867 were all as unpredictable as those both before and after. This was as true of the elections that followed the enfranchisement of the working class as of those that followed the enfranchisement of the middle classes, and as true of those that came in quick succession in 1922, 1923, and 1924 as of those that were delayed for as long as those of 1918 and 1945. It was equally true of Edward Heath's victory in 1970, Margaret Thatcher's in 1979, and John Major's in 1992. Each had its own story in which accidents of timing, electoral geography, external events, the state of the economy, and the strategies and tactics of the party leaders all played their parts: there is, for example, little doubt that Disraeli's dissolution in 1880 was as ill-judged as Gladstone's in 1874, or that Gladstone's commitment to the cause of Irish Home Rule split the Liberal vote, or that Michael Foot's leadership of the Labour Party was an electoral disaster. But whatever the contingent causes of the successive outcomes, and however dramatic their effects on the careers of individual politicians, they had no more influence on the distribution of political power within English society than had the results of the elections in which a small, venal, and wholly unrepresentative minority of the adult population had cast their votes in full view of observers in a position to bribe or intimidate them.

Although it was not until the second half of the twentieth century that sociologists had available to them the techniques with which to analyse in detail the correlates of party preference and quantify the extent of cross-cutting allegiances, contemporary observers in the late nineteenth and early twentieth century were already well aware of the diversity and complexity of the local environments within

---

[27] Sidney Webb, 'Historic', in *Fabian Essays*[6] (London, 1962), p. 71.
[28] G. R Searle, *A New England? Peace and War 1866–1918* (Oxford, 2004), p. 395.

which the number of working-class men admitted to the role of parliamentary elector had been increased to some two out of three in England and Wales by the time of the First World War. Disraeli was—characteristically—exaggerating when he wrote to his friend Lady Chesterfield that the measures passed by his administration after 1874 would 'gain and retain for the Conservatives the lasting affection of the working classes'.[29] The willingness of the Conservative Party to take account of working-class interests was only one of many influences that explain its continuing ability to win elections against both the Liberal and later the Labour Party. But the combination of sometimes disparate and sometimes overlapping environmental pressures—regional, religious, occupational, and familial—which historians have documented in detail secured for the Conservatives a significant minority of the working-class vote even after the connections between the franchise and ownership or rental of household property had been weakened or abolished and the registration of working-class electors was no longer constrained by either their poverty or the frequency of their moves from one rented living space to another.

A working-class elector who voted Conservative might, as detailed local studies have shown, be motivated by anything from an occupational interest in the arms industry or the drinks trade, to familial loyalty to a popular and long-serving MP, to a combination of religious and patriotic hostility to the other side. The diversity of pressures acting on working-class voters in their different constituencies was such as to invalidate any explanation resting on a presupposition that for them not to vote for the party claiming to speak in their name was a form of 'deviant' behaviour. Only the unusual environment of a homogeneous self-enclosed working-class community, whose members experienced severe economic hardship peculiar to a dominant local industry, favoured the diffusion and reproduction of atypical memes and practices in the process familiar to evolutionary theorists as 'niche construction': in the twentieth century, during the interwar depression, Mardy in Monmouthshire was one of a handful of 'little Moscows', as they were nicknamed, where communists were able to 'preserve and take advantage of the sense of cohesion and common purpose that was a feature of such mining communities',[30] and through existing associations including the local Miners Lodge and Workmen's Institute build up an unusually large and loyal following. But such niches never amounted to more than a handful. Even under universal adult suffrage at times of high unemployment, the overwhelming majority of the working-class electorate voted for parties that competed for their allegiance by appealing to their interests within a set of accepted practices which defined the roles of the competitors and the institutional rules which dictated how the competition was run. It was the same game that it had been two hundred years earlier.

[29] Robert Blake, *Disraeli* (London, 1966), p. 260.
[30] Stuart Macintyre, *Little Moscows: Communism and Working-class Militancy in Inter-war Britain* (London, 1980), p. 44.

To call the periodic constituency-based contests for seats in the House of Commons a 'game' is a literal statement of sociological fact, however different the histories of the various constituencies. As a distinctive category of behaviour within sociological theory, the practices by which games are defined have three common features, irrespective of the characters and motives of the individual players: first, they are serious—they are more than merely 'play'; second, they are inherently competitive—there are always winners and losers; third, they are ritualistic—they conform to conventional cultural norms acquired by imitation and learning which supplement the imposed practices defining the roles of the players of the game as such. Ostrogorski in 1902 characterized the emotions aroused during electoral campaigns as 'decidedly of a sporting character', and went on to recall that 'Many a time at elections I fancied myself at the Derby',[31] much as Salvador de Madariaga called it 'the sporting instinct of the British people, which leads them to view political campaigns as a match between rival teams'.[32] The losers all knew that in a few years, and perhaps sooner, there would be a rematch in which the score might be decisively different. Furthermore, both sides knew that the winning candidates would be taking their places in a House of Commons whose business was conducted through strictly refereed debates after which measures were either passed or rejected by majority vote, much as was done through similar practices in the trade unions and voluntary associations. It might be argued that not too much implication of moderation should be read into the reproduction of sporting terms and images, since these could equally be diffused and reproduced in an environment where physical violence was directed against members of rival factions (as, in some constituencies, it continued to be into the late nineteenth and early twentieth centuries). But the commitment among the elite to the culturally transmitted idea of fair play was strikingly illustrated when the first Labour government took office. Attlee, who remembered George V as 'a very fair-minded man', summarized the King's attitude to it as 'they are Socialists, I know, but they must have their chance'[33]—a sentiment explicitly avowed by the King himself when he wrote in November 1924 that 'they ought to be given a chance & ought to be treated fairly'.[34]

But as the plays and replays of the game returned one or another party to power, the mutant practices that facilitated the registration and turnout of new incumbents of the role of parliamentary elector in the environment of what was coming to be called 'mass politics' brought into being the increasingly influential roles of local party organizers and agents. Informal associations of like-minded supporters evolved into formal organizations like the National Union of Conservative and

[31] M. Ostrogorski, *Democracy and the Organization of Political Parties*, vol. 1 (London, 1902), p. 466.
[32] Quoted by Maurice Duverger, *Political Parties: Their Organization and Activity in the Modern State* (London, 1954), p. 217.
[33] Frank Field, ed., *Attlee's Great Contemporaries: The Politics of Character* (London, 2009), p. 72.
[34] Harold Nicolson, *King George the Fifth: His Life and Reign* (London, 1952), p. 389.

Constitutional Associations, the National Liberal Association, and the Primrose League. The Conservative, Liberal, and in due course Labour parties all bore out the implication of the subtitle that Robert Michels gave to his book *Political Parties* which was published in 1915: *A Sociological Study of the Oligarchical Tendency of Modern Democracy.* The party managers were under increasing pressure to adapt to the need for candidates to appeal across sectarian divisions, particularly in constituencies where the result might go either way. But the electors who duly turned out at the polling stations in their local constituencies were casting votes for candidates whom they had not directly chosen, who were advocating policies in which they had had no direct say, and whose behaviour once elected they were not in a position to control.

The rival parties' success in bringing the maximum number of supporters to the ballot box varied both from constituency to constituency and from election to election. Turnout was likely to be higher where and when the result looked likely to be close and there were clear-cut differences of policy between the contestants. But after no election could it be claimed that the nineteenth-century reformers' vision of a transfer of power from the state to the people through extension of the franchise was being realized as they had conceived it. There were visible changes in both the volume and the content of legislation reflecting working-class concerns, and in the number of parliamentary candidates of working-class origin. There was also a visible difference in the increased degree of control exercised by the party leaders and whips over their MPs: the role of the independent-minded member who would be described in the nineteenth century as 'sitting loose to party' was driven extinct. But the practices by which the role of 'MP' was defined were much the same as they had been before the electorate was expanded, the ballot made secret, and the cost of electioneering met from party rather than individual funds.

III

There was, at the same time, one other mutation in the practices defining the roles that governed the relations between rulers and ruled which did amount to an inter-systactic transfer of power. But it too was a change within the existing mode, not of it. Trade union leaders who in the 1830s and 1840s would have been exposed to the risk of arrest, imprisonment, and transportation were by the 1880s occupying roles close to or even within the ruling elite. Nobody at the time of the Combination Laws Repeal Act of 1824 foresaw how soon union leaders and officials would be not only standing for Parliament but being invited to serve on Royal Commissions and admitted in increasing numbers to the roles of alderman, councillor, magistrate, school board member, poor law guardian, borough auditor, and education committee member. That in no way precluded them from acting in their roles as officials and negotiators in ways directed to modifying or abolishing practices which they saw as perpetuating the unacceptable inequalities of reward and condition to which those whom they represented were subjected. Some remained as hostile as ever to their employers, and some of the stoppages that they engineered were both bitter and protracted. But it is, as always, necessary to focus on the practices rather than the people. Whatever the individual successes or failures of the more and less intransigent, the changes in their roles favoured the reproduction and diffusion of strategies of negotiation backed by the threat of selective and calculated withdrawals of labour rather than strategies of coordinated illegal activity backed by the threat of recourse to violence.

For as long as organizing a strike had exposed the organizers to a charge of criminal conspiracy, the roles of the trade union officers had been constrained within the legal limits governing the friendly societies and box clubs. That had not prevented workers from striking for higher wages in their ostensible roles as friendly society members, as for example the breeches-makers did in 1793, or from subscriptions being used to fund what was, in effect, strike pay. But once Parliament and the courts had legitimated the non-violent forms of collective behaviour which came to be labelled euphemistically as 'industrial action' and excluded attempts at peaceful persuasion from the legal definition of 'watching and besetting', consequential mutation of the practices defining the institutional relationships between government ministers and union leaders brought them into direct and increasingly habitual interaction with one another. Only when the state's authority as such was held to be under threat were the means of coercion mobilized against the unions, as in the general strike of 1926 and the miners' strike of 1984–85. It did not become a state that would concede to the unions whatever they might demand, whatever the political party in office. But nor did it become a state that gave them any reason to fear for their power to negotiate the terms and conditions of their members' employment and call them out as and when they judged it to their advantage.

The changed roles of the trade union leaders did not, on the other hand, do anything to weaken the long-standing resentment among the working classes of the practices through which the state intruded into their daily lives, even where, as for example with compulsory vaccination, the intrusion was demonstrably for their benefit. Compulsory schooling was not welcomed by parents for whom it came at a material cost in family income foregone even after it was made free. Demolition of substandard housing was not thought of as a benefit by occupants for whom no preferable alternative was available. Government-sponsored annuities were interpreted as an attempt to usurp the functions of the friendly societies. Labour exchanges were suspect as either a prelude to compulsory direction or a device to help employers find strike-breakers. As Lloyd George was made aware in 1911, there were many working-class people who preferred buying their industrial insurance and death benefits from the 'man from the Pru' to being compulsorily enrolled in a national system. The trade unions were for a long time explicitly opposed to family allowances as affording employers a pretext for reducing wages. Licensing laws were either opposed outright or thought acceptable only if administered by democratically elected working men. The desire for independence from the state extended also, in England and Wales (Scotland being different in this as in so many ways), to the Anglican Church which was identified with it. The memetic descent of these attitudes and beliefs can be traced back to the Levellers of the seventeenth century, and it helps to explain, among other things, the seemingly paradoxical recurrence, in the environment of an increasingly urban society, of periodic campaigns from the Chartists onwards for rural smallholdings cultivated by self-sufficient producers.

There is one obvious qualification to be made to the persistence of the resentment of the state among the working classes—their perception of it as a potential ally in their struggles with their employers for a larger share of their employers' profits. They might sometimes acknowledge that the payment of their wages depended on the solvency of the enterprises to which they were selling their labour: the *Poor Man's Guardian* of 26 April 1834 conceded that 'Thousands of employers can barely exist at the present rate of profits. Affect these profits by ever so slight an increase in wages, and they are ruined.'[35] Although 'ever so slight' may be an exaggeration, it has been estimated from the *London Gazette* and the 'docket books' held in the Public Records Office that 33,000 businesses failed in the course of the eighteenth century,[36] and after 1780 bankruptcies rose to a peak of over 3,000 in the disastrous year of 1826 alone. Four out of every five Manchester manufacturers failed between 1780 and 1815. But to many trade union negotiators, profits, and particularly distributed profits, were wages that their members were being denied. The unending fight for improved terms and conditions of work suggested both to some wage-earners and to an increasing number of commentators sympathetic to their cause that their interests would be better protected if the means of production were to be taken over by the state. 'This', as a historian of nationalization as a political issue put it in 1965, 'is how socialism has been defined in Britain by pioneer socialists who really meant what they said',[37] and as the Labour Party overtook the Liberals as the alternative party of government to the Conservatives the formula enshrined in Clause 4 of its 1918 constitution became a matter of more than academic debate both within and outside of the Labour movement. But beneath the noise and clutter, the trade unionists of 1918 were no more committed to socialism than those of 1913 had been. The enthusiasts for Clause 4 were the Fabians and guild socialists, not the union leaders for whom a capitalist mode of production provided their *raison d'être*. In the view of the historian of the evolution of the Labour Party between 1910 and 1924, it is the inclusion of the 'socialist objective' as in part a 'sop to the professional bourgeoisie' that 'helps to explain why the trade unions swallowed it as easily as they did'.[38]

[35] Quoted by Gareth Stedman Jones, *Languages of Class: Studies in English Working Class History 1832–1982* (Cambridge, 1983), p. 145.

[36] Julian Hoppit, *Risk and Failure in British Business 1700–1800* (Cambridge, 1987), p. 42.

[37] E. Eldon Barry, *Nationalisation in British Politics: The Historical Background* (London, 1965), p. 13.

[38] Ross McKibbin, *The Evolution of the Labour Party 1910–1924* (Oxford, 1974), p. 97.

The Liberal spokesman Ramsay Muir pointed out the inescapable trade-off as starkly as anyone when he said in 1925 that under public ownership 'The State would be the enemy against whom the workers were fighting'.[39] Some trade unionists saw in nationalization a potential for the state to subsidize the industry in question at taxpayers' expense and thereby pay higher wages than a privately owned company could afford (or, in the case of the mines, keep open uneconomic pits which a privately owned company would have no choice but to close). But here, the trade-off was that the state could afford a protracted withdrawal of labour which might have compelled a privately owned company to come to terms. How much difference did it make to the postal workers that the Post Office, with a quarter-million employees at the outbreak of the First World War and four-fifths of its postmen unionized, had always been a nationalized industry? Or to the workers in the royal dockyards and the ordnance factories? Or to the railwaymen and miners after the Second World War? The conclusion of a team of sociologists studying the lives and conditions of mineworkers following nationalization was that 'for the vast majority' their relation to the direction of work 'has not changed one iota'[40]—a conclusion that could equally be applied to municipal 'gas and water' socialism which, whatever the claims that Sidney Webb made for it, was no more, if no less, than 'the simple substitution of private investment with ratepayer investment'.[41] The practices defining the workers' roles as such—wage payment and managerial direction—went on being reproduced as before.

To some of the advocates of nationalization, its attraction was not the prospect of expropriating the current owners of the means of production, distribution, and exchange, so much as the prospect of an institutional transfer of power to workers or their chosen representatives who would assume control of the direction of the enterprises employing them. The shop steward who was reported to the Ministry of Munitions in 1918 as saying to his works manager, 'You have not much longer to run, and we are going to turn you out. We have the men ready to take your places', wasn't merely joking.[42] But a shop-floor worker who moves into the role of director or manager ceases to be a worker in the same sense of the word where a complex enterprise requires the coordination and supervision of a numerous and diversified workforce of wage and salary earners. Workers can of course be appointed or elected to the role of director on either a public or private company board. The question of the composition of boards of directors under 'socialization' (i.e. nationalization) was discussed at length by the TUC and Labour Party executive in 1931, and in 1975 the TUC assured a Committee of Inquiry on Industrial Democracy set up under a Labour government that 'there is no necessary

---

[39] Quoted by Michael Freeden, *Liberalism Divided: A Study in British Political Thought, 1914–1939* (Oxford, 1986), p. 196.

[40] Norman Dennis et al., *Coal is Our Life* (London, 1956), p. 76.

[41] D. Matthews, 'Laissez-faire and the London gas industry in the nineteenth century: another look', *Economic History Review* 39 (1986), p. 263.

[42] Bernard Waites, *A Class Society at War: England 1914–18* (Leamington Spa, 1987), p. 205.

contradiction between board level representation and collective bargaining'.[43] But the same individual cannot act simultaneously in two institutional roles defined by inherently adversarial practices. Even if the workforce is given statutory power to vote directors out and replace them with others more to their liking, it will not drive extinct the practices by which both their and the directors' roles are defined. Were 'worker-directors' to be imposed by statute (as in Sweden, which the Committee visited), they might or might not influence the decisions taken by company boards in the direction of readier concessions to employees' interests. But the roles of the employees for whose interests they were arguing would still be the same.

'Workers' control' was for many years a topic of debate among both Labour Party intellectuals and trade union leaders. But much of it was no more than noise. When and where the practices defining the roles that would put it into effect were explicitly addressed, it became immediately apparent that those practices, whoever their individual carriers, would be in direct competition with others which were among the proclaimed objectives of the Labour movement. If the workers—whether or not defined to include workers by brain as well as by hand—were to have power of decision over the allocation of the surpluses generated by the enterprise employing them, wage increases not matched by increases in productivity would necessarily be at the expense of their fellow-citizens in their roles of consumer or taxpayer (or both). Some trade unionists not only recognized but endorsed this. In 1936, the General Council of the TUC envisaged that a nationalized coal industry would set its prices at whatever was required to maintain the miners' wages at an acceptable level and be subsidized as necessary for the purpose. But how was this to be reconciled with the 'Socialist Commonwealth' of the Webbs in which there would be no conflict between sectional interests and the interests of society as a whole? Much of the Labour rhetoric was no more tendentious than the Conservative rhetoric in which 'responsible' trade unionism meant simply that negotiations on wages and conditions were to leave alone the prerogative of employers to manage their businesses and allocate their surpluses at their unfettered discretion. But it ignored the characteristics of a mode of production whose large workforces, complex division of labour, advanced technology, and graded managerial roles made workers' control, as opposed to bureaucratic control by agents of the state acting in the workers' name, sociologically impossible.

Throughout the twentieth century, therefore, the practices defining the relationship between the state and the trade unions were collaborative to the extent that the unions abided by the laws enacted by the state, and adversarial to the extent that any laws threatening free collective bargaining and the right to strike were resisted, not least when the state itself was the shareholder. There were still, both within and outside of the unions' membership, advocates of the use of the organized withdrawal of labour in pursuit of overtly political aims—a strategy with a well-documented history of its own which includes William Benbow's proposal

---

[43] *Report of the Committee of Inquiry on Industrial Democracy* (Cmnd 6706, London, 1977), p. 124.

of a 'general holiday' to be taken by the 'industrious classes', the Sorelian vision of an insurrectionary 'general strike' which would deprive the state of its ability to govern, and A. J. Cook, the miners' leader, shouting (as Beatrice Webb put it in her diary for 3 May 1927) that there must be 'a fortnight's cessation of work to coerce the Government'.[44] But for any such strategy to be successfully pursued, it had to outweigh the negative trade-off to its carriers who would have to bear the costs of challenging the mode of coercion as such when their individual interests would be better served either by free-riding or by local collaboration in pursuit of sectional arms.

Syndicalism was not wholly without influence. Noah Ablett's pamphlet *The Miners' Next Step* of 1912 influenced the young Aneurin Bevan among others and, according to the Webbs, 'created some sensation in the capitalist world'.[45] But underneath the noise of class-war rhetoric and clutter of industrial disputes, no evidence has been found by historians of the period that would justify either the hopes of left-wing observers or the fears of right-wing ones. The hostility of the rank and file was directed not against the institutions of the state but against the employers who were holding down wages and the union officials who were too ready, as the rank and file saw it, to settle with the employers on terms less favourable than more determined resistance could have won for them. As the practices defining the roles of the union leaders became increasingly bureaucratic, they could not but become increasingly likely to mobilize the rank and file against them—a trajectory which reached the point, in 1980, of the expulsion from the TUC of a union representing Labour Party employees to whom '"Management" became "the enemy" almost as though they were the Welsh coal owners of the 1920s, and even though in this period the NEC shared the same Leftwing perspectives as many of the union activists'.[46]

One consequence was the increasing adaptiveness of the practices defining the role of 'shop steward'. But its sociological significance was exaggerated by commentators from both ends of the spectrum of political opinion. After the Second World War, when governments as well as employers were concerned about the effect of unofficial strikes on the productivity of British industry, convenors were sometimes suspected of being the carriers of practices by which the authority of both managers and unions would be undermined as part of a concerted political attack on the capitalist state. The docks were one environment seen as particularly vulnerable to penetration by 'agitators': Bevan himself supported recourse to the Emergency Powers Act of 1920 to deal with a potentially damaging dispute in 1948. Another was the motor vehicle industry, which was singled out as being of particular interest to the Royal Commission on Industrial Relations of 1965

---

[44] Margaret Cole, ed., *Beatrice Webb's Diary 1924–1932* (London, 1956), p. 140.
[45] Sidney and Beatrice Webb, *The History of Trade Unionism*[2] (London, 1920), p. 657.
[46] Lewis Mishkin, *The Contentious Alliance: Trade Unions and the Labour Party* (Edinburgh, 1991), p. 589.

because of the role in the larger plants of shop stewards thought to be seeking to disrupt production as part of a deliberate campaign of subversion. But however ready the general body of unionized car workers was to stop work in defiance of union-negotiated procedures, and however vehemently their behaviour was deplored by employers and the right-wing press, they remained almost unanimously impervious to the efforts of communist (or sometimes Trotskyist) organizers to recruit them to their cause. At the time when, in the 1970s, union membership was approaching its peak, a team of sociologists examining what they called the 'fragmentary' class structure looked in vain for evidence to suggest that the 'polarisation of the working class into a revolutionary force' was anything other than 'very unlikely'[47]—a conclusion which the following decades did nothing whatever to disconfirm.

It is of course true that, however impervious to the rhetoric of Marxism, the working-class electorate ceased to identify its interests with the Liberal Party. The sequence of unforeseen events that led the Labour Party to displace it as the alternative party of government to the Conservatives has intrigued political historians no less than the story of franchise reform itself. But it is a symptom, not a cause, of the underlying evolutionary process. No historian has claimed that the Liberalism of a Liberal Party, whoever its leaders, which claimed to represent the fully enfranchised working class of the twentieth century, could be the same as the 'peace and retrenchment' and 'night-watchman' Liberalism of the 'People's William'. As the entire male working class was enfranchised and its employers came increasingly to identify with the Conservatives, even a strong and united Liberal Party whose leaders were willing explicitly to appeal to working-class interests and field working-class candidates in working-class constituencies could not have prevented the formation of *an* independent Labour Party (if not *the* Independent Labour Party formed in Bradford in 1893) by which it would be overtaken. But few working-class Labour voters then, or ever, envisaged a society in which a single-party state would control and direct the mode of production in the name of the ideological hegemony of the proletariat. However much it suited its Conservative opponents to pretend otherwise, the Labour Party posed no more threat than a successfully revivified Liberal Party would have done to the practices of a form of 'democracy' that socialists would continue to denounce as 'bourgeois'.

The Labour Party's moderation (or, in left-wing paradiastole, timidity or even cowardice) did not prevent it from gaining electorally from its association with a loosely defined 'socialist objective' which had a selective affinity with memes in the heads of middle-class as well as working-class voters. A long sequence of cultural selection made Labour, as the saying went, a very broad church. The revolutionary socialism of the far Left evolved alongside the ethical socialism of Ruskin and his followers, the Christian socialism of left-leaning clerics, and attachment in the name of socialism to causes including not only nationalization of industry but land

---

[47] K. Roberts et al., *The Fragmentary Class Structure* (London, 1977), p. 99.

reform, disarmament, redistributive taxation, food subsidies, full employment, economic planning, free health care, public works programmes, and abolition of fee-paying schools. If 'Socialism' meant a national health service free at the point of delivery, free primary and secondary schooling for all children, and old age pensions funded out of general taxation, many Conservatives were socialists too. But if it meant rationing, permits, wage restraint, 'snoopers', and 'red tape', many Labour voters were as opposed to it as Conservative ones. The trade-off was that both before and after the Second World War the Conservative Party, by 'democratizing the politics of anti-expropriation',[48] could assemble an electoral alliance united in opposition to any policy or programme that could be tarred with the socialist label and to use that label to disparage the record of Labour governments. The practices defining the roles that would constitute an authentically socialist mode faced not only a long history of working-class hostility to the state and a non-negotiable commitment to free collective bargaining and the right to strike, but also a tradition of working-class cooperation closer to the ideals of Mill than of Marx. The associational activities of the majority of manual workers and their families were of a studiously apolitical kind—to say nothing of the widespread and well-attested dislike and suspicion of middle-class socialists on the part of manual workers who wanted to send their own representatives to Parliament to defend their interests for themselves.

IV

It was never denied by even the most vehement of the mid-Victorian protagonists of *laissez-faire* that some things need to be done that only the state can do in addition to preserving or restoring public order, defending the realm, and projecting the nation's military and naval power overseas. It was no more than it had been in the eighteenth century a 'weak' state, even if the practices through which successive governments extended their control over the people evolved time and again through mutations whose sociological effects were disproportionately small in relation to policymakers' stated aims. In a rare example to the contrary, by 1855 the emigrant passenger 'was, in law, protected up to the hilt and the trade quite remarkably regulated' (perhaps in the hope of restricting emigration by making it more expensive).[49] But the statutes passed to protect the children who worked as chimney sweeps notoriously failed to do so despite the many sympathetic (not to say sentimental) descriptions of their plight. Legislation to control working conditions in mines could not hope to achieve its proclaimed objective when the role of inspector carried no effective sanctions, the mine owners could easily afford the

---

[48] David Jarvis, 'British Conservatism and class politics in the 1920s', *English Historical Review* 111 (1996), p. 82.

[49] W. L. Burn, *The Age of Equipoise: A Study of the Mid-Victorian Generation* (London, 1964), p. 166.

penalties, and there were in any case so few inspectors that their inspections could not be other than 'infrequent and desultory'.[50] The Apprentices and Servants Act of 1857, prompted by the scandalous ill-treatment of a pauper servant, was not going to safeguard all the others any better than the Obscene Publications Act of the same year was going to suppress pornography. Nor could a Lunacy Commission, statutorily empowered to inspect both licensed institutions and private houses where the mentally ill were detained, do much to alter behaviour when its salaried members consisted of three doctors and three lawyers.

It is the New Poor Law of 1834 that stands out in the writings of all historians of the period as both the most determined and in some ways most successful attempt by the rulers to impose on the ruled a novel set of practices with—it was hoped—specific and predictable effects on their behaviour. The fear and hatred of the workhouses was never in doubt. But the diffusion of the novel practices encoded in the legislation was constrained by the reactions not only of supposedly idle or improvident labourers to whom outdoor relief was now to be denied, but also of defenders of their own long-standing practices of investigation and dispensation through which the parishes had traditionally exercised local responsibility for the aged, the infirm, and the poor. The selective pressures generated by an increasing population within an increasingly urban environment, an increasing rate of internal migration, and an increasing disparity between the resources of different localities and regions were unmistakably apparent. But they did not displace the practices that ensured that recourse to the means of coercion to influence the behaviour of the ruled would be applied locally and that the legislation required would be permissive rather than mandatory. Centralization was, in the much-quoted words of Dickens's Mr Podsnap, 'not English'. To cite just three examples, the Public Health Act of 1875 was still full of permissive clauses; in the debates on the Workmen's Compensation Act of 1897, Chamberlain came out against compulsory insurance as unacceptably bureaucratic; and in 1908, when old age pensions began to be paid out of central government funds, legislation was also passed allowing but not requiring local subsidies to village post offices and local loans to fund purchases of rural smallholdings. In 1908, indeed, the first pensions were administered by voluntary committees whose members included both representatives of the friendly societies and local clergymen. And in the Education Act of 1944, the power attaching to the newly created role of Minister of Education extended to requiring local authorities to submit plans for reform but not to imposing them.

As always, it is difficult to sift out from the noise the culturally transmitted information that did significantly affect behaviour. But there is no mistaking the frequency of appeals to a memetic lineage congenitally resistant to what the sanitary

---

[50] P. W. J. Bartrip, 'State intervention in mid-nineteenth century Britain', *Journal of British Studies* 23 (1983), p. 77.

reformer Sir John Simon called the 'novel virtue of an imperative mood'.[51] The effect on the evolution of England's political institutions was a series of victories for permissive legislation and the self-replicating practices and roles that went with it. The mid- to late nineteenth- and early twentieth-century state could encourage. It could facilitate. It could require proposals to be prepared and submitted. It could insist on confirmation of local by-laws by a central department. It could pass (or obstruct) private bills giving local authorities powers not available to them under general legislation. It could incentivize, as when in 1856 police forces certified as efficient received grants to help cover the cost of pay and uniforms, or under the Code of 1861 grants were paid to schools on the basis of attendance and examination records. It could subsidize, as when in 1874 allowances per head were paid for the transfer of pauper lunatics from workhouses to asylums. But although there attached to ministerial roles statutory power to intervene by default when a local authority was deemed to have failed to exercise its functions as it should, there did not evolve, neither then nor thereafter, the practices and roles that would have led to a general replacement of elected local authorities and their officials by appointees and officials of central government. Nor did central government abolish the 'virtually unaltered medieval administrative units' with which it 'sped the country into the twentieth century'.[52] Counties, boroughs, county boroughs, districts, parishes, unions, and boards which were the products of separate path-dependent evolutionary sequences of variation and selection jostled, argued, and competed with one another under the oversight but not direction of incumbents of ministerial roles who could neither circumvent nor subordinate them.

This type of relationship between centre and periphery is familiar to comparative sociologists in examples that range all the way from small tribal chiefdoms to global empires. Indeed, it was all too familiar to the ministers and officials responsible for the administration of the British Empire who were forced to recognize the extent of their dependence on local elites whom they had to conciliate as much as command. There were the same trade-offs of practices between direct recourse to coercive sanctions, appeals to ideologically sanctioned prestige, and deployment of economic inducements and penalties, and between practices adaptive at the centre but mal-adaptive at the periphery and vice versa. The widening of the local franchise (including the admission to it of widowed or unmarried rate-paying women) and the creation of new bodies such as district and parish councils and the London County Council created an environment in which the competition for power between the political parties was variously cross-cut by religious differences over education, conflicts of both principle and policy over poor relief, and disagreements over the advantages (or not) of municipal trading. There was no more uniformity

---

[51] Quoted by John Prest, *Liberty and Locality: Parliament, Permissive Legislation, and Ratepayer Democracy in the Nineteenth Century* (Oxford, 1990), p. 210.

[52] P. J. Waller, *Town, City, and Nation: England 1850–1914* (Oxford, 1983), p. 249.

of practices between one region or district and another than there had been a century earlier.

The Association of Municipal Corporations which was created in 1872 and the County Councils Association which evolved out of the Association of County Clerks in 1890 had different relationships with ministers and central officials as well as different interests and priorities from one another. After the Local Government Act of 1888, many urban communities became county boroughs independent of the counties in which they were located, thereby depriving them of significant rateable value, while palpable mismatches between local boundaries and supra-local administrative imperatives could only be resolved by petitions to Parliament for special legislation. The Local Government Board created in 1871 brought within its remit a range of locally managed services which covered not only health and housing but workhouses, highways, food and drugs, and in due course old age pensions. But it operated, in the words of its historian, 'compromised, partial and pragmatic controls, which largely failed to secure a grip on local policy'.[53] Each local authority operated in its own environment in which different outcomes were influenced by different selective pressures favouring different practices imposed through the quasi-random decisions of different policymakers of different persuasions. Of these, Chamberlain in Birmingham was the most controversial, and has accordingly attracted the most attention from historians. But in the event, the impasse was resolved, to the extent that it was, not by the evolution of statutory prescriptions for what local authorities were to be compelled or forbidden to do but by the evolution of the fiscal practices of the state.

In any sociological comparison of the nature and extent of the power of different types of state, however classified, the practices through which they extract resources from their citizens or subjects need to be identified and their adaptiveness assessed. I have commented already on how the excise and the land tax between them enabled the eighteenth-century British state to function for the rulers' purposes as effectively as it did. But there is always a trade-off between practices that maximize yield and practices that minimize evasion. On one historian's estimate, 40 per cent of Britain's national income between 1700 and 1910 avoided tax by legal or illegal means.[54] At the close of the first decade of the twenty-first century, the Treasury was estimating an annual shortfall in tax receipts of over £40 billion from fraud, evasion, and underdeclaration, despite the categories of income from which tax was by then being deducted at source. Yet from the eighteenth century through to the twenty-first, the state continued to tax by agreement rather than force, both centrally and locally. The practices by which the different forms of tax were assessed and levied evolved through the standard process of variation and selection in a

---

[53] Christine Bellamy, *Administering Central-Local Relations 1871–1919: The Local Government Board in its Fiscal and Cultural Context* (Manchester, 1988), pp. 155–6.

[54] Patrick K. O'Brien, 'The political economy of British taxation, 1600–1815', *Economic History Review* 41 (1988), p. 6.

sequence so erratic, so inconsistent, and so haphazard that its leading historian is willing to endorse the verdict that by the last quarter of the twentieth century it could plausibly be said that 'No one would design such a system on purpose and nobody did' and that it demonstrated 'how seemingly rational individual decisions can have absurd effects in aggregate'.[55] But 'absurd' practices can be no less adaptive than their competitors. They continued to be reproduced down successive generations of assessors, collectors, and payers. In the last quarter of the nineteenth century, it was as obvious to Conservative as to Liberal ministers that the local authorities could not hope to raise enough from the rates to enable either the generous to do as much as they wished or the parsimonious to do as much as they ought. The resulting stand-off between the centre and the localities resisted all attempts of ministers and officials to resolve it, and by 1914 their disputes had been exacerbated by mounting demand on the Treasury to finance the simultaneously escalating costs of social welfare on one side, and military and naval expenditure on the other. But the critical practice that caused the relations between central and local government to be reproduced much as before was one whose subsequent history would have astonished its progenitors: a tax on incomes.

Once again, the successive mutations might as well have been random. Income tax, introduced by Pitt in 1799, reintroduced by Addington in 1803, and recodified by Peel in 1842, was not invented as a device enabling the state to transfer resources from the rich to the poor. Gladstone would have abolished it if he could. But in a classic example of evolutionary exaptation, it turned out to be the means by which, together with a tax on inherited wealth, the state was enabled both to increase its expenditure on naval construction and armament and to provide centrally directed and nationally applied welfare services on a scale that would (it was hoped) mollify an enlarged electorate among whom rising expectations and rising provision were reinforcing one another in an ascending spiral. It continued to be administered by locally resident commissioners, assessors, and collectors, and monitored but not levied by officials of the Board of Inland Revenue. By the fiscal year 1913–14, when it was bringing in over £50 million to the Exchequer, 60 per cent of government revenue was from direct taxation, and subventions to local authorities were being made, however reluctantly, through Treasury grants-in-aid.

The different local authorities in their widely different environments had always varied in the extent of their dependence on their ratepayers, and the practices through which they exercised their functions were selected accordingly. A few lucky boroughs such as Doncaster owned enough property not to be dependent on them at all. Others, such as Bristol, had enough to supplement them on a significant scale. Leeds, which did not, made profits out of gas. Birmingham made profits out of trams as well as gas. London enjoyed rateable values high enough to compensate for its higher level of expenditure. More important for them all was power to

[55] M. J. Daunton, *Just Taxes: The Politics of Taxation in Britain 1914–1979* (Cambridge, 2002), p. 5.

borrow, which made possible capital expenditure on infrastructure that would otherwise have been drastically limited: by 1914, their total debt had quintupled from what it had been forty years earlier. But that did nothing to reduce the competition between local and central practices. On the contrary, it brought the local authorities directly into conflict with ministers concerned not only with the total amount of borrowing that would in due course have to be repaid, but also with its impact on the money markets and on the government's own financing. A Royal Commission on Local Taxation which sat from 1896 to 1901 failed to offer any solution to the problems raised by the conflicts of interest and opinion that it disclosed.

The trade-off confronting local authorities was, as it was bound to be, particularly problematic in poorer areas where greater demands for expenditure on welfare coincided with correspondingly greater reluctance on the part of ratepayers to pay for it—a dilemma that was to enshrine in the histories of the period between the two world wars the names of Bedwellty, West Ham, and Chester-le-Street where Labour-controlled Boards of Guardians who had exceeded their borrowing powers were replaced by centrally appointed commissioners. Such episodes of 'Poplarism', as it was called, provided quasi-experimental confirmation of the power of central government to impose changes of local practice, as did rate-capping in Sheffield and the surcharging of councillors in Liverpool in the 1980s. But the trade-off continued to oscillate within an unstable institutional equilibrium as both Conservative and Labour governments continued to tighten central control but local authorities, supported by sections of public opinion still sympathetic to Mr Podsnap, continued to hold on to such independence as they could.

The evolution of local government and its financing during the twentieth century is accordingly a 'how come?' story of perpetual competition between alternative practices through which money is raised and spent. The sequence of variation and selection by which one practice displaced another was as erratic and haphazard as that which drove the evolution of the tax system itself. Rerating, derating, subsidies, rebates, proportionate grants, block grants, rate-capping, surcharging, compulsory purchases, expenditure targets, and a so-called 'community charge' (publicly dubbed a 'poll tax') and its withdrawal in the face of protest followed each other in bewildering succession, and were welcomed or deplored by those involved through their various roles in accordance with their various interests. The Local Government Act of 1929 was at the same time the successor to those of 1888 and 1894 and the precursor to those of 1972 (with a separate one for Scotland in 1973), 1985, and 1986. The Greater London Council was created in 1963 only to be abolished in 1986. The behaviour of different local authorities could be unpredictably affected not only by the results of general as well as local elections but also by factional disputes within dominant political parties and between councillors and their officials. However startled Defoe, Adam Smith, or the mid-nineteenth-century leader-writers for *The Times* and *The Economist* might be by the size and scope of the twentieth-century state, they would find the relationship of local to central government to be much the same as they remembered it and the controversies to which it gave rise.

For individual citizens, meanwhile, the practices determining the relation between central and local agencies of the state were seldom a matter affecting their own behaviour unless in consequence the state did more or less to interfere in their individual circumstances or to augment or diminish the power attaching to their individual roles. To be taxed or subsidized, prohibited or permitted, conscripted or exempted, debarred or licensed, arraigned or discharged, and more generally impeded or assisted by the state comes to much the same whether the sanctions attach to the roles of officials of local or of central government. For the rulers, there is always room for speculation about what set of alternative practices is, or has been, or might be more effective in influencing the behaviour of the ruled. There is also room for argument (and for paradiastolic redescription) among both rulers and ruled about what is preferable, and why, as a matter of moral principle. But the distribution of power at any one time is the outcome of an antecedent sequence of variation and selection of practices in which similar selective pressures have been at work at both levels. There is the same bureaucratization of officials' roles under pressure of the volume of business. There is the same ongoing reproduction of the practice of patronage. There is the same competition with both commercial and voluntary practices. There is the same perceived need to respond to the expectations of the electorate. There are the same environmental constraints on raising or transferring from elsewhere the resources with which to respond to them. And there are the same unintended consequences of mutations which their initial designers and carriers, whatever their motives or their talents, could neither anticipate nor reverse.

V

The part-adversarial, part-collaborative practices that defined the relationships between the incumbents of central and those of local political roles evolved in much the same way, and remained much the same under much the same selective pressures, in the institutions where the means of coercion controlled by the state were brought directly to bear on behaviour not only culturally defined as deviant but also socially sanctioned as unlawful. In the eighteenth century, although the role of policeman did not yet exist, members of local communities were carriers of practices that empowered them to deal with lesser misdemeanours themselves. By a process of what one historian has called 'administrative Darwinism',[56] Quarter Sessions had by then been invested with the power previously exercised by manorial courts. It was for constables, watchmen, gamekeepers, and property-owners

---

[56] David Eastwood, *Governing Rural England: Tradition and Transformation in Local Government 1780–1840* (Oxford, 1994), p. 44.

themselves to identify, restrain, and punish offenders who were likely to be personally known not only to those against whom they had committed the offence but also to those who tried and sentenced (or acquitted) them. No historian has argued that the system was then, any more than in previous or subsequent periods, an exception to Dr Johnson's dictum that no 'scheme of policy' in the world has 'brought the rich and poor on equal terms into the courts of judicature'. But the courts did offer ordinary citizens a measure of protection of their persons and property if they chose to have recourse to them: 'the key decision-maker in the eighteenth-century criminal law was the victim himself',[57] and farmers, traders, artisans, and labourers (who might on occasion receive a financial contribution from the court towards the expense involved) frequently instituted prosecutions against felons. Nor did either jurors or magistrates (including, from 1792, the London magistrates in their stipendiary roles) always side with the more powerful against the less so. The poachers, smugglers, gleaners, and wreckers were never viewed in the same way by their neighbours and friends as by those seeking to bring them to trial, and the game laws were hated not only by the organized gangs of persistent offenders against whom they were principally directed. Yet neither the deer-stealers in Whichwood Forest whose practices had become 'customary for being repeated generation after generation without challenge',[58] nor the petty (or not so petty) criminals in the dock at the Old Bailey, nor the rioters who destroyed the toll gates on Bristol Bridge in 1793 were threatening to overturn the institutions of the state.

On the other hand, the existing set of practices and roles could not continue to be reproduced exactly as they were in large, fluid, anonymous, urban (and 'suburban') environments where the identification, arrest, and successful prosecution of offenders were becoming more difficult year by year. There were always some niches in which informal sanctions remained adequate to control minor infractions, as with the 'rough music' and scapegoating rituals of rural and smaller urban communities. In, for example, a relatively isolated and homogeneous mining village in County Durham it was still possible as late as the second half of the twentieth century for young delinquents to be disciplined without involving the police because 'the pit was open, and if these kids' fathers didn't work there their brothers or their uncles would have done, and they'd have been left in no doubt about what was going on, and how people felt about it—and they'd have sharp done something about it'.[59] But already by the time that the London 'Peelers' had begun to be deployed on the model of Peel's own experience in Dublin, informal sanctions of

---

[57] Peter King, 'Decision-makers and decision-making in the English criminal law, 1750–1800', *Historical Journal* 27 (1984), p. 27.

[58] Michael Freeman, 'Plebs or predators? Deer-stealing in Whichwood Forest, Oxfordshire in the eighteenth and nineteenth centuries', *Social History* 21 (1996), p. 18.

[59] Mark Hudson, *Coming Back Brockens: A Year in a Mining Village* (London, 1994), p. 279.

this kind were, and could not but be, increasingly maladaptive, and the cultural prejudice against a police force increasingly untenable.

The distinction between metropolitan, urban, and rural police and the different practices adapted to their different environments was reflected in successive Acts of Parliament, from the Metropolitan Police Act of 1829 through the Municipal Corporations Act of 1835 and the County Police Act of 1839 to the County and Borough Police Act of 1856. The separate police forces were driven to cooperate with one another in an environment where the offenders they sought to detect and apprehend had become increasingly mobile and thereby anonymous. But they depended as much as ever on the cooperation of the local communities: the opening chapter of the *Report of the Royal Commission on Criminal Justice in England and Wales* of 1993 took it for granted that 'The proportion of crimes solved by the police without help of any kind from members of the public is negligible'.[60] In working-class districts, in particular, that help could no more be relied on in the twentieth than in the eighteenth or nineteenth century. The authorities were always aware that, in the words of a Home Office memorandum of 1921, it was especially but not only in the 'hereditary criminal classes' that there were 'many people who respect and would die for the old flag but would not on any account give information on any subject to the police'.[61] Whatever was laid down by statute or in ministerial directives, the practices defining the policeman's role were what the environment of his local community made them, not what Home Office ministers and officials might have liked them to be.

Historians of crime are unsure how far the fall in the annual rate of indictable offences in the second half of the nineteenth century should be attributed to more effective policing. Nor is it possible to measure with any precision how well the new police succeeded in overcoming the hostility that they initially encountered. But local and regional studies have shown in detail the extent to which the practices acted out in the relations between police and public varied in accordance with the different selective pressures that the different environments brought to bear on the policeman's role. Any generalization in terms of 'class' needs to be carefully qualified, not only to take account of different categories of offences and offenders but also to reflect the differences between the roles as well as the personal characteristics of the persons who came into contact with the police in different contexts. There were the young 'police baiters'; there were those who could be expected to turn out whenever there was the prospect that a public meeting, a march, a demonstration, or a strike might offer an outlet for what *The Times* in 1887 called 'simple love of disorder, hope of plunder, and the revolt of dull brutality against the rule of law';[62] there were the middle-class, and occasionally

---

[60] *Report of the Royal Commission on Criminal Justice in England and Wales* (Cm 2263, London, 1993), p. 7.

[61] Quoted by Keith Jeffery, 'The British army and internal security 1919–1939', *Historical Journal* 24 (1981), p. 7.

[62] Quoted by Donald C. Richter, *Riotous Victorians* (Athens, OH, 1981), p. 165.

upper-class, marchers and orators; there were the drunkards whose troublesome behaviour 'under the influence' was not confined within homes or clubs or pubs or messes; there were the vagrants kept under surveillance on suspicion of criminal intent; there were the ticket-of-leave men; there were the street bookmakers with their attendant touts, runners, and lookers-out; there were the prostitutes (and the respectable women sometimes mistaken for prostitutes); there were the strikers blocking access to mines, docks, and factories; there were the shopkeepers, publicans, and lodging-house keepers into whose premises the police were empowered to enter; there were the denizens of the 'rookeries' and 'no-go' areas into which the police were reluctant to venture alone if at all, like Jennings Buildings or, later, Broadwater Farm Estate;[63] and there were the casual bystanders who found themselves caught up in disturbances in which they had played no part. Whatever the legislators' intentions, only a small part of a policeman's role involved the detection of crime and the apprehension of a suspect. Members of the general public were more likely to encounter the police ensuring school attendance, directing traffic, moving on beggars and street traders, checking weights and measures, dispersing crowds, investigating complaints of noise or nuisance, or interfering in outdoor activities of one sort or another—to the point, on occasion, of trying to prohibit traditional bonfires and being physically attacked for their pains. Overall, even after due allowance has been made for the 'domestic missionary' role of the local policeman doing kind and helpful things, the journalist Stephen Reynolds was only slightly exaggerating when, in seeking to convey to his Edwardian middle-class readers the attitudes of his chosen working-class informants, he told them that 'In every direction, inside his home as well as out, the working-man's habits and convenience are interfered with, or are liable to be interfered with, or his property is invaded, by the police'.[64]

It is, however, in the control of popular protest that the difference made (or not made) to existing practices is of most sociological interest. Once a permanent police force, supplemented if necessary by pensioners or 'specials', is in existence, the military authorities can hand over to the civil the responsibility for the control of domestic disorder, the truncheon can replace the bayonet as the weapon of crowd control, and 'riots' can be tamed into 'demonstrations'. But in the event, the variation and selection of competing practices and the trade-offs between them resulted in a growing militarization of the police which evolved in parallel with the diminishing recourse by the governments of the day to the army or yeomanry. The means of coercion under the monopoly control of the state were made available no less to its civilian than to its military agents.

So-called 'riots' are complex events. Sociologists are well aware that panics are not necessarily irrational, outbreaks of violence not necessarily unorganized, and

[63] Jennifer Davis, 'From "rookeries" to "communities": race, poverty, and policing in London 1850–1985', *History Workshop Journal* 27 (1989), p. 75.

[64] Stephen Reynolds, *Seems So! A Working-Class View of Politics* (London, 1911), p. 86.

unlawful assemblies not necessarily subversive. They also know that no hard-and-fast line can be drawn between political and non-political protests, that rituals symbolic of collective aggression can be interpersonally boisterous but institutionally innocuous, that the terms 'crowd', 'rabble', and 'mob' need to be carefully deconstructed, and that processions and parades can either exacerbate or mitigate inter-systactic hostility. But this diversity is itself part of the problem facing the agents of the state in seeking to protect private property and retain control of public space in the face of behaviour which, if unchecked, might undermine their power to do so. Whatever might be written in complacent newspaper editorials, it was untrue that after the last Chartist demonstration in 1848 all subsequent disturbances were no more than anachronistic throwbacks to the eighteenth century or peaceful assemblies or marches which had been infiltrated by 'agitators'. Ministers and officials were well aware of the importance of the railway and the telegraph in enabling local authorities to summon and dispose troops by whom disorder could be prevented or contained;[65] and they were also as aware as General Napier had been during the Chartist disturbances that to authorize the use of force too soon might be as much of a mistake as to authorize it too late.

Every episode had, as in the riots of the eighteenth century, its own individual story of provocation and response. But there could be no mistaking the implications of the Murphy Riots of 1866 to 1871 which showed just how dangerous to public order an itinerant sectarian agitator could be; or of the North Lancashire cotton strike of 1878, which brought out the intense hostility to the police of workers who had no distinctive grievance but were, on the contrary, 'broadly similar in their composition to the average factory-working population';[66] or of the Llanelli Riots of 1911, where even after the troops had opened fire and two men had been shot, looting and arson continued until a further detachment had been brought in to clear the railway lines; or of the attack on Luton Town Hall and police station in 1919 in which the town hall was set on fire; or of the Carmarthenshire anthracite strike in 1925, when a violent and protracted confrontation between miners and police at Ammanford broke out after the surreptitious introduction into the colliery of a volunteer pumpsman; or of the ransacking mobs who attacked Italian property 'from Soho in London to Stonehaven in the north-east of Scotland' following Mussolini's declaration of war in 1940;[67] or of the Brixton riots of 1981, when the police were attacked by young black men with petrol bombs as well as stones and bricks; or of the 'Battle of Orgreave' during the miners' strike of 1984–85 in which shield-bearing ranks of riot police avenged the victory that had been won by Arthur Scargill's secondary pickets in the 'Battle of Saltley' in 1972; or

[65] David Kent, 'Containing disorder in the "Age of Equipoise": troops, trains and the telegraph', *Social History* 38 (2013), pp. 308–27.

[66] J. E. King, ' "We could eat the police!" Popular violence in the North Lancashire cotton strike of 1878', *Victorian Studies* 28 (1985), p. 459.

[67] Terri Colpi, *The Italian Factor: The Italian Community in Great Britain* (Edinburgh, 1991), p. 105.

of the looting and arson that broke out in parts of London and other cities in 2011 following the shooting by police of an allegedly unarmed suspect.

The acknowledged right of lawful assembly always carried the risk that a crowd of sufficient size, or a sufficient number of smaller groups acting in coordination at dispersed locations, could be neither controlled nor dispersed except by the direct application of force. Not that the police were unarmed: they were equipped initially with cutlasses and then with revolvers when and where it was deemed necessary. But despite the reluctance of the civil authorities to ask the military authorities for help and of the military authorities to provide it, the army was still on call in the same way as earlier as the ultimate guarantor of the state's ability to preserve the public peace, even if—as, not least, in the General Strike of 1926—in the hope that its visible presence would act as a deterrent before rather than after violence had broken out. The institutional difference from the years during which riots and their suppression by military force were as frequent as when Lord Barrington was Secretary of War was only that there was now a first line of defence. The truncheon did not do away with the bayonet: it was the sight of a detachment of the Grenadier Guards with bayonets fixed which caused the crowd to 'skedaddle' (in George Bernard Shaw's word, who was in it) from Trafalgar Square on the afternoon of 'Bloody Sunday' (13 November 1887). In any case, the effective deployment of the truncheon against large crowds refusing to disperse required the policemen equipped with it to operate under what was tantamount to army discipline. It was, in the words of a historian of Victorian policing, 'local political reality' which 'turned policemen into soldiers'.[68] They came under the orders of chief constables empowered on the authority of the Home Secretary to use their forces, supplemented as necessary by contingents supplied by either their colleagues or the Metropolitan Commissioner, to mount operations for the keeping of the peace which were military in all but name.

It was as always difficult both for the decision-makers at the time and for historians later to judge the risk posed to the stability of the state by forms of behaviour which are culturally defined as not merely deviant but dangerous and socially sanctioned as not merely unlawful but treasonable. Periodic rumours of plots and conspiracies could not be assumed to be without foundation when some, at least, turned out to be based on fact. It was generally more plausible in the English environment to interpret the figures for offences against persons or property as the sum of acts of individual misbehaviour than to read into them coordinated political aims. But persons of the type who committed such offences could still be potential recruits into bodies of protesters which might make the public peace unmanageably difficult to maintain. Might there have been significant Jacobite involvement in the Militia Riots of 1757? Was Pitt responding to a genuine danger when he argued in the 1790s for legislation that not only suspended

---

[68] Carolyn Steedman, *Policing the Victorian Community: The Formation of English Provincial Police Forces, 1856–1880* (London, 1984), p. 33.

Habeas Corpus but made trade unionism illegal? Could the Newport rising of 1839 have been the start of a wider insurgency? Might the powers which the government took into its hands in the Defence of the Realm Act of 1914 and the Emergency Powers Act of 1920 have turned out to be essential to ensuring public safety?

Many contemporary observers both within and outside of government answered all these questions in the negative. Concerns were, moreover, regularly voiced by the judiciary as well as the parliamentary opponents of the administration of the day about what they considered to be excessive and improper restrictions of individual liberty in the name of national security. The objections raised in the House of Commons in 1994 to a Police Bill that would have allowed police and customs to enter and bug selected premises without a warrant echoed the sentiments voiced by Lord Chief Justice Camden in 1765 when he questioned the government's right to order a search of the 'secret bureaus and cabinets of every subject of this Kingdom' suspected to be the author, printer, or publisher of a seditious libel.[69] In a celebrated episode in 1844, Giuseppe Mazzini, then a political exile in London, found that his mail was being opened by the Post Office; the resulting furore compelled the Home Secretary to confirm that it had indeed been opened, and in the following year, 'telling the truth in carefully chosen words',[70] to assure Parliament that the department formerly maintained in the Post Office by the Secretary of State for the Foreign Department had been abolished and that no similar establishment was maintained by the Home Department—an assurance that prompted Macaulay to denounce such practices as 'singularly abhorrent to the genius of the English people'.

Equally abhorrent was *espionage* (the word often used deliberately to imply the unEnglishness of the *espion*'s role) like that of 'Oliver the Spy', unmasked in 1817 as having infiltrated the conspiracy for which Joseph Brandreth and two others were subsequently tried and executed. It was strenuously disputed then, and has been since, whether or not 'Oliver's' language and conduct had been such as to have had the effect of 'encouraging those designs, which it was intended they should only be the instruments of detecting'.[71] But the agent provocateur was always an object of cultural distaste, even among those who abhorred the aims and activities of the enemies of the state whom the provocateur was being employed to provoke. Even in the closing decades of the twentieth century and the early decades of the twenty-first, by which time the existence of a much larger, more elaborate, and more professionally staffed security service had come to be accepted as a fact of political life, the practices whereby suspected groups and movements were infiltrated and informed on were periodically challenged by parliamentarians and judges as well as by civil-libertarian pressure groups. The long cultural tradition in which clandestine

---

[69] *English Historical Documents*, vol. 7, p. 259.

[70] Kenneth Ellis, *The Post Office in the Eighteenth Century: A Study in Administrative History* (London, 1958), p. 141.

[71] A. F. Freemantle, 'The truth about Oliver the spy', *English Historical Review* 47 (1932), p. 615.

surveillance, infiltration, and interception of communication directly by the government against its own citizens were regarded as either comical (if brought to light) or sinister (if not) survived through the two world wars of the twentieth century into a period when the principal enemy was first Irish Republican and then Islamic 'terrorism'. But the practices were reproduced as before. Whatever the Home Secretary may have said to Parliament at the time of the Mazzini affair, the Edwardian Post Office was opening the mail of suffragettes as well as suspected German agents, just as the early Victorian Post Office had been opening the mail of known or suspected Chartists, and later Home Secretaries were to authorize the tapping of telephone calls and interception of emails.

The evolution of the 'surveillance state' thus followed another quasi-random sequence of decisions about tactics and techniques taken ad hoc by whoever happened at the time to be the incumbents of roles to which there was assigned responsibility for the safety of the realm. It is a story full of fluctuating and sometimes confused responses to a changing international as well as domestic environment. The various agencies' success, or lack of it, is impossible to measure, and much of the relevant evidence is inaccessible. But the histories of MI5, Special Branch, and the rest are stories of a classic evolutionary arms race in which the variation and selection of alternative strategies and techniques is driven by the variation and selection of the strategies of the perceived opposition, and vice versa. The long shields, plastic bullets, and CS gas cartridges of the anti-riot police, like the tactics of crowd control in which they were now trained, were extended phenotypic effects of reactions to episodes in which they had been outmanoeuvred or compelled to retreat. Closed-circuit television cameras mounted on purpose-built vehicles were used to facilitate the identification of suspected troublemakers who would otherwise be difficult to locate and arrest. Road blocks were used to prevent the build-up of hostile crowds which might otherwise become too large to be effectively contained. Reliance on amateur informants was replaced by penetration by trained professionals of organizations thought subversive. The release of information to parliamentarians and journalists became increasingly restricted and its content increasingly carefully censored. The Official Secrets Act of 1911 was only one episode in the continuous 'intermingling of national security and bureaucratic convenience'.[72] Governments of different persuasions were sometimes more and sometimes less concerned to trade off their responsibility for the maintenance of public order against their obligation to respect the right of lawful assembly and protest. But no government had difficulty in passing through Parliament legislation in which the second gave way to the first.

No one, therefore, could dispute that the agencies of the state charged with security and order, like the domestic departments of state in general, had evolved into being both more bureaucratic and more centralized in their practices during

---

[72] David Vincent, 'The origins of public secrecy in Britain', *Transactions of the Royal Historical Society*, 6th series, 1 (1991), p. 231.

the twentieth century than they had been during the eighteenth. But neither the increase, however large, in the number of the state's employees, nor the extension, however intrusive, of the power attaching to their roles, significantly altered the institutional distribution of political power. To commentators on the Left, the state was never doing as much as it ought to curb the abuse of the system by the privileged, while to commentators on the Right, the state was never doing as much as it ought to curb the defiance of it by the unruly. Which of these views, or neither, you endorse or reject is up to you. But whatever the effects of the state's increasingly sophisticated methods of surveillance and control on the lived experience of the people, the society's mode of coercion did not evolve out of one into another kind.

VI

Since this book is an exercise in explanatory, not descriptive, sociology, it makes, as I emphasized in the Introduction, no attempt to convey to its readers what representative members of different groups or categories of the population felt about the changes in England's modes of coercion, persuasion, and production through which they lived. But in the course of assembling the evidence on which its proffered explanations are based, I have now and again come across an episode or incident or performance of the kind which anthropologists working in the field are always hoping to find in order to illustrate some central feature of the culture of the people they are studying. I accordingly end this chapter with a short descriptive account of a jury trial held in Bristol in 1868 which brings out to a revealing degree both the continuity of the practices defining the roles constitutive of England's mode of coercion and the difference between how they operated within that mode at the time and how they operated before and after.

The trial, as described by Montagu Williams QC in his *Leaves from a Life* published in 1899, arose out of the riots which had accompanied the recent parliamentary election under the newly enlarged franchise. The defendant, a Conservative solicitor named Watkins, had been charged with leading a portion of the rioters and inciting them to demolish a number of buildings in the town. Predictably conflicting evidence was heard in which prosecution witnesses claimed to have identified Watkins as 'the man on the white horse', but witnesses called by the defence swore that he was in a totally different part of Bristol at the time. The jury retired at six o'clock on the second day. It was known to the defence that one of the jurors (whom they were unable to challenge because it was a case of misdemeanour, not felony) was a local butcher who had declared his intention to get on the jury and 'have a leg cut off rather than acquit Watkins'. The butcher, however, denied that he had said it, stood on his rights, and refused to budge. The judge made no attempt to interfere beyond voicing the need for reliance on 'the gentleman's good sense' and the obligation attaching to his oath. When the jury, after deliberating for four hours, failed to agree, the judge told them that he would do everything in his power to compel them to come to a conclusion and that they would be locked up for the night. At one o'clock, when they had still not agreed, they were sent back again. At four o'clock, the usher announced that they had at last arrived at a verdict. But on their return, when their names were called out, only eleven answered. Not until the butcher's name was called out a second time did a feeble voice answer 'Here'. The judge didn't look towards the jury box. But Montagu Williams did, and what he saw was that the butcher's coat and waistcoat had been torn from his back, his shirtsleeves were tattered, and his face was smeared with blood.

3

Ideology and the Power of Prestige

I

Whatever their individual roles within English society, Defoe's contemporaries could all see for themselves that they were located somewhere in a rank order of social prestige that was headed by a hereditary monarchy, an established Church, and an aristocracy and gentry, and underwritten by the sanctions of commensalism, endogamy, and forms of interpersonal contact and address. They could also see that although they had, within certain explicit limits, freedom to articulate their chosen opinions and follow their chosen lifestyles, the institutional means of persuasion were almost entirely under the control of an almost exclusively male and native-born elite and its acolytes in the schools, universities, and churches, and what would later be called the 'media'. Indeed that, as has often been said, is what differentiates an ideology from a set of ideas. An ideologically imposed rank order need not be willingly accepted by those to whom it assigns a subordinate status any more than the poor need willingly accept their poverty or the unenfranchised their lack of the vote. But if the location of their roles in social space is to change, there will have to be mutations of the exclusionary practices imposed on them. In sociological theory, there are two contrasting ideal-typical modes of exclusion: in 'plural' societies, two or more separate hierarchies of internally ranked status groups coexist on mutually exclusive but equal terms, while in 'caste' societies every individual's role is embedded in a single ritually sanctioned hierarchy of endogamous communities in which lifelong membership and consequential occupational role are determined by birth. In English society, there were (and are) elements of both. But the critical mutations of information affecting behaviour, by which the evolution of its mode of persuasion has been driven, have to be identified and traced underneath the noise and clutter in the same way in the ideological as in the political and economic dimensions of power.

All sociologists can agree, however they choose to phrase it, that in a society with a capitalist mode of production social prestige will, to a significant degree, be determined by 'class' in the sense of the location of a person's economic role (or, if economically dependent, their secondary role) and consequential share in the distribution of income and wealth. In the 1730 edition of Nathaniel Bailey's *Dictionarium Britannicum*, it was taken as given that 'In our days all are accounted

Gentlemen that have money'.[1] More reflective commentators might echo the dictum that 'gentry is but ancient riches' and point out that admission to the role of 'gentleman' usually took more than one generation to achieve. But the source and amount of income of the head of a family or household was the readiest indicator of status among both the labouring people and the middling sort. The high-feed barrister owed his rank to his fees as well as to the prestige of the law, and the high-waged craftsman his rank to his wages as well as to the prestige of his craft. There were always exceptions, however, and differences in money and possessions could then as now be mitigated or overridden by differences of birth, religion, education, ethnicity, nationality, locality, and gender. Some roles were always more respected than others for reasons at least partly independent of inequalities in either economic or political power.

The sanctions underwriting the social practices by which respectability was culturally defined were matters of sometimes obsessional concern both to those whose prestige was being assessed and to those doing the assessing, and have been described as vividly by novelists as by historians. Among the middle classes, who was or was not to be admitted in company as a 'gentleman' or 'lady'? Among the working classes, how far did a well-tended home, a disciplined family, attendance at church or chapel, or conspicuously costly funerals of family members secure acceptance from members of a higher-ranked status group? As industrialization progressed, some contemporary observers of the more hardworking, thrifty, and prudent of the craftsmen and artisans predicted the evolution of a 'working class' more and more of whose members, even if still engaged in manual rather than non-manual labour, would adopt the lifestyle and come to share the prestige accorded to middle-class status groups. Different commentators, as was to be expected, viewed the prospect with very different feelings. Whereas Alfred Marshall, in a lecture given in 1875, had looked forward with enthusiasm to a time when every working man would be 'by occupation, at least, a gentleman',[2] Engels, in a much-quoted letter of 1889, complained that 'the most repulsive thing here is the "respectability" bred into the bones of the workers'.[3] But in the mid-twentieth century, a team of sociologists studied a selected group of 'affluent' assembly-line workers in the car industry in Luton in order explicitly to test Engels's view of 'the significance of the British worker's craving for "respectability" and enhanced social status which thus led to a willingness, indeed eagerness, to accept bourgeois social values, lifestyles, and political ideas',[4] and found that no such change had taken place.

It was a finding which, as their critics pointed out, might not have been replicated in every other industry, occupational group, and locality in Britain.

[1] Quoted by Peter Earle, *The Making of the English Middle Class: Business, Society and Family Life in London, 1660–1730* (London, 1989), p. 6.

[2] Alfred Marshall, 'The future of the working classes', in A. C. Pigou, ed., *Memorials of Alfred Marshall* (London, 1925), p. 102.

[3] Karl Marx and Frederick Engels, *On Britain*[2] (Moscow, 1962), p. 568.

[4] John H. Goldthorpe et al., *The Affluent Worker in the Class Structure* (Cambridge, 1969), p. 3.

But it disposed of any easy assumption that the difference between working-class and middle-class status groups was only a matter of the size of the wage packet. One social historian looking back from 1990 dismissed as 'absurd' the idea that in the 1960s and 1970s there would be 'any new mass membership by the working classes of what had hitherto been middle-class tennis clubs, bridge clubs, golf clubs and the like'.[5] No more in the twentieth than in the nineteenth or eighteenth century did rising real wages among the employed working class drive to extinction the persistently adaptive social practices as well as cultural conventions that separated the lifestyles of labouring and middling families.

Some assimilation of consumption patterns did naturally follow, as observers of all persuasions could see, from wages high enough to bring within the reach of manual workers possessions and pastimes which they had previously been unable to afford. By the mid-nineteenth century, it might mean a clock on the mantelpiece or a fob watch in the waistcoat pocket, a family outing to the seaside, window curtains, a musical instrument, and a few books in addition to a family bible. By the mid-twentieth, it might mean a car, a television set, and an annual foreign holiday. But there is nothing in the extensive evidence assembled by cultural and social histor-ians to license an inference of assimilation to 'bourgeois' status groups among the working men who gambled on horse races, drank beer in their local pub, went to the music or dance hall, watched football matches from the terraces, holidayed in Blackpool, took up angling or woodworking or cultivating an allotment or playing in a brass band or rock group, and shared with their mates and relations a repertoire of songs, jokes, and stories whose theme and point depended directly on the distinctiveness of working-class from middle-class lifestyles. Neither the memes in their heads nor the practices defining their roles were any more those of Mr Pooter in the Grossmiths's *Diary of a Nobody* or his latter-day counterparts than they were those of the 'rabble' as depicted by Robert Lowe in his campaign against the extension of the franchise, or by the skilled engineering worker Thomas Wright in his book *The Great Unwashed* of 1868.

The selective pressures that made the distinctive lifestyles of the late Victorian and Edwardian working classes what they were have been further obscured by the contested meanings attached to the idea of there being an 'aristocracy of labour' at the top of the skilled working class. This is yet another term which has given rise to more debate than it need because of failure to specify in sufficient detail the practices held to define the 'aristocratic' worker's role. In the 1830s, the author of a book about English coachmaking remarked of the body-makers that 'they are the wealthiest of all and compose among themselves a species of aristocracy to which the other workmen look up with feelings half of respect, half of jealousy',[6]

[5] Eric Hopkins, *The Rise and Decline of the English Working Classes 1918–1990: A Social History* (London, 1991), p. 271.

[6] Quoted by E. J. Hobsbawm, 'Custom, wages, and work-load in nineteenth-century industry', in Asa Briggs and John Saville, eds., *Essays in Labour History* (London, 1960), p. 116.

and in that sense there were always distinctions of status drawn between grades of skill and degrees of 'nicety of work' which lasted into the era of mass production and what came to be called 'automation'. But to the secretary of the British branch of the Friendly Society of Operative Cabinet-Makers in 1845 it meant whichever workmen 'maintained the price for their labour';[7] to Lenin, a generation later, it meant the exclusive group of unionized workers who, he believed, were benefiting from the dominant position of British manufacturers in an export market created by British imperialism; in one author's view, London's busworkers were 'radical aristocrats';[8] and to some mid-twentieth-century right-wing commentators, the phrase meant any and all unionized workers who were able to control entry, thereby raising costs and lowering both the wages and the status of the excluded.

When, however, their roles are looked at more closely, the high-skilled craftsmen, whatever the source of the demand for their labour, were never an endogamous status group; they differed among themselves in their degree of 'respectability' as well as their politics; and their lifestyles were always vulnerable to unstable markets, foreign competition, and seasonal shortages of demand. The practices that distinguished 'respectable' from 'rough' working-class status groups were far more widely diffused than either high and regular earnings or trade union membership. Until the upsurge in the recruitment of the unskilled in the 1880s, labour historians estimate that little more than one in twenty workers were trade union members. The role whose defining practices were much more adaptive was that of member of a friendly society, of whom there were an estimated 600–700,000 in 1801 and 'not far short of 1.5 million by 1850'.[9] If that is so, they covered by then some 30 per cent of the adult male population and thus a far higher proportion of working-class men than were trade unionists. All shared a culturally acquired norm of determination to avoid the indignity of a pauper's burial. It was not only the foremen, artisans, and apprenticed practitioners of the traditional crafts who were members of hierarchically ranked and residentially separated working-class status groups whose distinctiveness was sanctioned by the practices of derogation and ostracism. Those who imposed the sanctions were not doing so because they were taking either the 'bourgeoisie', or—still less—the status-conscious clerical workers in the lower-middle class emulating their 'betters', as a normative reference group.

The cultural forms in which working-class aspirations to, or demands for, higher social prestige were encoded emerge clearly from the behaviour of the Chartists during the 1830s and 1840s. The contingent causes of the Chartist movement's rapid rise, two short peaks, and virtual extinction after 1848 have been much debated by historians. Some have been readier than others to attribute its failure to

---

[7] Quoted by David Blankenhorn, 'Our class of workmen: the cabinet-makers revisited', in Royden Harrison and Jonathan Zeitlin, eds., *Divisions of Labour: Skilled Workers and Technological Change in Nineteenth-Century England* (Brighton, 1985), p. 32.

[8] Ken Fuller, *Radical Aristocrats: London Busworkers from the 1880s to the 1980s* (London, 1985).

[9] F. M. L. Thompson, *The Rise of Respectable Society: A Social History of Victorian Britain, 1830–1900* (London, 1988), p. 201.

the personal traits of its leaders and the quarrels between them; some have attributed its appeal more, and others less, to what contemporaries called 'knife-and-fork' grievances about low wages, tommy-shops, summary dismissal, and underemployment as distinct from the political grievances articulated in the Charter itself; and some have attributed its decline as much or more to Peel's willingness to make concessions to working-class demands (other, that is, than extending the franchise) than to his readiness to deploy the means of coercion directly in order to suppress it. But all are agreed that it was an authentically working-class movement. There was nothing incoherent in the responses of the strikers at a mass meeting in Ashton in 1842 who, when asked if they were striking for wages or the Charter, held up their hands to indicate both. In the aftermath of the First Reform Act, the New Poor Law, obstruction of the right of workers to combine in trade unions, more proactive methods of policing, restrictions on the unstamped press, and palpably inadequate statutory protection against exploitation in mines, factories, and mills gave manual workers at all levels ample reason to feel aggrieved. But the measures enacted, as well as those not enacted, by the reformed Parliament were perceived by the Chartists as attacks on the dignity as well as the living and working conditions of freeborn citizens for whom a still small and predominantly middle-class electorate had become not a normative but a comparative reference group. What the Chartists demanded of their 'betters' was not absorption but respect. In the dimension of social prestige, Chartism's rise as a political movement accelerated, and was in turn accelerated by, the diffusion of an aim which was 'democratic' in an ideological no less than a political sense.

Its sociological significance can thus be measured not only by the number of signatures to the two petitions for the Charter submitted to Parliament in 1839 and 1842 or the number of strikes called in its name, but also by the number of associational activities that it inspired. Many working-class women were, particularly at the start, involved alongside men despite their exclusion from the demand for the vote. There were Christian Chartists, Paineite Chartists, 'education' Chartists, 'household' Chartists, 'temperance' Chartists, Chartists who debated at Mechanics' Institutes, Chartists who taught children in Chartist day and Sunday schools, Chartists who drank together in inns and taverns, Chartists who held tea meetings in rooms decorated with Chartist banners, Chartists who turned out in crowds to listen to itinerant Chartist lecturers, and Chartists who came together regularly in each other's homes for readings from the latest issue of the *Northern Star*. What united them was not repudiation of the political power of the state as such but of the ideological power of those who controlled it.

There was some apocalyptic rhetoric deployed by some Chartist orators, and there were some advocates of 'physical-force' Chartism who disparaged 'moral-force' Chartism as 'unmanly'.[10] But the moral-force strategy was the more adaptive

[10] Anna Clark, *The Struggle for the Breeches: Gender and the Making of the British Working Class* (Berkeley, CA, 1997), p. 224.

not only because of the negative pay-off to physical force in the face of the means of coercion under the control of the state, but also because of the positive pay-off to moral force in respect, as was to be explicitly testified by Gladstone's proclaimed admiration for the conduct of the workers of Lancashire during the 'cotton famine' caused by the American Civil War. The cotton workers were, it could be said, atypical in their level of cooperation both within and between the households whose members worked alongside each other in the mills. But the working-class crowds who turned out in force in London and elsewhere in 1866 to demonstrate in favour of franchise reform deliberately demonstrated their respectability by their dress as well as their behaviour. In so doing, they were no more siding with their superiors than were the trade unionists who sat down alongside representatives of the employers on conciliation boards or met government ministers face to face in order to press their members' claims. An avowedly moderate leader like Robert Applegarth of the Carpenters and Joiners was as resistant in the 1860s to (in his own words) 'overbearing and tyrannical conduct' on the part of employers,[11] and as ready to call his members out on strike if he thought it to their advantage, as the once communist trade union leader Hugh Scanlon, who ended his career in the House of Lords, was to be a century later.

The longer-term outcome was a narrowing of social distance between working- and middle-class status groups of which both academic and non-academic observers were equally aware. In the twentieth century, it was visibly accelerated by the selective pressures generated by two world wars which affected the whole of the civilian population to an extent that no previous war had done. Both those who welcomed and those who deplored it agreed that it was becoming increasingly difficult to distinguish working- from middle-class men and women through their outward appearance, that manners were becoming less deferential, and that work-place relationships between workers and their employers were becoming less authoritarian. But it was equally easy to point to continuities in residential segre-gation, divergent uses of leisure time, status-group endogamy, distinctive domestic routines, and the disposition (some would say, determination) of middle-class men and (some would say, particularly) women to emphasize the differences 'subject-ively regarded'.[12] G. D. H. Cole, looking back from the 1960s to the opening years of the twentieth century, described the 'lower' classes as no longer feeling 'the same sense of exclusion from power and from equal intercourse as they used to feel', but he recognized at the same time that 'The class structure remains, not unaltered, but in its essentials the same'.[13] And there was always the all-important difference within the occupational role structure between the working-class 'job' and the middle-class 'career'. For incumbents of working-class occupational roles, improvement in

[11] Quoted by Asa Briggs, *Victorian People* (London, 1954), p. 197.
[12] Peter Willmott and Michael Young, *Family and Class in a London Suburb* (London, 1960), p. 122.
[13] G. D. H. Cole, *The Post-War Condition of Britain* (London, 1956), pp. 42, 41.

status, as in income, was as much as ever a matter of collective rather than individual upward mobility. For incumbents of middle-class occupational roles, it was as much as ever a matter both of raising the shared location of their occupational status groups and of enhancing their prospects of individual advancement within them. Hence the sociological significance of the variation and selection from the eighteenth century onwards of a set of practices critical to the evolution of the rank order of social prestige: those subsumed under the heading of 'professionalization'. Here, too, critical mutations can be identified and traced, which led to unmistakable changes in the way that 'professional' roles were performed. But they were changes within the mode of persuasion, not of it.

II

The practice generally taken to be the defining characteristic of a 'professional' role is training of a kind which qualifies the incumbent to be rewarded for a valued service performed, as opposed to being paid a market price for a manufactured or traded product sold or receiving a contracted amount of pay in return for a standard amount of labour. No lawlike trans-societal generalization follows about the professional's status: in Roman society in the time of Cicero, both doctors and architects were slaves whereas lawyers were not. But in Defoe's England, the three 'great' professions that enjoyed unchallenged social prestige were Divinity, Law, and Physic. Of these, Divinity was the one most permeated by the practice of patronage. Law was the one whose most successful practitioners were most highly remunerated. But it is Physic that offers the most instructive example of meme-practice co-evolution in operation.

From the early eighteenth century, the few hundred Fellows of the Royal College of Physicians were the acknowledged elite of the medical profession—holders of university degrees from Oxford or Cambridge, gentlemanly in deportment and manners, fluent in Latin, limited in their knowledge of either anatomy or chemistry, but in receipt from their prosperous clients of fees high enough to support a fashionable lifestyle. Below them, and the College's licentiates and ecclesiastically appointed extra-licentiates, ranked the shopkeeping 'apothecaries' who either themselves or according to a 'physician's' prescription prepared (as might also a 'chemist of trade' who 'might be defined the maker of medicines'[14]) and sold (as might also be done by a 'druggist') the cordials prescribed for the sick. The critical mutation dates as far back as 1704. Before then, the apothecaries had had no legal right to take a fee for consultation. But by an unexpected decision of the House of Lords they were then granted the right to diagnose and prescribe treatments as well as to compound and dispense medicines. In consequence, the practices defining their role gradually evolved to the point that apothecaries became the general

---

[14] *The Book of English Trades and Library of the Useful Arts*[7] (London, 1818), p. 96.

practitioners of the nineteenth and twentieth centuries, and the selling of medicines was delegated to retailers who then became designated chemists. For the surgeons, their traditional association with barbers and the use of the knife as the tool of their trade led them to be regarded as craftsmen whose skill, however valuable to their patients, was of a more banausic kind. But in 1800 they received their own royal charter, and after the passing of the long-gestated Medical Act of 1858 a General Council was institutionalized empowered to register successful examinees in either medicine or surgery who could then practise where they chose and sue for the fees they charged.

The selective pressure that gradually enhanced the social prestige of both the apothecaries and the surgeons came from a growing demand for increasingly valued services which they were perceived to be better fitted to meet. The apothecaries had not only more experience of dealing with a wider range of ailments than the physicians but a closer knowledge of the drugs, and particularly opiates, available for treating, or at least palliating, them. At the same time, the surgeons were expanding their knowledge of anatomy not only in the London teaching hospitals but in the army and navy during the extended periods when they gained their experience in an environment of international war. In the navy at the beginning of the eighteenth century, surgeons ranked only as petty officers on a level with bosuns and pursers. But by 1800, when army doctors ranked as captains and army surgeons as lieutenants, there were over 700 surgeons serving with the fleet, and Thomas Trotter, 'the most obdurate spokesman for naval surgeons', was making 'astonishingly outspoken claims for the professional authority of medically qualified practitioners in all that had to do with the health of seamen'.[15]

By then, too, higher standards in both surgery and medicine had been culturally acquired from practitioners educated in Scotland or continental Europe. To historians of medicine aware of how limited, by late twentieth-century standards, was the eighteenth-century practitioners' understanding of the causes of disease and the efficacy of the available techniques of prevention or cure, the willingness of the public to be purged and bled, and to pay for pills or potions of which many had no therapeutic value whatever, is the prologue to a cultural-evolutionary story of imitation and social learning which leads on to disinfectants, anaesthetics, x-rays, aspirin, antibiotics, the defeat of hitherto lethal infectious diseases, and a dramatic reduction in infant mortality. Sociologically, however, eighteenth-century medicine offered qualified practitioners without an Oxford or Cambridge degree entry into a role sufficiently prestigious as well as lucrative to attract an increasing number of younger sons from gentry families whose choice of career would otherwise have lain between a clerical living, a naval or military commission, and the bar (or, increasingly, an 'attorney at law's' or 'solicitor's' practice). 'Doctors' became familiar members of upper-middle status groups in both metropolitan and provincial

[15] Peter Matthias, *The Transformation of England: Essays in the Economic and Social History of England in the Eighteenth Century* (London, 1979), p. 266.

society. By the time of a sociological study of the town of Banbury carried out in the mid-twentieth century, the researchers located the doctors in what they called the 'upper frontier' group between the middle and upper classes, most of whom had the same sort of education and lifestyle as the 'upper' class and some of whom lived, like the 'county' families, outside the town.[16] Viewed in total, the medical, like the legal, profession continued to be internally differentiated in prestige as well as in earnings. The sometimes titled physicians and consultants who attended on the royal family in the twentieth century were replicating the roles of those who had attended on Queen Anne, and there were, as there had always been, practitioners of unorthodox (or alternative) forms of treatment who were excluded from the fully institutionalized associations by which the profession came to be controlled. But the practices defining the role of apothecary became maladaptive to the point that the chemists dispensed what the doctors prescribed.

In the course of this gradual evolution, the rising prestige of the surgeons was both reflected in, and enhanced by, a revealing mutation in the form in which they were addressed. At the beginning of the eighteenth century, the title of 'doctor' was reserved by custom to the physicians. The surgeons, like the apothecaries, expected to be called 'mister'. But to the growing number of patients who looked to an apothecary for a diagnosis and a recommended treatment as well as for the purchase of medicines, lack of a university degree was an irrelevance. Apothecaries, surgeons, and 'surgeon-apothecaries' came to be addressed in the second person, and referred to in the third, as 'doctor', whatever the fellows and licentiates of the Royal College of Physicians might think about it. But then, by one of the ironies characteristic of the evolutionary process, designation as 'mister' came to be the preferred mode of address for both surgeons and specialist consultants who wished to distinguish their by now more prestigious roles from those of the 'general practitioner'.

'Professionalization', however, is another of those words that are used in sufficiently different senses in different contexts to make it sometimes difficult to be sure which were the critical mutations of 'professional' practices that changed the social location of their carriers. In English society between the early eighteenth and early twenty-first centuries, it denotes distinguishably different mechanisms of variation and selection within the mode of persuasion with separate evolutionary trajectories of their own.

One is the ideological differentiation of the roles of the 'professional' and the 'amateur'. This has a well-documented history in sport, where the paid player was traditionally ranked lower in status than the gentleman for whom a game of cricket was a leisure pastime like pheasant shooting or riding to hounds. But in sport, as in both the sciences and the arts, the pressure of competition for public recognition made it increasingly difficult for the amateur, so defined, to outperform the professional. Reference to a 'professional' standard came to imply not merely monetary payment but a level of performance measured by acknowledged success.

---

[16] Margaret Stacey, *Tradition and Change: A Study of Banbury* (Oxford, 1960), p. 152 n.1.

Prestige attaching to outstanding individual performance in a role has always to be distinguished from prestige attaching to the role as such: the first is a matter of praise, whereas the second is a matter of respect. But the more often the outstanding performers who attracted the praise were seen to be the professionals, the less respect was accorded to the amateurs who were in consequence downgraded as such—unless, as when an occasional amateur jockey rode to victory in the Grand National steeplechase, the achievement was hailed as all the more praiseworthy on that account.

Professionalization, however, could also take the form of practices that resulted in combinations of fellow incumbents of similar roles for the explicit purpose of enhancing the prestige attaching to them, such as the Birmingham Law Society established in 1818 for the purpose of 'Promoting and encouraging a correct and liberal course of action in the Profession [note the capital P]; and of discountenancing and opposing all practices that may have a tendency to bring it into discredit or to lessen its respectability'.[17] It might be done either informally on the model of a learned society or formally on the model of the British Medical Association, which evolved in due course into an institutionalized negotiating body dealing directly with the government of the day. As more and more self-styled professionals came together in what might be called an association, but might equally be called a society or an institute or an institution or a federation or even a guild—the Engineers' Guild, founded in 1938, took as its objective to promote, among other things, the 'honour' of the engineering profession—the practices defining the roles of their officers and members varied increasingly widely. Sometimes, the selective pressures came from the structure of the market within which they operated and the sector of it within which their members plied their skills. But at other times, it was cultural selection that dictated repudiation of practices perceived as disadvantageously close to those of the trade unions.

Whereas, for example, the Chemical Society of 1841 was a learned society of an ideal-typical kind, the Institute of Chemistry was founded in 1878 for the specific purpose of endowing its members with a qualification which would be publicly acknowledged by prospective clients or employers who wished to make use of their skills. In the case of the architects, the Royal Institute of British Architects, which received its charter in 1837, was long divided between architects who wanted to see strict professional standards compulsorily imposed and architects who in their own eyes were artists more than professionals, with the professionals arguing that without a client, an architect could do nothing and therefore artistic autonomy had if necessary to be sacrificed to securing clients' favour.[18] Artists might also form their own associations such as the Contemporary Portrait Society or the Federation

[17] Quoted by Leonore Davidoff and Catherine Hall, *Family Fortunes: Men and Women of the English Middle Class 1780–1850* (London, 1981), p. 268.
[18] Barrington Kaye, *The Development of the Architectural Profession in Britain: A Sociological Study* (London, 1960), p. 92.

of British Artists. But there was always a trade-off in reproductive fitness between practices which raised the status of their carriers by securing for them higher pecuniary rewards, and practices which did so by dissociating their carriers from anything other than the enhancement of their social prestige.

Regardless of whichever of the two objectives the members of a professional association might attach the greater importance, restrictions on entry were inevitably suspect to prospective clients as threatening their freedom to choose for themselves. Why shouldn't we all be free to consult the doctor, dentist, druggist, bonesetter, osteopath, homeopath, or faith-healer of our preference? To the answer that the public needs to be protected from mountebanks and charlatans the rejoinder is that the trade-off of practices adaptive precisely because of their success in restricting entry is the discouragement of progress, the exclusion of talented outsiders, and the reproduction of self-selected elites. In 1858, Parliament did not make it a criminal offence for an unregistered person to practise as a doctor, but did make it a criminal offence to claim falsely to be registered or to have obtained registration under false pretences. The exclusionary practices of the increasingly institutionalized professional associations were no different from those of the skilled craftsmen's trade unions. But the apprenticed craftsmen, although they had a common interest in controlling the number of potential competitors for the work they were paid the going rate to do, were not competitors with each other for subsequent individual advancement. The professionals, on the other hand, although they might be content, once qualified, to offer their services to their clients at the going rate, continued to be potential competitors with each other for social prestige. The young clergy could see ahead of them the roles of dean and bishop, the young doctors higher qualifications with abbreviations to put after their names, and the young barristers silk and the judicial bench. They all had the same collective interest in the status of their profession relative to that of other occupational roles. But individually, they were rivals for prestige in the same way as the architects competing to design the buildings, the engineers competing to build the bridges, the playwrights competing to have their plays put on the stage, and the actors competing to perform the plays. Different selective pressures are at work.

The consequence was the acceleration of so-called 'credentialism'. Credentialism is an example of what is known in evolutionary theory as a 'runaway effect'. In the theory of natural selection, a textbook example is the peacock's tail, whose splendidly colourful expansion of plumage attractive to prospective mates comes at a cost in reproductive fitness to other and seemingly more adaptive genes. In the theory of cultural selection, a textbook example is the competition among the South Pacific islanders of Ponapae for growing larger and larger yams at the cost of what becomes a net loss in nutritional efficiency. In the social-evolutionary example of the professionalization of occupational roles, credentialism shows how competition for social prestige can defeat its ostensible purpose by recreating the problem that the competitors are seeking to solve—the trade-off being that new formal qualifications are introduced at the cost of diminishing the degree of differentiation which they encode. It was a problem already recognized in the last quarter of the nineteenth century. In 1976, the British sociologist Ronald Dore published a book to which he gave the title *The Diploma Disease*. But in 1894, the author of the preface to a book published in France about English education had said, in commenting on the system of local examinations controlled by the universities of Oxford, Cambridge, and London, 'I seem to see the examination disease, the certificate fever, more deadly, I am inclined to believe, than any of the plagues of Egypt, infecting the entire country'.[19] The analogy with the spread of a pathological virus needs to be cautiously construed, and Dore himself subsequently drew attention to the importance of the distinction between vocationally relevant credentials and the use of tests in general education for screening according to ability. But credentialism offers a classic demonstration of how evolution can produce maladaptive consequences for practices that emerged in an environment initially favourable to their reproduction.

Within the middling sort, there was always a difference between those who owed some or all of their social prestige to the possession or control of tangible assets, whether land, plant and machinery, houses, investments in government stock or speculative private ventures, or simply cash in the bank, and those who owed it to what sociologists would come to call 'human' capital. Wealth continued to confer status unless acquired by means culturally defined and socially sanctioned as irredeemably unrespectable: a twentieth-century train-robber might retain something of the ambivalent glamour of an eighteenth-century highwayman, but neither would be admitted on equal terms into polite society. But as the management of businesses became increasingly divorced from their ownership, the managers increasingly aspired to professional status. The claim that the 'real managers' are an 'expert professional class' was first advanced explicitly in the aftermath of the First World War,[20] and it led by a readily traceable sequence of meme-practice co-evolution to institutional qualifications extending from a National Certificate in Commerce in 1939 to the degrees awarded by the business schools of the 1960s and thereafter.

There remained observable differences in both lifestyle and party-political allegiance between managers (particularly in profit-making organizations) and professionals (particularly in the welfare professions): a study of male respondents to a questionnaire with an 81 per cent response rate addressed to supporters of the Campaign for Nuclear Disarmament in 1965 led its author to conclude that 'occupational self-selection on the part of radicals' explained the much higher percentages of supporters found among middle-class employees in non-commercial, non-profit-making organizations (including freelances) than in commercial, profit-making ones.[21] But these were pluralistic differences, not differences of caste. In the

---

[19] Quoted by Elie Halévy, *A History of the English People in the Nineteenth Century*, vol. 5: *Imperialism and the Rise of Labour* (London, 1961), p. 150 n.1 (first published in 1926).

[20] John Lee, *Management* (London, 1921), p. 2.

[21] Frank Parkin, *Middle Class Radicalism: The Social Bases of the British Campaign for Nuclear Disarmament* (Manchester, 1968), pp. 188–9.

late twentieth century, a solicitor working in the legal department of a large commercial, industrial, or financial organization ranked no differently in prestige from one working as a partner in an independent firm or in the employment of the state. Both men and women moved freely between managerial and professional roles in the course of their careers,[22] and intermarriage between them was commonplace. The threefold division between upper-middle, middle-middle, and lower-middle was within the two categories, not between them.

I suggested in Chapter 1 that Defoe would have no difficulty either in reconciling his sociological vocabulary with ours or in extending it to include occupations that did not yet exist in his day. He might be sceptical about the number of professional associations, cynical about the restrictions imposed on recruitment, and scornful of credentialism. He might be intrigued that engineers and surgeons are academically rather than mechanically trained, dismissive of some of the branches of learning in which students are awarded university degrees, and amazed that jockeys and footballers are awarded honours in the gift of the Crown. But if invited to compare the gradings devised by sociologists in the second half of the twentieth century with Gregory King's Table from the close of the seventeenth, he would be unlikely to conclude that the rank order of social prestige had been drastically modified, let alone reversed. There is only one pervasive difference that he might detect in the nature of the relationship between the incumbents of occupational roles ranked higher or lower in social prestige. The word encoding this critical mutation is 'servant'—a cultural as well as social construction whose behavioural effects extended far more widely than the roles of domestic servant or servant-in-husbandry. Through a sequence of meme-practice co-evolution of which the decline of domestic service was one but by no means the only part, the role of servant evolved into the role of employee.

The practices defining a servant's role imply subordinate membership of a household in which the master or mistress is the acknowledged head and the servant is lodged and fed or, if living apart, is still at the beck and call of the employer. A descriptive sociology would need to cover a wide range of divergent experiences and their subjective interpretation on both sides. Social historians have documented in detail how much these varied between one household and another. The cooks and butlers presiding over their own subordinates in the houses of the rich and great were inhabitants of a different world from the pauper children farmed out from the workhouses to be singly employed in the houses of local farmers or shopkeepers or clerks. It would, moreover, be a mistake to assume that even in the eighteenth century female domestic work was not recognized at all as a form of 'labour and employment':[23] servants could and occasionally did take

---

[22] John H. Goldthorpe, 'The service class revisited', in Tim Butler and Mike Savage, eds., *Social Change and the Middle Classes* (London, 1995), p. 320.

[23] Carolyn Steedman, *Labours Lost: Domestic Service and the Making of Modern England* (Cambridge, 2009), p. 151.

disputes over their wages and conditions before the magistrates. But to work for, and under the direction of, another person in their home or in quasi-domestic premises under their ownership, as did not only the apprentices in the masters' workshops but the shop assistants of whom only the most senior in a few of the larger establishments were allowed to marry and live off the premises,[24] was to forfeit the social prestige implicit in the role of the independent worker whose contractual relationship is with an employer who has no power to regulate the worker's domestic life.

There is a nice illustration of the direction in which the role was evolving in the late nineteenth century in a legal decision of 1880 (*Yewens v. Noakes*) where the court ruled that a salaried clerk could not be a 'servant' but was more clearly akin to 'persons in the position almost of gentlemen'.[25] The Amalgamated Society of Railway Servants, established in 1871, only became the National Union of Railwaymen in 1913. By the beginning of the twenty-first century, the word had largely dropped out of use except in the context of domestic service, and even there 'servants' had by then been almost entirely replaced by independent non-residents and semi-professional contractors. But in the 1931 census there were still over 1½ million of them, and only after the Second World War did the proportion of women in paid employment whom the census classified as resident domestic servants fall below 10 per cent. Culturally, 'Domestic service humour was still viable in Britain in the 1960s and 1970s.'[26] It took time for the vocative use of 'sir' and 'madam' to die out in relationships between payers and receivers of wages, and for the terminology in which it was conventional to speak of a railway company's employees as its 'servants' to be, like references to factory employees as 'hands', driven extinct. As late as 1947, a general manager in Hoovers was voicing surprise that the 'factory' as opposed to 'office' worker 'is still called a "hand" by many who ought to know better',[27] and it is always difficult to be sure what inferences about changes in actual behaviour can be drawn from the evidence for changes in vernacular discourse. Nor can the exclusionary practices of commensalism and endogamy be assumed to have been driven extinct simply because 'in public, at least' working men are treated with 'much more respect' by the 'well-off' than hitherto.[28] But Defoe, even while recognizing a familiar rank order of occupational prestige, would at the same time have no difficulty in detecting the narrowing of social distance within it which followed from the separation of employees' places of residence from their places of work.

[24] Christopher P. Hosgood, ' "Mercantile manservants": shops, shop assistants and shop life in late-Victorian and Edwardian Britain', *Journal of British Studies* 38 (1999), p. 337.

[25] Quoted by Simon Deakin, 'The contract of employment: a study in legal evolution', Working Paper 203 (ESRC Centre for Business Research, University of Cambridge, 2001), p. 29.

[26] Lucy Delap, 'Kitchen-sink laughter: domestic service humour in twentieth-century Britain', *Journal of British Studies* 49 (2010), p. 641.

[27] Quoted by Ross McKibbin, *Classes and Cultures: England 1918–1951* (Oxford, 1998), p. 138.

[28] Richard H. Trainor, *Black Country Elites: The Exercise of Authority in an Industrialized Area, 1830–1900* (Oxford, 1993), p. 363.

III

The most widely observed and intensively discussed change in England's mode of persuasion between the early eighteenth and early twenty-first centuries was the declining authority of the Established Church and concomitant decline in the social prestige of the clergy. But however many of the people of Britain had ceased either to 'believe' or to 'belong',[29] the decline did much less to disturb the social order than many observers either hoped or feared.

By the late eighteenth and early nineteenth centuries, there was ample evidence of heightened participation by both men and women in increasingly secular and open discussion of issues of public concern which bore directly on the traditional criteria of social prestige. The earlier environment of courtly patronage, restricted communication, and clerically imposed indoctrination had become one of circulating libraries, newspapers, debating societies, and inns, taverns, and coffee houses to which access was restricted only by individual choice. But the proliferation of premises where coffee or alcohol was freely on sale and both political and religious topics freely discussed did not eliminate differences of social prestige either among their customers or between themselves. Women were present more in the roles of servants or occasionally proprietors than of patrons, and politicians and their hangers-on chose venues to meet not in order to debate with opponents but to mingle with like-minded equals. Macaulay, in chapter 3 of his *History of England*, commented that although nobody was excluded who 'laid down his penny at the bar', nevertheless 'every rank and profession, and every shade of religious and political opinion, had its own headquarters'. The 'jumbling of ranks' observed in the debating societies that flourished in London in the 1780s was limited and transitory.[30] Much of the expanded volume of public discussion and debate in the provinces as well as in London reflected a dissatisfaction with the dominant ideology which was variously articulated by dissident freethinkers, reform-minded radicals, disgruntled gentry, censorious Nonconformists, and status-hungry professionals. But however forcefully they expressed it, and however much both their opinions and their opportunities for expressing them differed from those of their fathers and grandfathers, the practices defining the roles constitutive of the mode of persuasion continued to be reproduced much as before.

The Established Church was, however, confronted by extensive and continuous competition from the early eighteenth century onwards. It 'found itself especially subject to frequent and potent intellectual threats after the Glorious Revolution',[31] including Arianism, Socinianism, and Deism, as well as having to contend with its

---

[29] David Voas and Alasdair D. Crockett, 'Religion in Britain: neither believing nor belonging', *Sociology* 39 (2005), pp. 11–28.

[30] Donna T. Andrews, 'Popular culture and public debate: London 1780', *Historical Journal* 50 (2007), p. 436.

[31] Julian Hoppit, *A Land of Liberty? England 1689–1727* (Oxford, 2000), p. 227.

long-standing antagonist the Catholic Church, whose members included recusant aristocratic families whose social prestige was as high as that of any of their Anglican counterparts. But Catholicism was as much 'not English' as centralization to Mr Podsnap. Aggressively and sometimes virulently anti-Catholic memes were not only encoded and transmitted in sermons, speeches, tracts, songs, stories, plays, cartoons, and ceramics, but acted out in rituals such as burning in effigy and riots against 'Popish' persons and property. Anglicans who converted to Catholicism were well aware that to 'go over to Rome' was widely regarded among their compatriots as defection to the enemy. Opponents of Irish Home Rule readily equated it with 'Rome Rule'. It was not from that quarter that the Anglican pastors had cause to fear for their hold over their flocks but from Protestant rivals whose anti-Catholicism was as far beyond doubt as their own.

Any detailed history of religion in eighteenth- and nineteenth-century England has to address the much-disputed and sometimes contradictory influence of Methodism, whose effect on the behaviour of its converts was as subversive of the existing rank order in some local environments as it was supportive of it in others. The different selective pressures which favoured different cultural mutations were as readily detectable in the environment of rural East Anglian districts dominated by alliances between squires, farmers, and parsons, or among the coalminers in the pit villages of County Durham, as they were among the urban congregations drawn from the 'upper echelons of the lower orders, and lower income groups within the middle ranks',[32] who made what they could, saved what they could, and gave what they could. In rural environments not under the control of large landowners and established clergy, female preachers were often the carriers of the 'cottage religion of sectarian Methodism'.[33] But Methodism was one among many variants of Protestant Christianity separating not only Dissent from Anglicanism but New Dissent from Old and Low Anglicanism from High. Sociologists of religion are familiar from many cultures and societies with the sometimes hectic pace of variation and selection which drives runaway sectarian fission and generates new memetic lineages analogous to the genetic lineages of natural selection. In nineteenth-century England, at the same time that the Anglican clergy were becoming concerned about their weakening hold over their working-class congregations, intra-Protestant rivalry was finding expression in increasingly intense competition between rival status groups whose unintended effect was to accelerate the diminution of the social prestige attaching to all clerical roles.

The rivalry between Methodists, Baptists, Congregationalists, Unitarians, Quakers, and (after 1837) Mormons was heightened by further doctrinal and liturgical mutations which brought into being sometimes tiny Protestant subsects with

[32] David Hempton, *Religion and Political Culture in Britain and Ireland: From the Glorious Revolution to the Decline of Empire* (Cambridge, 1996), p. 29.

[33] Deborah M. Valenze, *Prophetic Sons and Daughters: Female Preaching and Popular Religion in Industrial England* (Princeton, 1985), p. 101.

intriguing if short-lived histories of their own. Within the Established Church, Tractarians quarrelled with Evangelicals, and Ritualists with Anti-ritualists (to the point even of occasional riots calling for the intervention of the police). The Christian Social Union, itself in competition with the Christian Socialist League and Christian Fellowship League, was irreconcilably divided between the 'respectable' and the 'extreme'. But the competition between them for adherents was always about more than differences in their rival interpretations of the Christian message. It was acted out by carriers of both irreconcilable memes and incompatible practices who were no less protective of their social standing in relation to one another than they were eager to retain or reclaim for Christ the indifferent, the alienated, and the sceptical.

Dissenters generally shared a common feeling of relative deprivation of status when they compared themselves with Anglicans. But within Dissent, Quakers outranked Unitarians, who outranked Congregationalists, and within Methodism 'New Connection' Methodists outranked 'Wesleyan' Methodists who outranked 'Primitive' Methodists. With increased respectability came not only declining missionary zeal but alienation from a working class to whose members the churches had less and less to offer beyond a venue for the rituals surrounding marriage and death. As a writer in the Congregationalist *British Weekly* lamented in 1892, 'There are three unwritten laws, unchristian but yet held by many church-members, which run thus—(1) whosoever goes to church must be well-dressed, (2) whoever goes well dressed to church is respectable, (3) whoever is respectable is a worthy church-member.'[34] At the same time that it was an 'incontrovertible fact' that 'Protestant sects were training-grounds for working-class leaders',[35] one prominent cleric identified 'the principal belief of the working man', as 'a sense of injustice' among the causes of which 'he was inclined to classify the churches'.[36] Ecclesiastical historians of all persuasions are agreed that by the time of the First World War, only a small minority of the population, of whom the great majority were middle rather than working class, could be counted as active and committed members of any Christian church or sect. Even the Catholic bishops, whose celibate, plain-living priests were more closely in touch with their immigrant Irish working-class parishioners than either the Anglican or the Nonconformist clergy were with theirs, were worried about what they called 'leakage'.

From a social-evolutionary perspective, it is particularly revealing that this weakening of the various churches' ideological power did not come about through a lack of conscious effort to retard or reverse it. Indeed, the vigour of the effort provides quasi-experimental confirmation of the strength of the selective pressures,

---

[34] Quoted by K. S. Inglis, *Churches and the Working Classes in Victorian England* (London, 1963), p. 116.

[35] Robert Moore, *Pitmen, Preachers & Politics: The Effects of Methodism in a Durham Mining Community* (Cambridge, 1974), p. 3.

[36] A. F. Wilmington-Ingram, as cited by Owen Chadwick, *The Victorian Church*, vol. 2 (London, 1970), p. 267.

both cultural and social, with which it had to contend. Extensive material, personal, and intellectual resources were invested in the attempted revivification of Christianity in both its Anglican and its Nonconformist forms by protagonists who did so in something of the conscious spirit of an experiment. If enough churches and chapels could be built in the towns and cities, would that not bring the workers and their families back into them? If enough priests and ministers could be sent out to live the Christian life among the working classes, would that not restore the social relationships which urbanization and industrialization had broken? Would re-evangelization not revivify the respect of the working classes for their traditional betters? But the answer to all these questions was no.

In 1818, the parliamentary grant of a million pounds, which supplemented some £200,000 privately subscribed, was the beginning of what one historian of Victorian England called 'the flood of money to be poured into church building'.[37] Prosperous Dissenters were equally willing to fund the construction of thousands of chapels or meeting halls, or the conversion of existing structures for the purpose. But the idea that working-class families would be dutiful attenders at places of worship once there were enough such places for them to go to was as much wishful thinking as was the idea that missionary 'settlements' such as the Anglican Toynbee Hall, the Nonconformist Mansfield House, or the Catholic St Philip's House would bring clergy and appropriately motivated laity into active and fruitful contact *de haut en bas* with the working classes. The settlements did something to heighten the awareness of churchmen, politicians, and local government administrators of the circumstances of the urban poor. But both contemporary observers and subsequent historians are agreed that their impact on the working classes themselves was negligible. The First World War, when it came, may have brought those who fought in it back to Christianity to the extent that they joined willingly enough in the services held for them by military chaplains before they went into battle. But to a historian of the political significance of Nonconformity in British society, it is a 'commonplace' that the First World War 'dealt a shattering blow to organized religion. The churches never recovered from the ordeal, either in terms of communicants or self-possession.'[38]

Yet there was always more to Christianity than either culturally acquired beliefs or socially imposed attendance at divine service. Attendance may have been integral to the relationship between the roles of priest and parishioner in the pre-industrial communities where the resident clergy (if there were such, which in many parishes there were not) were agents as much of social control as of spiritual guidance. But empty churches did not necessarily preclude continuance of 'a general if passive acquiescence to semi-Christian doctrine'. That phrase is taken from a detailed study of the London borough of Lambeth between 1870 and 1930 by a historian who argues that 'a general addiction to Anglican rites of passage, the obtrusive presence

---

[37] G. Kitson Clark, *The Making of Victorian England* (London, 1962), p. 155.
[38] Stephen Koss, *Nonconformity in British Politics* (London, 1975), p. 155.

of ecclesiastic philanthropy, the universality of Sunday Schools, the spread of professional religious education in the Board Schools after 1870, and the popularity of occasionally attending popular festivals' amounted to 'a very impressive religious presence in Lambeth's pagan slums'.[39] The language and rituals of political and public life continued to be permeated by Christian metaphors, symbols, and motifs. Successive monarchs continued to be crowned to nationwide acclaim in Westminster Abbey, and successive Archbishops of Canterbury to sanctify them. Journalists and in due course broadcasters continued to disseminate news and views within a tacit presupposition that their audiences were citizens of a nominally Christian society. Voting behaviour continued to be influenced by inherited denominational allegiances long after the weakening of the selective affinities of the decades prior to 1886 between Liberalism and Nonconformity on one side, and Anglicanism and Conservatism on the other. Neither the trade unions nor the Labour Party were anti-clerical. Public discourse in which appeal was made to conventional morality was still informed by culturally transmitted norms recognizably similar to those that the clergy preached, however horrified Victorian churchmen of all denominations would have been by the twentieth-century relaxation of sexual mores condoned by governments and churches alike.

It might be that many English people would have said the same to a doorstep interviewer a century earlier when 'Churches, chapels, and other organs of religious life dominated—indeed, to a large extent *were*—the mass media of mid-Victorian Britain'.[40] But over the period, the cultural reproduction of the Christian message underwent a selective process of memetic dilution which discarded the traditional invocation of the divine authority of the Bible and threats of divine retribution after death while continuing to reproduce the traditional injunctions about good behaviour. With the advent of broadcasting, the BBC under John Reith used its monopoly of the medium to preserve what Reith explicitly called a 'high moral tone' which was avowedly Christian in inspiration. Under pressure from audience feedback and (after 1933) competition from continental radio stations, religion, along with educational talks and concerts of classical music, began to be displaced by human-interest stories, jazz, and audience-participation programmes, with the result that Reith, for all his acknowledged authority and force of character, 'lost and the audience won'.[41] But it hardly needs saying that there did not result the collapse of social order which nervous agnostics as well as disheartened clerics had feared would follow the waning of culturally transmitted Christian belief in the collective English mind.

The troubled speculations of intellectuals such as Leslie Stephen and Henry Sidgwick, like Matthew Arnold before them, are a biographically illuminating part

[39] Jeffrey Cox, *The English Churches in a Secular Society: Lambeth 1870–1930* (Oxford, 1982), p. 104.
[40] José Harris, *Private Lives, Public Spirit: A Social History of Britain 1870–1914* (Oxford, 1993), p. 162.
[41] W. G. Runciman, *A Treatise on Social Theory*, vol. 3 (Cambridge, 1997), p. 163.

of the cultural history of the nineteenth century. But they are of no social-evolutionary significance. The authority of the Bible was undermined by scholarly criticism and scientific discovery without any noticeable effect on the behaviour patterns of either the middle or the working classes. Sidgwick's fear that without the expectation of an afterlife, for which he was unable to find any rational basis, human beings wouldn't conduct their lives as they ought, invited the obvious rejoinder that this hadn't ever been the case in the past. Strategies of cooperation and defection, or free-riding and altruism, continued to be acted out in competition with one another, as in every human population, in sequences of the kind to be later modelled in detail by evolutionary game theorists. Agnostics could endorse Tom Paine's dictum that 'my religion is to do good' whether or not they shared his politics. Culturally transmitted visions of the good society which had nothing to do with Jesus of Nazareth inspired members of the Social Democratic Federation, and later of the Communist Party of Great Britain, no less than the followers of William Morris who agreed with him that socialism had 'an ethic and religion of its own', or the evangelical humanists of the Workers Education Association, or the 400,000 members of the League of Nations Union who were described in one of its publications in 1938 as 'a body of men and women pledged to a life of devotion to the ideal of a world order, based on justice collectively administered and enforced'.[42] Few of the late twentieth-century supporters of Oxfam shared the beliefs of the Quakers who had founded it in 1942 as the Oxford Committee for Famine Relief.

As the clergy lost their traditional standing, nominal religious affiliation ceased to be a matter of socially imposed ideology and became a matter of culturally acquired preference for one or another leisure activity and choice of congenial company. Couples who chose to get married in church now did so only because they 'wanted to show that they were serious about their relationships and felt that an old ritual in an old building conferred more dignity and solemnity on the event than did a civil ceremony in the local council offices'.[43] In 1839, a Bishop of London could still declare the Established Church to be 'the recognized and authorized instrument of education in this country'.[44] But a century later, its position had been so severely weakened by the combination of Nonconformist competition, the assumption by the state of responsibility for religious education in the board schools, and the hostility or indifference of the laity in general that the role of the Anglican clergyman had evolved from one of preceptor and pedagogue to one of social worker ministering to the needy of his parish alongside both his denominational competitors and the agents of the 'welfare state'.

---

[42] Helen McCarthy, 'Parties, voluntary associations, and democratic politics in interwar Britain', *Historical Journal* 50 (2007), p. 897.

[43] Steve Bruce, *Secularization* (Oxford, 2011), p. 86.

[44] Quoted by John Hunt, *Education in Evolution: Church, State, Society and Popular Education 1800–1870* (London, 1971), p. 18.

It took longer than might have been expected against that background for Christian memes to be driven towards extinction in the formulation of educational policy. The part that religious instruction was to play in the schools continued to provoke controversy long after the quarrels between Anglicans and Dissenters over rate aid for church schools which led to the Education Act of 1902. Although the Bill's opponents in the Labour movement were concerned that the abolition of School Boards, which were to some degree, at least, under popular control, would become subject to undue clerical influence under the Local Education Authorities replacing them, they did not seek, neither then nor thereafter, to have instruction in the Christian faith removed from the curriculum of the schools that the children of working-class parents would attend. It continued to be taken for granted up to and beyond the Education Act of 1944. In the run-up to that Act, the Norwood Report of 1943, after invoking the ideals of truth, beauty, and goodness, went on explicitly to assume that 'the recognition of such values implies for most people at least, a religious interpretation of life, which for us must mean the Christian interpretation of life'.[45] Only in 1959 was a report of the Central Advisory Committee for Education (England), in its discussion of the Sixth Form curriculum for fifteen- to eighteen-year-olds, content to recommend that they should 'understand the central affirmations of the Christian faith so that (whether they believe it or not) they at least know what Christians believe'.[46] In 1963, another report by the same body, while claiming that in the classrooms 'there is much common ground that Christian and agnostic may travel together', conceded that 'No review of the world situation can fail to show boys and girls how strong and how various are the faiths by which men live'.[47] This was to become true in a manner unforeseeable by the authors of these reports as the religion of Islam and the contentious issue of faith schools entered the agenda of policymakers in the twenty-first century. But the cultural environment had by then become one barely recognizable to the early members of the Society for the Promotion of Christian Knowledge and the evangelical philanthropists who founded charity schools in order to diffuse the Word of God among the lower ranks of the people.

There was at the same time, in the story of the Established Church's decline, one variant that offers a textbook illustration of evolutionary exaptation. By another irony of meme-practice co-evolution, Anglican Christianity survived and flourished within the institutional catchment area of the educational system which was furthest from the Sunday schools where working-class children were introduced to God the Father, His Son Jesus Christ, and the Holy Ghost. Anglican Christianity was central to the curriculum of the expensive 'public' boarding schools to which an increasing number of English upper- and middle-class parents were

---

[45] Quoted by Corelli Barnett, *The Audit of War: The Illusion and Reality of Britain as a Great Nation* (London, 1986), p. 300.

[46] Ministry of Education, *15 to 18*, vol. 1: *Report* (London, HMSO, 1969), p. 275.

[47] Ministry of Education, *Half Our Future* (London, HMSO, 1963), pp. 54, 168.

sending their sons from the 1860s onwards. It is true that during these same decades, the Sunday school movement was expanding to the point of drawing in at its peak an estimated three-quarters of five- to fourteen-year-olds. But this cannot be taken as evidence of serious commitment to the Christian faith on the part of the parents any more than of the children: it was, rather, evidence of working-class parents' recognition of the benefit of having their children minded outside the home for a few hours on Sundays by teachers from whom the children might be helped 'to avoid "getting into bad ways"',[48] and by whom they were not infrequently encouraged to attend by offers of excursions and treats. The pseudonymous C. H. Rolph recalled in his old age how his was 'always the quietest group in the place' because what they got instead of biblical instruction was a reading from something like *Treasure Island.*[49] The public schools, on the other hand, exemplify the evolutionary process sometimes analysed by sociologists under the rubric of 'neo-institutional theory' in which formal organizations are shown to adapt to their environment by linking culturally acquired legitimating myths to socially imposed disciplines. Each school had its own individual history and its own succession of more and less charismatic headmasters. But the codes, customs, and ceremonies that were replicated and transmitted in all of them both acted out and reinforced a Christian ethos whose sermons, hymns, prayers, Bible readings, and divinity lessons are as vividly described in the testimony of pupils who reacted aggressively against them as in that of pupils who unquestioningly accepted them. The members of the hundred-strong Headmasters' Conference of 1900 were as firmly and explicitly committed to the Established Church as were the chaplains conducting the services in the ubiquitous school chapels at which attendance was compulsory.

   This was not a Christianity whose message was the plight of the weak and sinful soul redeemable only by acknowledging the prospect of eternal damnation awaiting those who refused to give themselves to Christ. It was a Christianity whose message legitimated the prestige to be accorded to a status group of young men—sons not only of the 'rich and great' but also of the professional and mercantile classes, minor landed gentry, naval and military officers, and the non-clerical as well as clerical intelligentsia—who were to be the carriers of a tradition going back by long memetic descent to the medieval ideal of the good Christian knight. The good knight is, and cannot but be, superior in rank to those whom he protects. But he is not only physically courageous. He is also courteous, truthful, loyal, and immune to the temptations of avarice and pride. It hardly needs saying that in this there was much of what in the eighteenth century was called 'cant', in the nineteenth 'humbug', and in the twentieth 'bullshit'. But it was a construction that the reverse engineer will at once recognize as designed, whether consciously or not, to be adaptive in an environment very different from the one in which it first evolved. This is one institutional catchment area that was directly influenced by the fact of

---

[48] Richard Hoggart, *The Uses of Literacy* (London, 1957), p. 118.
[49] C. H. Rolph, *London Particulars* (London, 1980), p. 101.

Empire. As has been pointed out many times, both then and since, the public schools were peculiarly well adapted to the need to fill the roles by which subordinate populations overseas were being administered and defended. In the words of a book published in 1901 about the influence of the public schools on English history, 'If asked what our muscular Christianity has done, we point to the British Empire'.[50] It was a legitimating myth as adaptive in its way, for as long as the Empire lasted, as those which had justified to the elites of pre-Christian Rome their rulership over alien peoples including, among others, the natives of what later came to be called 'England'.

By the end of the nineteenth century, however, the 'kind of sanctified, but discreetly manly, social discipline' known in its 'cruder manifestations' as 'muscular Christianity' had lost such influence as it had had earlier.[51] An Old Etonian looking back from 1955 to his Victorian boyhood wondered at how it had been 'common ground' for the headmaster (Dr Warre), as much as himself (Jones minor), that an omnipotent, omniscient male God had created the universe, decided after billions of years to people an insignificant planet in a minor galaxy with a race of potentially immortal (but sinful) spirits, sent his son to earth some 2,000 years before the present to atone for human guilt by his death and resurrection, and thereby enabled those fortunate enough to have been born since then in parts of the world where they could be baptized to be redeemed from sin and enjoy, after death, everlasting life.[52] This reaction is perhaps atypically explicit. Not all Jones minor's contemporaries actively repudiated in later life the doctrines preached to them in chapel. But neither the public schools nor the ancient universities were exempt from the general secularization of the national culture. The extent of the change might have surprised the agnostic Victorian intelligentsia no less than it would the Anglican bishops and clergy so readably depicted in the novels of Trollope. But both might have been equally surprised by how little difference it made to the behaviour of the people. It was no longer a Christian culture in more than a historically vestigial sense. But that had no effect on the distribution of power between English society's constituent roles or the rank order of social prestige that the Anglican clergy had legitimated and upheld for so long.

IV

Whether with or without (but usually with) the help of a dominant religious ideology, children in societies of many different kinds acquire by imitation or learning from parents and mentors information that will weight the probability of their entry into one or another of the more or less prestigious occupational (or, as it

---

[50] J. G. Cotton Minchin, *Our Public Schools: Their Influence on English History*, p. 113, quoted by J. A. Mangan, *Athleticism in the Victorian and Edwardian Public School* (Cambridge, 1981), p. 137.
[51] John Chandos, *Boys Together: English Public Schools 1800–1864* (London, 1984), p. 266.
[52] L. E. Jones, *A Victorian Boyhood* (London, 1955), p. 203.

may be, secondary) roles that they will occupy in their adult lives. Educational institutions not only reflect but reproduce the ideological rank order of roles, and did so as much in English society in the twentieth century, when formal schooling was both universal and regulated by law, as in the eighteenth, when it was neither. The evolution of England's educational institutions was never so narrowly constrained that they functioned only to preserve the mode of persuasion unchanged. But the variation and selection of the memes transmitted from teachers to children, and of the practices defining the roles of the teachers who transmitted them, followed a co-evolutionary trajectory which sometimes assisted but sometimes, on the contrary, impeded educational reform.

No historian of the English educational system disputes that until the late nineteenth century, England's schools not only failed to enrol many working-class children at all but also failed to teach very much to those whom they did enrol. Before the Education Act of 1870 took effect and attendance was (from 1876) made compulsory, as many as a third of all men and half of all women are estimated from marriage registers to have been unable to sign their names. It was not only the standard of elementary education, as it was called, in the dame schools, ragged schools, private adventure schools, trade schools, charity schools, industry schools, and workhouse schools that was of concern to policymakers. Both the leading public schools on which the Clarendon Commission reported in 1864 and the endowed schools on which the Taunton Commission reported in 1867 were found to be falling short of what was expected of them. This is another of the topics on which commentators then and since contrasted English institutions unfavourably with Scottish ones, not only at the elementary level but all the way to the universities (or, as was possible in Scotland, directly to university from a parish school). But the practices that the would-be reformers sought to introduce faced an environment which was at once politically, ideologically, and economically hostile to their diffusion and reproduction. It was not merely that interdenominational rivalry between the Christian churches frustrated all attempts to find an acceptable compromise. Governments did not have the power to impose educational practices from the centre; middle-class parents were more concerned to have their children educated separately from the children of their inferiors in status than to raise the intellectual content of what they were taught; and the provision of financial resources was limited not only by ministerial and official parsimony but also by the haphazard distribution of endowments, the vested interests of headmasters and trustees, and the costs of upkeep of buildings of which many were ill-sited, under-repaired, and out of date.

A detailed history of English education since the eighteenth century would disclose a wide range of variation in local performance of the teachers' roles as well as in the practices defining them. Examples of impressive individual achievement against unfavourable odds can be matched against examples of mismanagement of a kind from which paradiastolic redescription would be hard pressed to extricate those convicted of it. But the education provided for successive generations of pupils, whatever their individual traits, evolved in selective affinity with the social prestige both of their parents and of their presumptive adult roles. Mill, in his *Principles of Political Economy*, took it for granted that occupational roles at all levels would be filled chiefly by children whose parents were in employments ranked the same in what he called 'social estimation'. It was common ground to the makers of educational policy that the instruction given should be appropriate to the pupil's rank. To educate working-class and middle-class boys and girls in the same way and to the same standard would be to instil into recalcitrant learners information which the working-class children would not be capable of absorbing and which would be of no use to them if they were.

After the extension of secondary education to all children and the progressive raising of the school-leaving age, the competition for alternative curricula for different grades of pupil continued to reflect the same selective pressures as previously. After the passing of the 1944 Education Act, there was much noisy talk of the 'parity of esteem' which it was hoped would be achieved between the three levels of the tripartite secondary system inaugurated by the Act. But as a speaker bluntly put it to the 1953 Congress of the TUC, 'All of you who have got children round about the age of 11 will know whether there is equal esteem or not.'[53] At the same time, the prestige attaching to a university degree was maintained or even heightened. Neither academics nor policymakers questioned that 'the increasing educational requirements of the developing professions and of the upper branches of governmental and industrial administration have made university education a technical as well as a cultural necessity for occupations of high social prestige'.[54] A slowly increasing number of sons, and a still smaller number of daughters, of working-class parents began to win places at institutions of 'higher' education. But those institutions, like the occupational roles for which they qualified their graduates, continued to be ranked as before.

There runs through the history of English education at all levels from the early eighteenth century to the early twenty-first the same selective affinity between the prestige of the teachers and the prestige of the subjects they taught, from the professors of Greek and Latin at Oxford or Cambridge down to the teachers by rote of the multiplication tables. By the end of the nineteenth century, there were some quarter-million schoolmasters and schoolmistresses in the elementary schools of England and Wales, attendance had risen above 80 per cent, and illiteracy had been virtually eliminated. But the mutant practices which evolved from a monitorial system through a pupil–teacher system to payment by results under the Revised Code of 1862 did nothing for the status of teachers denied the recognition accorded to the teachers of more 'advanced' subjects for which their national associations unsuccessfully campaigned. A partial exception was to be found in the local environment of Wales, where 'nonconformity had a widespread national and

[53] Trade Union Congress, *Report* (1953), p. 315.
[54] D. V. Glass, 'Introduction', in D. V. Glass, ed., *Social Mobility in Britain* (London, 1954), p. 17.

patriotic appeal with which the teachers were associated'.[55] But in England, they were subordinate to a clergy whose social standing was higher than theirs and who were empowered in the roles of inspector or manager to assess and report on their performance. The introduction after 1846 of the practice of certification by examination did something both to raise the pay of the certificated by way of government grants and to enhance the status of elementary school teaching more generally. But the trade-off was that the government controlled the criteria of certification. After both the Revised Code of 1862 and the Education Act of 1870, the standard was deliberately lowered in order to encourage recruitment. During the twentieth century, the social prestige of the teachers improved as the standard of instruction rose, recruits were attracted from the grammar schools and universities, and the working environment of the primary schools, as they were now called, became increasingly congenial. But the status of the secondary school teachers rose at the same time in parallel. 'Parity of esteem' was as elusive as ever.

Reproduction of this persistent disparity was sustained throughout by the selective pressures brought to bear from within the mode of production. Parents who were ready and able to pay to have their children educated shopped around as might be expected for the best bargains they could find. This was as true of working-class parents who spent a few pennies for a son to learn to keep a set of account books in a clear pen-and-ink hand as it was for middle-class parents saving on their own domestic expenses in order to send a child (typically, a son) to a public boarding school. But no working-class parent could afford the freedom of choice that many middle-class parents could. The headmaster of Repton reported to the Schools Enquiry Commission in 1868 that wealthy parents invariably asked 'what is the character, station, and position of the home boarders?' and when they were given the answer 'of all classes down to the sons of blacksmiths and washerwomen' they 'immediately withdrew their applications'.[56] Later, as the concerns of middle-class parents were increasingly directed to formal qualifications and university entrance, the pressure of competition forced the fee-paying schools to enhance the quality of the product they offered sufficiently to justify the fees that they charged in order to do so. Those which failed to adapt, including some of the preparatory boarding schools which offered preparation for entry to the public schools, were driven out of business in classic Darwinian fashion. In the second half of the twentieth century, a Labour government set up a commission charged with considering the integration of both the public and the direct grant schools into a national comprehensive system—a measure that had already been considered but then discarded during the run-up to the coalition government's Education Act of 1944. But how were parents to be prevented from paying teachers or private tutors

---

[55] Asher Tropp, *The School Teachers: The Growth of the Teaching Profession in England and Wales from 1800 to the Present Day* (London, 1957), p. 35 n.23.

[56] Quoted by Brian Simon, *Education and the Labour Movement 1870–1920* (London, 1965), p. 99 n.1.

of their choice to educate their children as they wished to see them educated? Where the state-run secondary schools were able to offer what middle-class parents wanted, middle-class parents were ready to take advantage of it. But now, the trade-off was, as it came to be colloquially put, in the postcode, that is in the price of the houses into which the middle-class parents moved in order for their children to be eligible for admission to the local schools which they judged to be best for them.

At the tertiary level, there were no less visible selective pressures that favoured the continuing reproduction of existing practices after the number of institutions offering higher education was increased in the second half of the twentieth century. The Robbins Report of 1963 assumed 'as an axiom' that 'courses in higher education should be available for all those who are qualified by ability and attainment to pursue them and who wish to do so' and expressly hoped for 'the removal of any designations or limitations that cause differentiation between institutions that are performing similar functions'.[57] But as a directly involved contemporary observer was later to put it, this meant that 'parity of esteem was to be the principle whatever the reality'.[58] The thirty-two 'polytechnics' created under the so-called binary system did not achieve parity with the degrees awarded by the universities, and when they were subsequently promoted to being universities they reproduced in less prestigious forms many of the practices to which they might have offered competing alternatives. The same questions as ever continued to be debated among both policymakers and commentators about the form and content of tertiary education that would best serve the national economy. But whatever the answers, the institutions of post-compulsory education continued to reflect the criteria of social prestige of the wider society in which their credentialed graduates pursued their subsequent careers.

Viewed in retrospect, it was astonishing that in 1937–38 the percentage of Cambridge graduates from public schools should have been, at 68 per cent, higher by 6 per cent than the percentage given by the statistician J. A. Venn for the years 1752–99.[59] Although the number of students at English universities doubled between the two world wars, no more than half a dozen per thousand came from elementary schools (and of the total, under a quarter were women). When the time came that Oxford and Cambridge could no longer be viewed as little more than finishing schools for the sons of the gentry and recruiting stations for the Church, 'inequality of access to the universities became an almost commonplace illustration of distributive injustice'.[60] But a multitude of sociological studies documented the continuing extent to which educational achievement at all levels was correlated with the occupation of the child's father, and children of parents who had themselves

---

[57] Committee on Higher Education, *Report* (London, HMSO, 1963), p. 8.

[58] Noel Annan, *Our Age* (London, 1990), p. 373.

[59] Hester Jenkins and D. Caradog Jones, 'Social class of Cambridge alumni of the 18th and 19th centuries', *British Journal of Sociology* 1 (1950), p. 103.

[60] A. H. Halsey, *Decline of Donnish Dominion: The British Academic Profession in the Twentieth Century* (Oxford, 1992), p. 65.

been to university were likelier to succeed in the competition for acquisition of a prestigious positional good which excluded others from its possession.

Even at the end of the twentieth century, these issues concerned only a minority of the relevant age-cohort. But in the late nineteenth and early twentieth centuries, the diffusion of literacy among almost the entire population through universal state-funded primary education impacted on the daily lives of the working classes in ways which cultural historians have documented in detail, including not only the curricula of the schools but also both the fiction and the journalism that the pupils used their literacy to read. But it did not disturb the order in which the roles of the population were ideologically ranked, any more than had the eighteenth-century diffusion of the new conventions of discussion in the 'bourgeois' public sphere. Nothing prevented the mass-circulation newspapers of the late nineteenth century, any more than the ubiquitous television programmes of the late twentieth, from questioning that ideology—as, indeed, they sometimes did. But more often, they reflected it in their treatment of the topics that they chose for the entertainment of their readers and viewers. The 'partnership', as one historian puts it, 'between the schoolmasters and the capitalist proprietors and editors, bound together by mass literacy',[61] was widely credited by commentators on the Left with a function of 'social control' in crowding out, if not actually suppressing, the dissemination of messages subversive of established institutions. But that is a commonplace if construed to mean that the messages most frequently transmitted in print, as later by radio and television, were more supportive than otherwise of the dominant ideology, and a falsehood if construed to mean that any questioning of the dominant ideology was excluded.

In the environment of a formally free market, the controllers of the means of persuasion were engaged in continuing and strenuous competition for readers, listeners, and viewers. It has been estimated that in the aftermath of the Second World War over half the British working class was reading at least some part of the *News of the World* every Sunday. If, by contrast, not only the communist *Daily Worker* but even (despite being subsidized by the TUC) the Labour *Daily Herald* were failures, it was because they did not provide their intended readers with enough of what they wanted to read. This may make it the more remarkable that Robert Blatchford's *Clarion* had been selling 80,000 copies a week in the 1890s. But Blatchford's genial, unpatronizing, and anti-puritanical version of Socialism, with its combination of full-blooded patriotism and nostalgic anti-industrialism, was far more appealing to its audience than either the doctrinaire Marxism of Hyndman and the Social Democratic Federation or the hardly less doctrinaire Fabianism of the Webbs.

The trade-off critical to the success of the mass-circulation newspapers was between circulation and price. For the proprietors' investment to be profitable, prices low enough to attract working-class readers had to attract enough of them,

---

[61] David Vincent, *Literacy and Popular Culture: England 1750–1914* (Cambridge, 1989), p. 236.

with the consequential risk of a runaway effect that would bankrupt any who were not in a position to subsidize their papers from other sources of revenue. The dilemma was solved by advertising, which in due course led to the selling for free of papers or magazines able thereby to increase their circulation to the point that advertisers would compete for space in their pages: instead of readers buying newspapers, 'newspapers bought readers'.[62] The advertisements then came to influence working-class lifestyles as much as, if not more than, anything else that the papers contained, whether by meeting readers' perceived daily needs or by encouraging them to aspire to the ownership of goods previously restricted to middle-class status groups. But whatever change resulted in patterns of consumption among working-class households, they did not alter the criteria by which individuals, families, and households continued to be ranked in accordance not only with the occupational role of the family or household head but also with the culturally constructed distinctions of ethnicity and gender which, in both their factual and their fictional messages, the media purveyed.

V

Psychologists have yet to devise a technique for measuring precisely the extent to which messages favourable or unfavourable to the image of a group, category, or community culturally defined as 'other' increase or reduce the extent and degree of exclusionary behaviour towards its members. How far did 'the most viewed television programme for much of its six-year life'[63]—the BBC series *Till Death Us Do Part*—reinforce, undermine, or merely reflect the place in the rank order of social prestige of members of ethnic minorities that it portrayed? There are abundant examples in the literature of comparative sociology where stigmatizing memes and the practices in which they are acted out are either reproduced with consistent fidelity over many generations or diffused across a whole population with extraordinary speed within a single one. But there are also abundant examples where, despite their best efforts, neither propagandists nor policymakers are able to change popular attitudes and consequential patterns of behaviour in the direction they wish. Cultural historians are generally agreed that in some respects, at least, the English became a more tolerant people between the early eighteenth and early twenty-first centuries. But no historian has claimed that discrimination against either women or ethnic minorities became a thing of the past to the extent that religious discrimination did.

The psychology of stereotyping is a well-researched topic in evolutionary theory. Its long history can be traced back to the environment in which our hunting and

---

[62] A. J. P. Taylor, *English History 1914–1945* (Oxford, 1965), p. 309.

[63] Gavin Schaffer, 'Till death us do part and the BBC: racial politics and the British working classes 1965–75', *Journal of Contemporary History* 45 (2010), p. 457.

foraging ancestors were first forming relationships with out-groups on which they depended but could not control. Given the lack of reliable information about the 'others', a stereotype based on such limited inferences as can be drawn from preliminary observation of their behaviour provides a basis for predicting the out-group's subsequent actions and reactions and adopting a strategy with which to respond to them. As the relationship evolves, and impressions culturally transmitted are supplemented by recognition of differences in the power attaching to social roles, stereotypes function to endorse the evolving exclusionary practices by which the 'others' are institutionally disprivileged. The probability of reproduction of the stereotype is likely to be enhanced if the out-group is physically distinguishable (which it does not have to be, as is strikingly illustrated by the example of the 'invisible race' of Japanese *Burakumin*[64]). It is then enhanced if the distinguishing characteristics are directly associated with a stigmatized role. The stereotype will continue to be culturally adaptive for as long as the 'others' have attributed to them traits that exclude them from social roles in which, were they admitted to them, their behaviour would reveal the stereotype to be baseless. Significant change in their social location requires a break in the feedback loop between the exclusionary practices and the stigmatizing memes whose probability of reproduction both increases and is increased by theirs.

From the perspective of comparative sociology, England is a society which, although it could not possibly be classified as a 'caste' society, still retained some castelike practices which continued to compete with pluralist ones. Explanation of their relative fitness is complicated by overdetermination from a multiplicity of selective pressures in local environments where residential segregation, occupational specialization, language, physical appearance, religion, and lifestyles perceived as alien combine to sustain exclusionary behaviour patterns between unequally ranked status groups. Some incomers from more or less distant societies of origin were more, and others less, easily absorbed. Anti-Semitism in more and less outspoken forms is abundantly documented at all systactic levels throughout the period in a complex interplay between cultural construction of differences and exclusionary social practices. In the eighteenth century, the prejudice encountered by Scots who came south after the Act of Union was dissipated in part by the roles made available to them through the commercial and military expansion of the British Empire. In the nineteenth century, the prejudice encountered by Irish immigrants was for some time exacerbated by their Catholicism but then diminished as religious differences lost their earlier salience. After the Second World War, as the number of Asian and Afro-Caribbean immigrants from formerly dependent territories grew and they were increasingly concentrated in particular areas of major cities, they could not but be perceived as intruders by members of the indigenous population from whom they were differentiated by colour as well as lifestyle.

[64] George De Vos and Hiroshi Wagatsuma, *Japan's Invisible Race: Caste in Culture and Personality* (Berkeley, CA, 1966).

Among the Jews, of whom over 150,000 from Eastern Europe settled in Britain between 1881 and 1914, money often brought social prestige: the rich eighteenth-century 'Jew-broker', Samuel Gideon, did not himself acquire a title but his son became a baronet. Lionel Rothschild, having been elected to Parliament in 1847, was denied his seat only when he refused to take the Oath. Disraeli's unabashed (if idiosyncratically self-defined) Jewish identity and physical features deliberately accentuated by opposition cartoonists did not prevent his climbing to the top of the greasy pole,[65] even though in his case the money he needed was borrowed rather than his own. But the persistent association of Jews in the English mind with money-lending and money-making accounts for Cobbett's reference to the 'Jew-like race of money-changers' and the Chartists' denunciations of 'Jewocracy', as later for Rupert Brooke's complaint in a letter written to his friend Eddie Marsh after his return from the South Seas that 'another Jew has bought a peerage'.[66] In the 1930s, the arrival of Jewish refugees from Nazi Germany was met with sympathy but also with resentment of so-called 'Refujews'. They were more easily either assimilated or ranked alongside their Gentile counterparts on the 'pluralist' model than were the 'coloured' minorities. But the stereotype was never driven all the way to extinction.

By the third quarter of the twentieth century, 'race relations' had become an academic discipline of its own. The 'facts of racial disadvantage',[67] particularly in employment and housing, were unmistakable. It was hardly possible to deny when, for example, researchers found that in the West Indian population of the West Midlands in the 1960s nurses were four times as numerous as white-blouse workers but in the general population there were sixteen times as many white-blouse workers as nurses.[68] After discrimination on grounds of race became a matter of legislation as well as widespread public debate, field experiments using controlled applications for advertised vacancies confirmed the persistence of bias on the part of employers.[69] A survey of people of Indian, Pakistani, Bangladeshi, black Caribbean, and black African background carried out after the general election of 2010 found second-generation immigrants to be not only those most disadvantaged in the labour market but also 'the ones who feel most alienated from the political process'.[70] But the ethnic minorities, as defined, made up no more than 8 per cent of the resident adult population of England and Wales in the 2011 census. The

---

[65] David Feldman, 'Conceiving difference: religion, race and the Jews in Britain c. 1750–1900', *History Workshop Journal* 76 (2013), p. 175 & fig. 3.

[66] Quoted by Philip Larkin, *Required Writing: Miscellaneous Pieces 1955–1982* (London, 1983), p. 180.

[67] David J. Smith, *The Facts of Racial Disadvantage: A National Survey*, PEP Broadsheet 560 (1976).

[68] E. J. B. Rose and associates, *Colour & Citizenship: A Report on British Race Relations* (London, 1969), p. 166.

[69] Colin Brown and Pat Gay, *Racial Discrimination 17 Years after the Act* (London, 1989).

[70] Anthony F. Heath, Stephen D. Fisher, Gemma Rosenblatt, David Sanders, and Maria Sobolewska, *The Political Integration of Ethnic Minorities in Britain* (Oxford, 2013), p. 8.

change that affected a whole half of the population and might (I have suggested) strike Defoe more than any other was the decline in the stereotyping of women.

The relative neglect of women in the academic literature by male sociologists and historians has been convincingly interpreted by feminist critics as itself symptomatic of stereotypes transmitted down successive generations by patriarchal family and household heads and an exclusively male clergy, judiciary, professoriate, and Parliament within a gendered division of labour. No historian denies that women were widely and persistently subordinated to a husband, father, or male household head through whom they were assigned secondary rank in accordance with the status group to which the husband, father, or household head belonged. In the nineteenth century, although not taken so wholly for granted as in the eighteenth, this subordination was reproduced even in legislation passed in response to the acknowledged concerns of married women. It was symptomatic that although the Infant Custody Act of 1839 vested custody of children under seven with the divorced mother, this was subject to the proviso that she had not been ruled adulterous, and that the Matrimonial Causes Act of 1857 allowed men but not women to petition on the grounds of adultery. Likewise, the Married Women's Property Acts of 1870 and 1882 were framed explicitly in terms that presupposed that the power of decision-making was vested in the husband, and the Guardianship of Infants Act of 1886 gave more power to fathers than to mothers.

It would, however, be an exaggeration to claim that English women were ever totally powerless. They inherited, accumulated, managed, lent, and bequeathed property of their own and acted in the roles of both executor and trustee. Women who were born or married into families within the ruling elite could exert informal but acknowledged political influence (not to mention that the monarch could be a queen). Middle-class as well as upper-class women exploited the practice of coverture to their own advantage and working-class women represented their husbands in county courts to negotiate small debt claims. No doubt there were submissive wives of domineering husbands at all levels of English society: the placing of property in the hands of trustees to avoid coverture did not prevent a husband from being a trustee or from bullying his wife into giving him control.[71] But in the eighteenth century, 'Masculine authority was formally acknowledged but practically managed' by 'genteel' women,[72] and in the nineteenth, 'Much talked about in Victorian circles, the angel in the house was nowhere to be found among living women'.[73] As the intellectual arguments for patriarchy became increasingly discredited in both parliamentary and extra-parliamentary debate, a growing number of women became involved in local politics in the roles of both voter and candidate,

---

[71] Ben Griffin, *The Politics of Gender in Victorian Britain: Masculinity, Political Culture and the Struggle for Women's Rights* (Cambridge, 2012), pp. 82–3.

[72] Amanda Vickery, *The Gentleman's Daughter: Women's Lives in Georgian England* (New Haven, CT, 1998), p. 285.

[73] M. Jeanne Peterson, 'No angel in the house: the Victorian myth and the Paget women', *American Historical Review* 89 (1984), p. 708.

even if the variation and selection of practices arising from the quasi-random decisions of policymakers sometimes enhanced their involvement (as when a parliamentary amendment extended the franchise to female ratepayers in 1869) but sometimes reduced it (as when a court decision restricted it to unmarried women in 1872). By the end of the nineteenth century, a million women were enfranchised on a county or borough register and politically active women were organizing, canvassing, serving on committees, and speaking on public platforms. Male commentators were frequently provoked to condescension, disparagement, or ridicule. But their reactions were a testimony to the threat these women were seen to pose to the accepted stereotype.

Two alternative strategies were then in competition for reproduction and diffusion within the groups and associations making up what came to be called the 'women's movement'. Neither was directed to altering the distribution of power between the roles to which women were denied access. Once admitted to the masculine hierarchy of social prestige, women largely reproduced it. There were of course individual women at all systactic levels who did wish to see it altered, just as there were others who wished to see it remain unchanged. But their common objective was to alter the beliefs and attitudes that legitimated the denial of the 'perfect equality between the sexes' for which Mill had pleaded in 1869. Their difference was over how that phrase was to be construed. To some, it implied a 'separate-but-equal' ideology whereby women's distinctive attributes and capabilities were acknowledged but accorded the same respect as the distinctive attributes and capacities of men. But to others, that implied an ongoing reproduction of a cultural stereotype which was inherently demeaning and had to be comprehensively overturned.

Some feminists explicitly distanced themselves from the role of wife and mother. But others agreed with Violet Markham that 'the man as worker, the woman as homemaker remains my ideal of society'.[74] She was not implying by this that she saw the homemaker as the inferior of the worker any more than did an upper-middle-class woman for whom 'wifehood, as she exemplified it, was a profession in itself'.[75] In the working classes, many women who were 'increasingly defining themselves as housewives' were as such being entrusted by their husbands with all aspects of household management.[76] The gendered division of labour which for some women was the badge of inferior esteem was for others the route by which they could not merely affirm equality with men but demonstrate capacities and skills of higher value which, if carried into masculine roles, would benefit society as a whole. Josephine Butler argued that if women were to have 'unrestricted liberty to

---

[74] Quoted by Jane Lewis, *Women and Social Action in Victorian and Edwardian England* (London, 1991), p. 293.
[75] Pat Jalland, *Women, Marriage and Politics* (Oxford, 1986), p. 7.
[76] Joanna Bourke, 'Housewifery in working-class England 1860–1914', *Past & Present* 143 (1994), p. 167.

engage in any employment' it would 'lead to the restoration of true home ideals'.[77] But this, it could then be argued, implied an endorsement of the cultural stereotype which differentiated 'masculine' and 'feminine' temperaments, talents, and tastes, and thereby helped to perpetuate the 'institutionalized deference' of, for example, the 'personal secretary-boss relationship, where deference and "femininity" are an important part of the job-training'.[78] 'Separate spheres' could not, on this view, be equal spheres unless and until women were occupying political, professional, financial, commercial, entrepreneurial, judicial, academic, military, artistic, managerial, supervisory, administrative, and proprietary roles alongside of men in proportion to their numbers in the general population.

Competition between the rival strategies was clearly discernible throughout the long campaign for the parliamentary vote. Not all women felt relatively deprived of social prestige by the lack of it. Some of its most articulate opponents were themselves women, like the Duchess of Atholl who spoke so well that 'her audience could not understand why, whatever she might say, such a woman should not vote'.[79] As narrative history, the story has its full share of intriguing might-have-beens. What, for example, would have happened if Gladstone had shared the opinion of Mill, or Asquith that of Lloyd George? It might not have required a four-year war in the course of which suffragette militancy waned, a coalition government was formed in which Labour was represented, women were recruited in growing numbers into 'war work', and the case for votes for women became linked with the case for votes for hitherto unenfranchised servicemen. Even then, women under thirty had to wait a further ten years. But when it finally happened, it turned out to be yet another contested event whose sociological consequences were less than its advocates had hoped and its opponents had feared. Female voters merged with male in an electorate whose behaviour was determined by much the same interests and constrained within much the same limits. There was never a women's party as such, any more than women ever formed a 'class'. The members of associations such as the Women's Labour League and Women's Cooperative Guild found that they were neither treated like men nor accorded separate but equal status as women. It was not unusual for activists' experience to be of 'men doing most of the talking and decision-making in the constituency parties and leaving them to make tea and organize the Christmas party'.[80] The selective pressure which did most to undermine the fitness of the cultural stereotype came

---

[77] George W. and Lucy A. Johnson, eds., *Josephine E. Butler: An Autobiographical Memoir* (Bristol, 1909), p. 81.

[78] Kate Purcell, 'Gender and the experience of employment', in Duncan Gallie, ed., *Employment in Britain* (Oxford, 1988), p. 162.

[79] Brian Harrison, *Separate Spheres: The Opposition to Women's Suffrage in Britain* (London, 1978), p. 113.

[80] Pamela M. Graves, *Labour Women: Women in British Working-Class Politics 1918–1939* (Cambridge, 1994), p. 75.

not from the political but from the economic environment—not, that is, from the world of electioneering but from the world of work.

When G. K. Chesterton said that the women of England rose up with the cry that they would not be dictated to and proceeded to become stenographers, he was making a valid sociological point as well as a typical Chestertonian pun. Nineteenth-century women were not institutionally debarred from working outside their homes, and many unmarried women depended for their livelihoods on doing so. But the extent to which the division of labour was gendered is attested not only by the statistics of occupational distribution but also by the idiom in which the occupational roles were designated—seamstress (or needlewoman), laundress, governess, parlourmaid, charwoman, schoolmistress. The most highly ranked of the 1¾ million women employed as domestic servants in 1881 worked in their employers' houses as cooks, not as butlers. Young children might be taught by women, but it was unthinkable that university students should be taught by a woman or that a woman should take holy orders and conduct services in church. Cooking, clothing, caring, cleaning, mending, minding, and nursing were culturally defined as women's work, not fighting or pleading or preaching. From the 1880s onwards, women might be sat down to operate a typewriter or answer a telephone, but the feminization of office work was almost exclusively confined to the lower grades.

During the First World War, women moved into roles which there were not enough men to fill. But the historians of the period are agreed that government, employers, trade unionists, and the women themselves all saw this as a temporary phase of so-called 'dilution' which would come to an end when the war was over. Moreover, women were in any case more likely to be found in service jobs (including bus conductresses or 'clippies') than in the male-dominated manual trades. The composition of the female labour force as reported by the Registrar General in 1931 was much as it had been in 1901: it was so far made up of single women (including the widowed and divorced) that of the occupational roles covered by the census only some 15 per cent of it were occupied by married women. Despite the Sex Disqualification (Removal) Act of 1919, many employers, public authorities included, operated a marriage ban by which primary responsibility for home and family was socially imposed on wives and prospective mothers. Employers continued to pay women less than men for the same work, and when women were recruited into 'skilled' trades the work was likely then to be reclassified as 'unskilled'.

It was only in the environment of near-full employment that followed the Second World War that the stereotype of man as worker and woman as homemaker ceased to be reproduced as previously. The nearly trebled proportion of married women in the female labour force from the 15 per cent of the 1931 census to the 40 per cent in the census of 1951 is in part a function of an increase in the number of women marrying, and doing so at an earlier age. But when the participation rate for married women is cross-tabulated by age, the rate for those aged twenty to twenty-four rises from 18.5 per cent in 1931 to 36.5 per cent in 1951,[81] before rising further through the 1960s and 1970s to the point that by 1977 the Department of Employment calculated that 59 per cent of married women aged twenty to twenty-four were in paid work. Much of this work was part-time, and much of it in the expanding service sector of the economy. But by 1990, the total number of women in employment was 94 per cent of that for men. Behind the overall rates, there had always been different selective pressures at work. Some married working-class women had never wanted factory work, particularly if they had small children to care for, while others 'would rather be in a factory than in the house because the comparative isolation gave them the dumps after being used to the company of hundreds of workmates'.[82] More wives in textile towns worked and had on average fewer children than in mining villages where there were fewer opportunities for paid work and they had on average more children. In upper-middle status groups, Nonconformist families were more likely than Anglican families to encourage daughters as well as sons to become educationally qualified and take up professional careers. Among the three 'great' professions, women faced exclusionary practices for longer in the Church than in the law and for longer in the law than in medicine. But by the last quarter of the twentieth century, the unprecedented extent to which women had entered the non-domestic labour force was such that the interwar period came to be viewed in hindsight as the by now outdated 'high water mark of the privatized little domestic unit'.[83]

The change was thus the outcome of an evolutionary trajectory in which expanded opportunities within the same market-driven division of labour heightened the frequency with which women took advantage of them, which led in turn to their being increasingly seen occupying and performing roles, including 'professional' roles, from which they had previously been excluded and thereby to the progressive abandonment of the culturally transmitted stereotype that had functioned to perpetuate their exclusion. Frequency-dependence requires that genes, memes, or practices that were initially rare in the population increase disproportionately to the rate at which they would otherwise do so. But in an environment in which that condition is fulfilled, their diffusion will follow the S-shaped logistic curve familiar to sociologists from behaviour patterns that range from the wearing of seat belts to child-bearing outside marriage, which by the year 2000 reached 40 per cent.[84] Whether Defoe would welcome that change or, on the contrary, be outraged by it, he could not but immediately appreciate the magnitude of its impact on the lived experience of its beneficiaries.

---

[81] Guy Routh, *Occupation and Pay in Great Britain 1906–60* (Cambridge, 1965), p. 46.
[82] Allen Clarke, *The Effects of the Factory System* (London, 1899), p. 58.
[83] Ray Pahl, *Divisions of Labour* (Oxford, 1984), p. 73.
[84] John Ermisch, 'The puzzling rise in childrearing outside marriage', in Anthony F. Heath, John Ermisch, and Duncan Gallie, eds., *Understanding Social Change* (Oxford, 2005), p. 33.

VI

In the search for a descriptive vignette that might convey the extent of both continuity and change in the rank order of roles in the dimension of social prestige, domestic service offers a multitude of revealing examples. Even if resident domestic servants were still a staple of jokes after the Second World War, it was in the aftermath of the First that the jokes began to reflect a recognition that neither their availability to any prospective employer who could afford them nor their acquiescence in the deferential forms of conduct and address expected of them could be taken for granted to the extent that they had been up to 1914. It would have been astonishing before 1914 to hear a Minister of Labour remarking in the House of Commons, as happened in 1921, on 'the amount of heat to which this domestic servants' question gives rise on both sides of the House',[85] or, as happened in 1923, for a non-parliamentary committee to be set up by the Ministry of Labour to investigate complaints about the payment of unemployment benefit to women suitable for domestic work. Domestic service remained on the agenda of public policy until 1945, when the government published a report on its post-war organization. But by then the role, although not entirely extinct, was enough of an anachronism for the question put by prosecuting counsel to the jury in the *Lady Chatterley's Lover* case of 1960, about whether they would wish their servants to see the book in their house, to provoke immediate and widespread ridicule.

No historian or sociologist will claim that cartoons in *Punch* are a reliable guide to actual patterns of social behaviour. No middle-class host ever said to a guest 'with Socialistic opinions', as depicted in a cartoon of 18 June 1919, 'I hope you'll be careful what you say about the moneyed classes. Our maid is very sensitive.' But they can be a revealing pointer to the nuances and subtleties of attitude and belief which distinguish the subjective experiences of representative members of different status groups in different environments. Not only the captions but also the draughtsmanship are expressions of aspects of the stereotypes assumed to be somewhere in the heads of the prospective readers. They may have no influence whatever in either moderating the stereotype or reinforcing it. But however minimal their explanatory value, they have a unique descriptive value of their own.

On 2 June 1920, *Punch* carried a full-page cartoon under the heading MANNERS AND MODES entitled 'The Domestic Servant Shortage' in which the daughters of the house are depicted dressing up as maids. The caption reads 'How the Misses Marjoribanks De Vere (with the assistance of a perruquier) uphold the dignity of Her Ladyship their Mama's afternoon "At Homes"'. It is the type of cartoon that tempts cultural historians to read into the drawing and the caption overtones that may or may not have been present either in the minds of the cartoonists or in those of the contemporary readers of *Punch*. But what, for a

---

[85] 147 H.C. Deb., *c.*476 (Hansard).

start, about the chosen family name? Marjoribanks is the surname of a family ennobled as Tweedmouth, and the second Lord Tweedmouth had got into trouble in 1908 when as First Lord of the Admiralty he was said to have disclosed details of the naval estimates to Germany. De Vere, by contrast, is the name of a Norman family which received its lands in Essex from William the Conqueror himself. Perhaps Marjoribanks was chosen simply as one of those upper-class surnames that nobody quite knows how to pronounce, like Cholmondeley. Perhaps De Vere was chosen to echo the extinction of the original line, the last of whom died in 1703 as twentieth Earl of Oxford after fighting at the Battle of the Boyne. At all events, the mother has to be 'Mama'—'Mum' would be out of the question. As for 'At Home', the ritual was not unique to the aristocracy: the wife of a prosperous provincial millowner in Edwardian England could be expected to receive on designated days in the month visitors who would on entry put their calling-cards on a silver tray in the hall. But such visitors would always have had to be let in by a maid. So if, in 1919, the daughters of the house were to pass as maids, they would have to look the part. Hence the need for the professional perruquier who, as if for a performance of amateur theatricals, is brought in to make sure that the hairdo is right.

How funny you find any of this is up to you. But the cartoon could no more have been thought up and published a century earlier than a century later. It captures the flavour of a stage in the evolution of the rank order of social prestige in which members of the topmost status group, for whom a resident domestic staff was a matter of course, face the prospect (which was in due course to become a matter of course itself) that daughters of working-class parents would no longer be available for such employment in the way that they had been since the time of Aubrey De Vere, twentieth Earl of Oxford, and the tradesman and journalist Daniel Defoe.

4

Economics and the Power of Markets

I

Defoe's England was neither an industrial nor an urban society. But it was a society whose central economic roles were defined by practices through which the purchase and sale of property (or rights to property), raw materials (or access to them), labour and the products of labour, commodities, credit, personal and household possessions, and perquisites of diverse kinds were negotiated and concluded under recognized institutional rules—not forgetting the lucrative traffic in slaves in which numerous Englishmen and Scotsmen were actively involved overseas. There were of course many divergences from the ideal type: theft and extortion were no more market transactions than the imposition of customs and excise duties, or the seizure of merchant seamen by the press gangs, or donations to charitable causes freely made by wealthy philanthropists. But, as one historian of eighteenth-century England puts it, 'Getting and spending was everyone's business—at least everyone's who could afford it',[1] and in a period of expanding foreign trade as well as domestic demand there were more and more opportunities both to get and to spend. Native and foreign observers concurred in seeing a society in which the rich were as rich and the poor as poor as was only to be expected, but the social space between them was being filled by an increasingly large and commercial middling sort and an increasing number of labouring people getting and spending above the level of bare subsistence.

A market economy need not be a cash economy, despite the unquestioned importance of monetized practices in the evolution of capitalism as a mode of production. Economic historians are agreed that in England, full-time wage labour was far from universal in Defoe's day among those who worked with their hands. Even if during the eighteenth century a majority of working-class households came to receive at least part of their income in wages, much labour (particularly the domestic labour of women and children) was not waged at all, many wage workers raised their own livestock and cultivated their own plots of land, and, as Defoe himself remarked, many of the poor took rights of 'commonage' to be as much their property as rich men's land was theirs.[2] The environmental pressures that restricted

---

[1] Roy Porter, *English Society in the Eighteenth Century* (Harmondsworth, 1982), p. 202.
[2] Defoe, *Tour*, vol. 1, p. 395.

the diffusion of the practice of wage labour were of several kinds. In remoter districts, some employers were unable to pay cash because it was not until 1821 that the Mint began 'at last' to produce sufficiently large amounts of small coin.[3] The practice was constrained in some rural environments by manorial controls, and in some urban environments by guild regulations. The culturally acquired conception of the 'just price' was sometimes socially imposed by the decision of local magistrates, particularly in response to the 'vagaries' of international trade and domestic demand,[4] which affected the market for provisions as well as labour to the point of provoking local riots. But all this took place within the institutional catchment area of a market where sellers were selling for as much as they had the power to charge to buyers buying for as little as they could help.

Economic historians are also well aware that the diffusion and reproduction of the practice of wage labour long pre-dated the evolution of large-scale factory production. But a striking quasi-experimental illustration of its fitness is to be found not in agriculture or manufacturing but in the difference between the roles of English and Scottish coalminers. In the time of Defoe, Scottish miners, unlike their English counterparts, were neither tenants nor wage workers but serfs. Not only they but also their children were bound to landowners empowered to prevent them by force from withdrawing their labour and to move them at will from one colliery to another. They were excluded from the Scottish equivalent of Habeas Corpus. Escape was difficult because the mining communities were small, the work was underground, and the miners were kept under close supervision. Whereas many English miners had worked leased land where they had rights to dig and sell, Scottish miners had never had such entitlement. Yet serfdom became increasingly maladaptive under selective pressure from a market that generated a threefold increase in the demand for coal in the second half of the eighteenth century. Enserfed miners weren't sufficiently productive, and had to be supplemented by imported free labour. The Scottish practices were accordingly outcompeted by those encoded in one-year bonds which were by then customary in the mining communities of North East England (which differed in their turn from the similar but not identical practices that had evolved in the different environments of the coal mines of Yorkshire or South Wales or the lead mines of Derbyshire or the tin mines of Cornwall). Scottish serfdom has an evolutionary trajectory of its own, including the practice of 'arling' by which a present was given to a collier and his wife at the time of a child's christening in return for a promise that the child would be brought up a miner. But it did not secure for the lairds the supply of labour which only the offer of wages at the market rate could do. Some employers responded by adopting the practice of requiring miners to produce formal proof

[3] M. J. Daunton, *Progress and Poverty: An Economic and Social History of Britain 1700–1850* (Oxford, 1995), p. 426.

[4] Dale Edwards Williams, 'Morals, markets, and the English crowd in 1766', *Past & Present* 104 (1984), p. 59.

of discharge from their previous bonds. But the trade-off was that annual contracts afforded the miners a regular opportunity to bargain between rival employers for higher pay.

As in all capitalist societies, market practices were encoded in ostensibly binding agreements, whether oral or written. All the players, therefore, had a potential interest in strategies by which they could vary or evade the terms. The winning strategies were underwritten partly by trust and ideological sanctions and partly by threat and coercive sanctions. In Defoe's England, as since, there were debtors refusing to pay their bills, shopkeepers selling shoddy goods, promoters offering false prospectuses, suppliers giving short measure, professionals charging inflated fees, apprentices neglecting their duties, contractors embezzling the property of the state, and workers pilfering from their employers. But none of these generated runaway spirals of defection. They did not retard the diffusion and reproduction of market practices in parallel with the growing capacity of the economy to generate purchasing power. Defoe was not alone in his disapproval of what it was used to buy. But the strictures of self-appointed moralists against useless, wasteful, or immoral expenditure did little to curtail what they deplored, any more in the eighteenth century than they were to do in the nineteenth and twentieth. Active interference was chiefly directed to the drinking habits of the lower orders, as in the draconian but unenforceable Gin Act of 1736. Whatever their interest to cultural historians, the fulminations against 'luxury' were no more than noise. Despite the lack of precise and reliable statistics for household incomes, probate inventories, and the volume of domestic and foreign trade, the historians of the period have endorsed the views of 'a whole category of contemporary commentators making the same point',[5] as did David Macpherson in his *Annals of Commerce* in 1805. Buying and selling at prices dictated by what the seller was able to charge and the buyer to pay were intrinsic to the behaviour not only of the rich and great and the middling sort but also of Defoe's 'mere' labouring people.

The competing practices that significantly restricted the reproduction and diffusion of market practices were of two kinds: practices internal to the mode of production itself, and the political or ideological practices interacting with them from the society's modes of coercion and persuasion. In a free and open market where information is shared and transaction costs are nugatory, both the return on capital and the price of labour and services are under constant downward pressure. But markets are always imperfect, even where—and sometimes because—there is little or no intervention by the state. There were in the eighteenth century, as after it, players whose strategies enabled them to skew the terms of exchange in their favour, whether would-be monopolists of scarce materials, inventors keeping secret new discoveries, dealers cornering market sectors, merchants hoarding scarce supplies, workers joining together to withhold their labour, employers joining

[5] Neil McKendrick, John Brewer, and J. H. Plumb, *The Birth of a Consumer Society: The Commercialization of Eighteenth-Century England* (London, 1982), p. 24.

together to refuse employment, or producers combining to keep up the price of finished goods. All were acted out in contests of a kind as familiar in Defoe's day as at any time since.

In the course of the eighteenth century, the practices defining the roles of wage labourers and their employers began to evolve under novel selective pressures generated by an unforeseeably but drastically altered ecological environment in which the exploitation of the energy stored in fossil fuels was transforming both the nature and the conditions of work in ways totally inconceivable in Defoe's lifetime. But whatever its impact on individual lives, the mode of production was reproduced as before. As other societies, both capitalist and in due course socialist, began to industrialize through sequences of variation and selection of practices that followed very different trajectories, sociologists came to distinguish among others the '*sauve qui peut*' capitalism of the United States, the 'social-democratic' capitalism of Sweden, the 'socialized' capitalism of France, the 'authoritarian' capitalism of Japan, the 'coordinated market' capitalism of post-1945 Germany, the 'state' capitalism of post-Maoist China, and the 'clientist' capitalism of Saudi Arabia. But whatever the reasons why the 'industrial revolution' originated in England, it did so in an environment where market practices faced less competition than they were to do in many societies that industrialized later. Whatever qualifications are necessary (some of which were touched on in Chapter 2) to the once conventional opinion that 'By 1850, so the story goes, the triumph of the *laissez-faire* philosophy of government was virtually complete in Britain',[6] no historian has argued that the British economy in 1850 should be labelled dirigiste.

The extensive and detailed researches of economic historians since the phrase 'industrial revolution' first gained currency have provoked, as they were bound to do, new controversies at the same time as settling old ones. There are, and will no doubt continue to be, competing explanations of the timing and extent of its effects not only on output, productivity, trade, and standards of living but also on art and literature. There is also a large and growing body of evidence documenting the procedures, techniques, and organizational forms of late twentieth- and early twenty-first- as opposed to late nineteenth- and early twentieth-century capitalism. But these are marginal to the explanation of the effects that the industrial revolution did (or didn't) have on the relative location in social space of the roles constitutive of the economic institutions of the society in which it began. The rich and great, the middling sort, the labouring people, and the underclass remained as distinctive as ever; the middling remained divided between upper, middle, and lower; the labouring people remained divided between skilled, semi-skilled, and unskilled; and there were always self-employed traders, artisans, and smallholders who were neither quite middling nor labouring.

It is hardly controversial in any version of the story to treat as the dominant carriers of the practices on which the evolution of the capitalist mode of production

---

[6] Phyllis Deane, *The First Industrial Revolution*[2] (Cambridge, 1979), p. 225.

depended the capitalists themselves—that is, the owners and controllers of the means of production who brought together the raw materials, machinery, and labour which enabled the resulting products to be sold at a profit. They did so in very different ways, of which the arch-paternalist Robert Owen's mills at New Lanark, with their model village and schools and village store, their shortened working hours, their singing and dancing classes, their colour code for good and bad behaviour, and their strict prohibition of alcohol were for a short time thought by some observers to offer the model that others could, would, and ought to copy. Contemporaries were as aware as subsequent historians of the differences in practices and roles between, for example, Birmingham with its wide range of products and its active service and commercial sectors, and Sheffield, with its more isolated and specialized place in the division of labour. Some entrepreneurs took higher risks in pursuit of higher rewards, some were more successful than others in securing credit within a fragmented banking system, and some developed more and others less collaborative relations with their workforces. But whatever might be envisaged in the critiques of radical artisans, pioneer socialists, or nostalgic romantics, no alternative practices to those of the capitalist mode emerged in effective competition with them. The critics of capitalism were agreed that it was functioning, in conjunction with an insufficiently reformed political system, to enrich idlers and parasites, protect practitioners of force and fraud, substitute destructive competition for constructive cooperation, and deny to workers their fair share of the fruits of their labour. During the nineteenth century, various combinations of anti-capitalist memes, each with their own more and less eloquent carriers, pressured the defenders of the capitalist mode into formulating increasingly explicit counter-arguments of their own. But capitalist practices continued to be reproduced decade after decade across all sectors of the economy, however different the performance of their social roles by the individual capitalists of the nineteenth century by comparison with those of the eighteenth, or those of the twentieth by comparison with those of the nineteenth, and to whatever extent control of the means of production attached to the role not of private employers but of employers who were agents of the state.

　　To stress the adaptiveness of market practices is not to imply that there evolved a progressive harmonization of interests between the buyers of labour and its sellers. But the ability of employees to raise the price that their labour could command from their employers depended on the employees' acquiescence, however reluctant, in the practices defining their respective roles. Employees' bargaining power might be strengthened on occasion by the state, whether as earlier by decision of local magistrates or as later by ministerial interventions or negotiations which might involve even prime ministers themselves, as when in 1893 a sixteen-week lockout in the coal industry was settled by a conference chaired by Lord Rosebery at Gladstone's request. But, both before and after the trade unions were politically and ideologically incorporated, they were competitors on behalf of their members in a market within which their *raison d'être* was to sell their members' labour on the best attainable terms.

The standard measure of trade union power is density—that is, the ratio of the total of members to the total potential membership (including the unemployed as calculated by the Department of Employment). Labour historians accept that it is impossible to estimate for the eighteenth and early nineteenth centuries when workers were first coming together in the parlours of local inns to coordinate withdrawals of labour, organize tramping from one house of call to another, and pool funds for mutual protection which were often entrusted to the innkeeper. Nor is it much easier to do for most of the Victorian era. But by the end of the nineteenth century, official figures for the number and distribution of trade union members are sufficiently reliable, thanks to the Board of Trade, for meaningful comparisons to be drawn. The subsequent fluctuations in overall density from roughly half in the aftermath of the First World War, to a quarter in the interwar depression, to over a half at its peak in 1979, to a quarter at the end of the twentieth century, was as unpredictable by academic researchers as by either politicians or trade union leaders. But union membership was always the exception rather than the rule across the total employed population. It was higher where the union's practices corresponded to those of the professional associations mentioned in Chapter 3. But it remained persistently lower among women than among men, domestic servants continued to be impossible to organize, and workers in retailing or catering hardly less so. Agricultural workers who could be recruited in good times were particularly difficult to retain in bad times. The police as well as the armed services were debarred from forming one. Although the skilled were better able than the semi-skilled, and the semi-skilled than the unskilled, both to impose restrictions on entry and to retain the members on whom their bargaining power depended, the fortunes of individual unions were as unpredictable by their officials as by their members' employers.

High density was no guarantee of survival. Nobody could have guessed in 1910 that the cotton spinners, with a density then close to 100 per cent, would have ceased to exist two generations later. Practices adaptive in the short term could be maladaptive in the long, as when the successful imposition of a closed shop caused employers to start up elsewhere on greenfield sites with non-union employees. Some employers refused to recognize unions but ensured that their workers were paid above locally negotiated union rates. Some union negotiators overplayed their hand—a metaphor that has a literal meaning in evolutionary game theory where a more aggressive strategy can be shown under specified conditions to have a measurable negative pay-off. Whatever the organizing abilities of individual trade union leaders and officials, the recruitment of dues-paying members depended on what the individual members could see accruing to themselves, including funeral and sickness as well as unemployment benefits. There were always free-riders. The effect of intimidation was not negligible, even if seldom amounting to what became known as the Sheffield Outrages of 1866. But membership was unlikely to be diffused among workers who gained no protection against wage cuts or redundancy, or even faced immediate dismissal. Where a union was recruiting clerical workers, some employers responded simply by promoting, or awarding a salary increase to, all and only those who declined to join. It would be as mistaken to assume that once trade unions were free to recruit, organize, and call out on strike it would be 'deviant' for vendors of their labour not to belong to one as to label 'deviant' any who, once there was a 'Labour' party, failed to support it at the polls.

No amount of research will yield an uncontroversial assessment of the net effects of the trade unions on the performance of the national economy. In the verdict of some commentators, they stifled innovation, held back productivity, undermined competitiveness, and won benefits for their members at the expense of other workers (particularly women). In the verdict of others, they compelled employers to attend to the health and safety of their employees, curbed the abuse of managerial prerogatives, accelerated the introduction of more efficient working methods, and heightened the level of consumer demand by winning for their members a larger share of employers' profits. Nor was agreement ever going to be reached between Conservatives for whom the function of the state was to curb the influence of 'extremists', Liberals for whom it was to 'hold the ring' between contestants whose 'mutual dependency' gave them a joint interest in conciliation, and socialists for whom it was to divert workers from their 'real interest' in their struggle with the 'dominant fraction of capital'. But there is no difficulty in identifying in hindsight the combinations of unforeseeable contingent events and selective environmental pressures which strengthened or weakened the relative bargaining power of employers and unions across the different sectors of the economy and between the different enterprises within them.

Unions could not but gain from a tightening labour market, a sudden increase in demand for the relevant product (as was particularly likely in wartime), the ability of employers to pass the cost of wage increases on to the customer, the sensitivity of employers to short-term interruption to their supply chains, the accumulation of members' subscriptions out of which to fund strike pay, the availability of support from other unions, and the vulnerability of employers' premises to picketing. They could not but lose from rising unemployment, employers' ability to substitute semi-skilled for skilled labour, lockouts which exhausted their reserves, adoption by employers' associations of inter-trading rules, inflows of immigrants seeking work, decisions of the courts limiting the effectiveness of stoppages, and police protection for blacklegs willing to cross picket lines. Foreign competition or technological innovation could undermine a strong negotiating position almost overnight. Public opinion and what would later be called media coverage could improve the bargaining position of either unions or employers. Government initiatives could either promote or discourage recruitment. But the practice that consistently retained its reproductive fitness was collective bargaining over the terms and conditions on which different groups or categories of unionized workers sold their labour to whoever was paying for it.

No reader of either the general histories of the trade union movement or the detailed studies of individual unions can fail to be struck by the ubiquity and persistence of inter-union competition within the labour market which the rhetoric of working-class solidarity could do little to conceal: the 'language of Marx', as an American observer somewhat overstated it in 1982, 'cannot mask the desperate Hobbesian struggle of union against union'.[7] The rivalry could lead either to mergers, federations, and alliances or to the extinction of the weakest. But the larger unions faced a trade-off between gain in size and loss of cohesion. Labour historians are as familiar with the breakaway of the Associated Society of Locomotive Engineers from the Amalgamated Society of Railway Servants (as it still was) and divisions within the National Union of Mineworkers (as the Miners Federation of Great Britain became) as they are with the formation and consolidation of the Amalgamated Union of Engineering Workers (AUEW) and the Transport and General Workers Union—assisted, in the case of the latter, by the creation of the role of trade group secretary. Competition was also endemic between central headquarters and local branches, between leaders and would-be leaders aiming to displace them, and between officials and the rank and file. Many union leaders and members alike were more concerned with protecting demarcation lines and differentials in earnings than with securing gains across a wider front. Collective agreements arrived at through the increasingly widely diffused practices of formal consultation, conciliation, mediation, and arbitration could either be flouted when the local environment changed or ignored from the outset. As the mid-twentieth-century miners' leader Joe Gormley said in reference to the AUEW, 'True, they negotiate across the board for a flat rate increase they think should apply. But when you get a little shop with twenty or thirty engineers in it they can negotiate what the hell they like.'[8]

The underlying process of variation and selection of practices was as little grasped by those trade unionists who saw any victory over employers as a sign of an onward march towards Socialism as by those employers who saw any defeat for their side as a sign of an impending surrender of their traditional right to conduct their businesses as they chose. More perceptive was Charles Booth, to whom it was obvious in the late nineteenth century that trade unionism was an 'expanded form of individualism'[9]—a judgement echoed a century later by a historian of the 'Industrial Age' to whom it was equally obvious that the nineteenth-century trade unions were 'not an expression of collectivism, but of individualism'.[10] The practices that did generate collaboration and promote solidarity within the trade union movement evolved elsewhere than in the clutter of strikes, lockouts,

---

[7] Samuel H. Beer, *Britain Against Itself: The Political Contradictions of Collectivism* (London, 1982), p. 62.

[8] Joe Gormley, *Battered Cherub* (London, 1982), p. 193.

[9] Quoted by T. S. Simey and M. B. Simey, *Charles Booth, Social Scientist* (Oxford, 1960), p. 134.

[10] Charles More, *The Industrial Age: Economy and Society in Britain 1750–1985* (London, 1989), p. 201.

settlements, agreements and disagreements over piece rates, sliding scales and overtime, refusals of employers to re-engage strikers, and refusals by union members to work alongside anyone who had refused to come out on strike. They were to be observed not where collective bargaining was taking place on the ground but in the relations between the industrial and political wings of the 'Labour Movement'—particularly, in the 1930s, in the National Labour Council which, by meeting before each year's party conference, was able to 'marshal the Trade Union battalions behind the official policy'.[11] Union leaders who might agree about little else could agree in wanting statutory protection for picketing, compensation for injury at work, safety regulations in factories or aboard ship, a shorter working day, and fair-wage clauses in local authority contracts. Hence the importance of the roles of the members of the Trade Union Congress and its Parliamentary Committee. The Webbs were—characteristically—rather scornful of the TUC. But for as long as union leaders saw no threat to free collective bargaining and the right to strike, they were unlikely to oppose lobbying for measures which, even if they benefited workers in only one sector of industry, did nothing to reduce the bargaining power of the rest.

On the railways, for example, where relatively high union density was accompanied by relatively low pay and long hours, and where the safety of the travelling public was of as much ministerial concern as the safety of the railway workers, the Railway Servants (Hours of Labour) Act of 1893 was followed in due course by episodes when Lloyd George in 1907, and again in 1911, put direct ministerial pressure on the railway companies to settle under threat of compulsory arbitration. But in the mining industry, by contrast, the hewers in the north-east coalfields were, as a result of previous local agreements, staunchly resistant to statutory imposition of an eight-hour day. Nor was compulsory arbitration any surer a guarantee of stability than other practices of conciliation, mediation, or arbitration whose variation and selection were determined by different local and sectoral pressures. In iron and steel, where there was—unusually—some scope for promotion within the manual workforce, groups of workers 'gradually evolved their own version of conciliation boards . . . with the result that iron and steel was able to retain its reputation for industrial peace well into the twentieth century'.[12] In a highly automated sector of the oil industry in the third quarter of the twentieth century, a sociologist comparing British with French unions found that at the British sites management 'facilitated union organization' where the trade-off was 'a certain amount of help in controlling the aspirations of the workforce',[13] in contrast to French management where more effective control over decision-making was traded off against more antagonistic and politically combative industrial relations.

---

[11] G. D. H. Cole, *The People's Front* (London, 1937), p. 293.
[12] Alastair J. Reid, *United We Stand: A History of Britain's Trade Unions* (London, 2004), p. 194.
[13] Duncan Gallie, *In Search of the New Working Class: Automation and Social Integration within the Capitalist Enterprise* (Cambridge, 1978), p. 254.

One union might occasionally offer support to another in a dispute not its own, and all be as conscious as each other of the adversarial aspects of their relationships with employers. But that is not the same as a joint commitment to a strategy of confrontation within which competing sectional interests are dissolved.

Meanwhile, increasingly visible selective pressures were coming to bear on the employers also. Although the Royal Commission on Labour set up in 1891 saw formal employers' organizations as a response to the growing strength of the trade unions, combinations between 'masters' were already, as Adam Smith had put it, part of the 'natural state of things' in the eighteenth century. The difficulties that they faced nonetheless, including the recurrent risk of self-replicating defections from agreements made, were as evident in the course of the institutionalization of employers' associations as of workers' unions. The General Chamber of Manufacturers of 1785 was as little likely to resolve the conflicts of interest among its actual, let alone prospective, members as would be the Grand National Consolidated Trade Union of 1834. But during the late nineteenth and early twentieth centuries, the increasing power of the unions and the increasing (if sometimes reluctant) willingness of ministers (although not of the judiciary) to ease the legal restrictions on them did put employers under growing pressure to trade off some of their autonomy in return for more effective joint defence of their common interests. By the time of the First World War, there existed across British industry 'a formidable phalanx of employers' organizations'. But it was a phalanx that subsequently had to contend, in the same historian's words, with 'powerful centrifugal forces, working to undermine collective organization and to relocate regulatory power at the level of the individual company, rather than the collective organisation'.[14] As another historian puts it, British business was 'atomistic in its associational politics as in its underlying economic structures'.[15] In the case of the individual trade unions, the selective pressures that promoted or inhibited the growth of one or another employers' organization and the reproduction of the practices of which its officials were the carriers are not difficult to detect in hindsight. But the office-holders of the Federation of British Industries and its successor the Confederation of British Industries, however strongly motivated they were individually, could no more speak with authority on behalf of their overall membership in anything other than the broadest terms than could those of the TUC.

During the twentieth century, the increasing intervention in, or regulation of, the market by the state evolved into different organizational forms, and operated through different practices and roles, under selective pressures generated both nationally and internationally. By the end of the century, the reproduction and diffusion of the practice of second-order bargaining over economic policy covered a

---

[14] Arthur J. McIvor, *Organised Capital: Employers' Associations and Industrial Relations in Northern England 1880–1939* (Cambridge, 1996), pp. 270, 271.

[15] F. Trentmann, 'The transformation of fiscal reform: reciprocity, modernization, and the fiscal debate within the business community in early twentieth-century Britain', *Historical Journal* 39 (1996), p. 1030.

range of institutional bodies, with their own histories and functions extending from the Arts Council to the Civil Aviation Authority, the Licensed Trade Training and Education Committee, the Manpower Services Commission, and to the Securities and Investments Board (later to become the Financial Services Authority and later still the Financial Conduct Authority). Their objectives ranged from vocational preparation and training to consumer protection, subsidies and tax incentives for undercapitalized industries, and to the promotion of recreational activities of favoured kinds. There was nothing new about lobbying. There was only a difference in the expanded number of organizations involved in it and their relation to the sociological distinction between corporatism of the traditional kind going back to the practices of the medieval corporations and the more recent practices involving negotiation between governments on one side and pluralities of organizations with mutually antagonistic interests on the other. As in the comparative sociology of industrial capitalism itself, different societies can be classified in terms of different varieties of corporatist practices and roles. Each has its own evolutionary trajectory with its different relative weights to be assigned to the convergent evolution of practices under common selective pressure, their homologous descent in a path-dependent sequence, and their lateral diffusion by imitation. In an economy extensively exposed to international competition with a long history of established markets in commodities and labour, second-order exchanges of privileges accorded by the state in return for compliance with government policy were increasingly adaptive. But they had no necessary implications in either direction for the distribution of market power between the economy's constituent roles.

As before, the outcomes of these second-order transactions continued to reflect the bargaining position of the two sides within an environment that sometimes favoured the one and sometimes the other under the influence of the quasi-random choices of strategy of governments of different persuasions. As in the relations between central and local government, there evolved a bewildering succession of mutant practices through which the state sometimes exercised more and sometimes less control over different sectors and regions (Scotland having once again a distinctive evolutionary trajectory of its own). With the appearance of new practices defining new roles with new titles, new credentials, and new functions, old arguments continued as previously over whether the efficiency of the national economy was increased or diminished as a result. But whatever the answer to that perennially controversial question, the new roles and their defining practices evolved within a mode of production which they did little if anything to disturb and nothing whatever to overturn.

II

The twentieth-century expansion in both the absolute number of non-manual occupational roles and the proportion of the total workforce which they comprised was unmistakable to both academic and non-academic observers. But there was no agreement among sociologists either about the 'basic model' linking trade unionism to the stratification of occupational roles,[16] or about the distinguishing character-istics of the 'new middle class' (or was it a 'new working class'?) of 'white-collar' workers joining trade unions and the consequences of their doing so. Wherever similar routine tasks were performed by workers brought together in large estab-lishments with few prospects of promotion, there was created an environment favourable to the practice of collective bargaining, particularly where government policies accorded with the spirit and recommendations of the Whitley Reports of 1917. In the aftermath of the Second World War, although the increase in density of non-manual unionism was not enough to offset a decline in that of manual unionism, in the public sector it rose to over 80 per cent, and by the end of the century the demand for 'white-blouse' labour had increased to the point that the female density rate had risen to a similar proportion relative to that for men. These figures would no doubt have amazed the leaders of the early white-collar unions such as the Railway Clerks Association or the National Union of Clerks, both founded in 1897, at the same time that they would have gratified the Webbs. But whatever the Webbs or others might hope or predict, it did not follow that the workers by brain were 'coalescing' with the workers by hand in the manner confidently claimed by a German historian of British Socialism, well-informed though he was, writing in the immediate aftermath of the First World War.[17]

Some sociologists continued to insist that the workers by brain were proletarians who, whether they realized it or not, were being exploited, and their skills down-graded, by the bourgeois class (and the state as its executive committee) in the same way, for the same purposes, and with the same impending outcome as the workers by hand. But to others, they were an increasingly well-educated workforce who were being released from the outdated routines of the office stool and the hand-written ledger into more skilled and responsible roles supported by new technology which increased rather than diminished their opportunities for promotion. Both sides could, and did, draw on empirical evidence favourable to their arguments. But it was difficult to equate the diffusion of the practice of collective bargaining among non-manual occupational roles with proletarianization. The general practitioners whom the British Medical Association called out on strike in 1974 and again in 2012 were no more 'coalescing' with manual workers than were barristers protest-ing about reduction or withdrawal of fees under government-funded legal aid. It could, on the one hand, be demonstrated that the new technology offered little to lower-grade clerical workers, many of whom were women who would leave the labour force on marriage, in large financial or industrial establishments where the work was routine and their discretion minimal. But, on the other, the readiness of

---

[16] George Sayers Bain, David Coates, and Valerie Ellis, *Social Stratification and Trade Unionism: A Critique* (London, 1973), p. 8.
[17] M. Beer, *A History of British Socialism*, vol. 2 (London, 1920), p. 347.

journalists, teachers, civil servants, cinema technicians, and airline pilots to bargain collectively with their employers, whether private or public, was symptomatic more of the value they placed on their skills than of a sense that they were losing them. Nor were the technical, clerical, and sales workers recruits to the ranks of an increasingly homogeneous and disaffected working class any more than they were 'part of a "new middle class"' willing to endorse unambiguously the reward structure embraced by existing socio-political arrangements'.[18] However different the nature and conditions of their work from the time of their fathers and grandfathers, the location of their roles in the inter-systactic distribution of economic power was much the same.

As critical as ever to the continuing sociological significance of the middling/ labouring distinction was the difference in 'work situation' as defined in 1958 by the sociologist David Lockwood—that is, 'the set of social relationships in which the individual is involved at work by virtue of his position in the division of labour'.[19] One aspect is, as it has always been, the closer and more frequent personal contact with the managers or proprietors (including partners in professional firms) responsible for the direction of the enterprise. But another is that office workers are generally, given the practices that define their roles, associated with managerial authority and the transmission and recording of the instructions that emanate from the directors. It does not follow that they command a higher price for their labour than some manual workers can do: it was possible in the period when Lockwood was writing for a highly skilled metal spinner not yet displaced by new technology, in a small engineering plant, to be taking home more than his works manager. But neither does it follow (nor did Lockwood suggest that it did) that by joining trade unions, workers by brain were joining the workers by hand in a common front against the purchasers, whether public or private, of their labour.

An argument advanced in the 1980s by the authors of one among many sociological studies of white-collar trade unionism was that in the public sector, where such a high proportion of workers were union members, 'market principles are clearly more attenuated, if they apply at all', and that this could be expected to 'ensure a greater degree of sympathy than might otherwise be anticipated with the broader aims of the labour movement in the general provision of resources'.[20] But employees of the state were selling their labour to an employer who might be under no less pressure than a private-sector employer to hold labour costs down. It is true that governments can, and sometimes do, override the market by using funds raised from loans or taxes to create occupational roles which are then remunerated in excess of market rates: some overmanning in the public sector in the 1970s was

---

[18] Gordon Marshall, Howard Newby, David Rose, and Carolyn Vogler, *Social Class in Modern Britain* (London, 1988), p. 274.
[19] David Lockwood, *The Blackcoated Worker: A Study in Class Consciousness*[2] (Oxford, 1989), p. 15.
[20] K. Prandy, A. Stewart, and R. M. Blackburn, *White-Collar Unionism* (Cambridge, 1983), pp. 150, 151.

deliberately designed to keep down unemployment through an 'employment subsidy policy' and 'variety of "job-creation" schemes' which attracted predictable criticism from indignant commentators on the Right.[21] But the upsurge of militancy among white-collar trade unionists on which many contemporaries remarked was a response to pressures from a labour market environment which threatened them with lower real incomes, higher risks of redundancy, imposed restructuring, and reduced opportunities for promotion—threats which impacted on employees of the state no less, and sometimes more, than on their private-sector counterparts.

There was, moreover, one institutional area where the work situation of the employees of the state created an environment that made them less rather than more likely to identify their interests with those of the working class. As the number of civil servants grew, so did the number of white-collar trade unionists. But 'the notions of public service and of professionalism militated against an oppositional form of collectivism, as did the generally favourable economic position which these public servants enjoyed';[22] and many of them were in roles that involved administering benefits and services provided to recipients drawn from among members of the working class least likely to share the circumstances, lifestyles, and attitudes of the officials from whom they were receiving them. Culturally, memes prejudicial to the distribution of public funds to recipients stigmatized as undeserving had lost none of their fitness. Mutual antagonism between unionized lower-middle-class civil servants staffing the benefit offices and job centres and the working-class claimants with whom they dealt were compounded by the element of discretion inescapable within a system where no bureaucratic rule-book could be devised from which decisions could be extrapolated by formula. Not all claimants were working class. But middle-class claimants were better equipped to negotiate within the system, which was why, in the opinion of the Chairman of the Supplementary Benefits Commission, 'middle-class people often defend discretion so fiercely'.[23] Furthermore, middle-class people were less likely to be claimants for the same reasons that continued to separate the middle from the working classes—work situation, lifestyle, credentials, opportunities for promotion, access to credit, relatively greater security of employment, and the prospect of more valuable informal help from family and friends.

By the last quarter of the twentieth century, British sociologists had available to them an abundance of empirical evidence on which to base their conclusions about the change (or lack of it) in the relative location in social space of the middle and working classes. But the arguments that it provoked (or prolonged) were little different from those that could be traced back before the nineteenth century to the

---

[21] Martin Holmes, *The Labour Government, 1974–79: Political Aims and Economic Reality* (London, 1985), p. 183.

[22] Robert Price, 'White-collar unions: growth, character and attitudes in the 1970s', in Richard Hyman and Robert Price, *The New Working Class? White-collar Workers and Other Organizations* (London, 1983), p. 161.

[23] David Donnison, *The Politics of Poverty* (Oxford, 1982), p. 64.

period when the vernacular terminology first began to distinguish more and less highly located 'classes' rather than 'ranks'. The inequalities deriving from the relation of working-class roles to the means of production which for some sociologists provided the defining criterion had always to take account of those deriving from ideological distinctions, including ethnicity and gender and the exclusionary practices in which these were acted out. Moreover, to focus exclusively on vertical differentiation between classes, or fractions of classes, was to ignore the horizontal differentiation which there had always been within them: writing in 1995, Lockwood drew attention to the volume of contemporary debate 'in which a chief issue is the usefulness or otherwise of counterposing to the idea of a unitary service class that of there being three middle classes—namely, the entrepreneurial, managerial, and professional, differentiated mainly by their respective command of property, organizational and cultural assets'.[24] There was also the same small but enduring systact of self-employed artisans, smallholders, and sole traders who could be classified according to preference as 'intermediate', 'upper-proletarian', or 'petty-bourgeois', but was not taken to include 'freelance' authors and artists who, however impecunious, were assigned to the 'middle class' on the grounds of social prestige. And whatever the schema adopted, there were always some sociologists ready to question 'both the existence of the actual boundaries and the homogeneity of the groups contained by them',[25] thereby echoing those eighteenth-century observers who had insisted on the smooth gradation of differentiated ranks which they saw as distinctively characteristic of the structure of English society.

The narrowing of the gap in incomes between the upper-working and lower-middle classes was documented with increasing precision. But it did not abolish the difference in opportunity to borrow on more or less favourable terms. It was symptomatic that when the Post Office Savings Bank was established in 1861, it gave working-class savers rates below market, and that 'differential treatment [was] meted out to debtors from different classes'.[26] In difficult times, the pawnshop (as later the 'pay-day lender') was often the only source of credit available to wage-earning households. There was a long cultural tradition of mutual support in working-class communities, but its extent was inevitably limited—'a little bit of tea, a little bit of sugar, a shilling'[27]—by comparison with the networks of support to be found among middle-class families. Homeownership was not beyond the means of all working-class families. It has been estimated at 10 per cent at the beginning of the twentieth century, rising to 20 per cent by the outbreak of the Second World War, and the Cooperative Permanent Building Society used

[24] David Lockwood, 'Introduction: marking out the middle class(es)', in Tim Butler and Mike Savage, eds., *Social Change and the Middle Classes* (London, 1995), p. 1.

[25] Kenneth Prandy, 'Class and continuity in social reproduction: an empirical investigation', *Sociological Review* 46 (1998), p. 343.

[26] Paul Johnson, 'Class law in Victorian England', *Past & Present* 141 (1993), p. 151.

[27] Elizabeth Roberts, *A Woman's Place: An Oral History of Working-Class Women 1890–1940* (Oxford, 1984), p. 191.

'an extensive network of cooperative retail schemes' to the extent that 70 per cent of its borrowers were working class, of whom more than half were semi-skilled or unskilled.[28] In some local environments such as mining communities or cotton towns as many as a quarter of manual workers might own their own homes. But in the interwar years, although the unintended consequence of government policy on rent control was that 2½ million houses were built for private sale and 'anyone with a secure salary of around £190 or above could aspire to home ownership',[29] 'anyone' meant in practice, as the word 'salary' implies, a prospective borrower from a building society who was much more likely to be in a non-manual than a manual occupation.

Even a manual worker who in good times was taking home £5 a week might find it difficult to keep up the mortgage repayments in the face of the risks of illness, unemployment, and fluctuating earnings. The contrast became less marked in the decades following the Second World War, when the increasing assimilation of lifestyles was furthered by the increasing availability of credit (or hire purchase) to working-class families, particularly when both husbands and wives were in work. But the practices defining middle-class roles continued to place them, as it always had, in both market and work situations that differentiated them from manual and routine lower-grade service workers not only in what the market paid for each hour of labour over the course of a working lifetime but also in what proportion of it was saved rather than spent and what, when spent, it was used to buy. And it was also a difference in the ability to withstand the cyclical downturns inseparable from a capitalist mode of production in which the less credentialed, experienced, trained, or well-connected were relatively disadvantaged, just as they always had been.

Not all workers were dependent on wages or salaries paid by either a private employer or an agency of the state. As well as the self-employed, there were members of producer cooperatives whose roles were defined by the joint practices of common ownership and common participation in the making of the decisions on which the policy of the enterprise depended (with the possible option of 'value-added sharing' through 'partnership' as opposed to 'full co-operation'[30]). But the diffusion and reproduction of those practices were constrained by an environment from which, however strongly motivated their carriers, there was no realistic prospect of escape. They were not driven extinct. But the number of cooperatives never expanded beyond a modest number—105 in the year 1900[31]—of middling-sized enterprises in a limited number of industries where the founders could construct a niche within which they were spared the three trade-offs between

[28] Luke Samy, 'Extending home ownership before the First World War: the case of the Cooperative Permanent Building Society, 1884–1913', *Economic History Review* 65 (2012) pp. 189, 178.

[29] Alan A. Jackson, *The Middle Classes 1900–1950* (Nairn, 1991), p. 31.

[30] Alasdair Clayre, 'The political economy of a "third sector"', in Alasdair Clayre, ed., *The Political Economy of Co-operation and Participation* (Oxford, 1980), p. 7.

[31] Robert Oakeshott, *The Case for Workers' Co-Ops* (London, 1978), p. 59, citing Derek Jones in Ken Coates, ed., *The New Worker Co-operatives* (Nottingham, 1976), p. 36.

practices which confronted them as soon as they started to expand. The first was between effective decision-making and comprehensive consultation in other than very small groups. The second was between efficient coordination of productive functions and consensus over the allocation of rewards. The third was between the need for fresh loan or equity capital and the increase or retention of market share. As the enterprise prospers (if it does), all three become steadily more exigent. The choices become wider, and the attendant risks higher. If the workers are free to sell their shares, as some will do, they cease to be proprietors, but if they are not they are exposed to potential loss of savings and retirement incomes if the enterprise fails. The equity can, as in the retail company John Lewis since 1928, be held by an independent trust out of which the employees (always referred to as partners) are allotted bonuses based on each year's profits. But the role of trust beneficiary is not the same as the role of co-proprietor. Although there is no necessary contradiction between the practices that continue to define the role of worker-owner, the combination, adaptive as it might be in an economy of rural smallholdings, artisan production, self-administering professional partnerships, and family-owned corner shops, was increasingly maladaptive as the 'corporate economy' evolved into its late twentieth-century form.[32]

III

Powerful as market forces were, there were always cultural pressures acting on both employers and employees which moderated what would otherwise be the effects on the practices defining their roles of unfettered economic competition. On one flank were those who wanted the imperatives of supply and demand to be tempered by custom and precedent, the political influence of newly made wealth to be curbed, and social prestige to be withheld from families whose money was made in trade. On the other were those who wanted the commanding heights of the economy to be occupied by agents of the state, the rich to be punitively taxed, and social prestige to be denied to anyone buying it with profits made at the expense of the workers' rightful share. During the twentieth century, discussion of market forces in 'Labour circles' took place within a 'moral register, in which the normal view was that any form of competition was seen as antithetical to the good society'.[33] The opprobrium directed against plutocracy before the First World War and against profiteering after it was not confined to the Left. It was shared with practising capitalists who had no wish to see the existing mode of production overturned but were concerned about the damage being done to its public image, like the industrialist Lord Weir who worried in the 1930s that 'profiteering' in the aircraft

---

[32] Leslie Hannah, *The Rise of the Corporate Economy* (London, 1976).
[33] Jim Tomlinson, 'Labour and the economy', in Duncan Tanner, Pat Thane, and Nick Tiratsoo, *Labour's First Century* (Cambridge, 2000), p. 73.

industry would put at risk 'all Private Enterprise'.[34] Both those who deplored it and those who were relieved by it had reason to wonder how it was that market practices continued to resist attempts to restrain their reproduction and diffusion as successfully as ever.

In the twentieth century, the disjunction between contemporaries' culturally acquired perceptions of the mode of production on the one hand, and the underlying process of variation and selection of economic practices on the other, was as marked on the Left as on the Right. But it was, in a seeming paradox, the opposite in the aftermath of the Second World War of what it had been in the aftermath of the First. In 1914, the makers of government policy neither planned nor expected any major institutional changes before the war was prosecuted to its conclusion. But after 1915, as the influence of the state on the national economy extended beyond anything envisaged hitherto, both those who welcomed and those who deplored it could see that it had come about without either causing or being caused by a modal redistribution of economic power. Observers who doubted how far it would outlast the return of peace were largely vindicated by the unimpeded reproduction of the same pre-war practices and the roles defined by them. There was much noisy rhetoric about 'reconstruction'. But neither demobilized manual workers who experienced falling wages and rising unemployment, nor women returning from the factories to their unpaid domestic roles in the home, nor families all too aware of the emptiness of the promise of 'homes fit for heroes to live in', nor ex-officers unable to find jobs (let alone careers) commensurate with their military rank were likely to feel that such hopes as they may have had of a new and better world had been realized.

Conversely, many businessmen who had feared for their autonomy as decision-makers as well as for the profitability of their enterprises could not feel other than relieved at the return of what came to be called 'normalcy'. To commentators on the Left, it all went to show that capitalism was as unreformed as ever, and the same ruling class was still in charge. To commentators on the Right, it all went to show that measures that might have been necessary in time of war could be allowed to lapse in time of peace. There were, as all observers could see, some changes that were not reversed, including those which followed the Trade Union Amalgamation Act of 1917, the Education Act and Maternity and Child Welfare Act of 1918, the Housing Act of 1919, the Unemployment Insurance Act of 1920, and the Railways Act of 1921. All of these were responses to selective pressures which had been generated by the war. So were the creation of a Ministry of Transport, and the survival of the Ministry of Labour despite the Geddes Committee's attempt to abolish it. So too were the increased rates of income tax which at the top level had been 8 per cent before the war but quadrupled after it, as did the rate of estate duty. In the field of health policy, there was after 1918 'a gradual erosion of

---

[34] Quoted by Chris Wrigley, 'The trade unions between the wars', in Chris Wrigley, ed., *A History of British Industrial Relations* (Brighton, 1987), p. 118.

market-related mechanisms'.[35] A textbook example of a mutation whose long-term adaptiveness was entirely unforeseen was the introduction of 'uncovenanted' unemployment benefit in 1921 which set a precedent then taken as a matter of course as much as local relief at parish level had been. But all these were changes within a capitalist mode of production whose constituent roles were defined by the same practices and performed in the same way as previously.

After 1945, on the other hand, when the Labour Party held for the first time an impregnable parliamentary majority and half of the gross national product was controlled by agencies of the state, it suited commentators on both Left and Right to exaggerate the extent of change in the mode of production. If this was particularly evident in the rhetoric of both the supporters and the opponents of nationalization, it applied also to the extent to which the government was perceived as replacing the so-called anarchy of private production with the practices and roles subsumed under the rubric of planning. This is yet another of those words that meant different practices to different people. To some, planning meant allocation by government of labour and raw materials, to others a national council staffed by independent experts empowered to take decisions on capital spending, to others restrictions on imports and the convertibility of sterling, to others price controls and subsidies, to others transfers of industry to regions of high unemployment, and to others large-scale state-financed public works. The historians of the period from 1945 to 1951 disagree among themselves, and will no doubt continue to do so, about the effects on the national economy of the Attlee government's policies and the difference that might have been made to productivity per head if others had been adopted in their place. But they are not in disagreement about the lack of unanimity about what planning was to be taken to mean and the absence of detailed proposals setting out where, how far, and with what aim in view intervention in the workings of the market was to go. However convinced Attlee's ministers or their supporters might have been in 1945 that wartime controls could and should be retained, and however much they disapproved in retrospect of how rapidly they had been dismantled after 1918, they presided over a steady retreat from the practices and roles of a command economy.

The selective pressures unfavourable to reproduction of the practices of central planning came from both the national and the international environment. Although food rationing, for example, was retained after the war, it was not because it had the effect, to whatever extent it did, of narrowing the gap in living standards between the rich and the poor, but because of continuing scarcities and the cost of imports. Whatever the appeal of the slogan 'fair shares for all' to Labour supporters in their roles as wage- or salary-earning producers, in their roles as consumers they wanted no less than eighteeenth- or nineteenth-century wage and salary earners had done, the freedom of choice which the market was there to provide. No historian

---

[35] Charles Webster, 'Conflict and consensus: explaining the British Health Service', *20th Century British History*, vol. 1 (1990) p. 150.

has claimed that the 'bonfire of controls' which had already been lit before Churchill returned to power in 1951 was unpopular with the general public. There was the usual noisy comment both attacking and defending what consumers used their money to consume, whether alcohol, tobacco, football pools, beauty products, visits to the cinema, dog racing, or unhealthy foods. But it had no more effect on behaviour than similar comments had ever done in any period of rising real incomes from the eighteenth century onwards. Whether from a left-wing or a right-wing perspective it could not be disputed that it was the market, not the state, that was determining on what goods and services consumers spent their money and by whom the goods and services were supplied.

In what to many observers on both Left and Right was a self-evident contrast, the roles constitutive of the institutions of the so-called welfare state as it evolved during the twentieth century were defined by practices explicitly designed to meet the needs of the population independently of the market. Its often-told history is full of unanticipated contingencies and unforeseen changes of both tactics and strategy. But its historians are all agreed that it would not have taken the form that it did without Beveridge's celebrated report of 1942, published under the title *Social Insurance and Allied Services*, which was based on the principle of contributory insurance supplemented to whatever limited extent might be necessary by taxpayer subsidy. The change was neither as sudden nor as drastic as it suited some of its supporters and its opponents alike to claim: already in 1939 the British social services 'taken all in all, were the most advanced in the world'.[36] It was part of a long sequence of variation and selection within which the practices defining its constituent roles continued to be influenced by market forces from both without and within.

As in other societies undergoing the shared experience of industrialization and urbanization, the local practices that had traditionally protected the 'really miserable' from starvation and provided the elderly and infirm with a roof of some kind over their heads had long ceased to be adaptive. Whatever the effects, whether intended or unintended, of the New Poor Law, by 1850, when over 40 per cent of the population of England and Wales were living in towns of over 10,000 inhabitants as against an estimated 13 per cent in 1700, it was palpably impossible for the parishes to continue to perform the functions that they had in the seventeenth century. Culturally, however, it was as unacceptable as it always had been that the poor should be left to die from starvation without any attempt being made to provide for them. Although the potato blight of the 1840s was beyond the means of the authorities to remedy, and deaths from malnutrition extended beyond Ireland (where they are estimated to have exceeded a million) to the Highlands of Scotland, not even the most doctrinaire advocates of the New Poor Law denied as a matter of principle all claims for assistance to those who would otherwise be left

---

[36] Paul Addison, *The Road to 1945: British Politicians and the Second World War* (London, 1975), p. 33.

without shelter or food. The divisive questions were the same three as ever: how should those in work or in possession of property subsidize those without either, how should the subsidy be paid for, and what conditions should attach to it? Among higher-paid and independent-minded craftsmen in skilled trades unable to find work in times of economic recession, the practice of national insurance was culturally as well as socially adaptive, and a line of homologous descent can be traced from Lloyd George's scheme of 1911, in which the young Beveridge had had a hand, to that advocated by Beveridge himself in 1942. Traceable too is the lateral influence of the German practice of compulsory insurance against age and illness introduced by Bismarck before the beginning of the twentieth century. The novel mutation was a commitment to a universal minimum funded out of general taxation, the unforeseen consequences of which were to prompt a sequence of policy responses whose effects were equally unforeseen in their turn. Beveridge's reliance on the 'contributory principle', however appealing to both policymakers and recipients, was unrealistic from the outset. The poor had, as always, to be subsidized somehow by funds raised in one way or another from fellow-citizens more fortunate than they.

Time and again, the practices through which successive ministers and officials sought to expand coverage and improve the quality of welfare services, while keeping costs under control, turned out to be maladaptive for reasons apparent only in hindsight. It was not simply that in the political environment of universal suffrage competitors for office were likely to promise more than they would be able to deliver. Nor was it simply that the chopping and changing of policy was often based on over-optimistic assumptions about the money that would be available to pay for such services. From the 1950s onwards, there was a continuing trickle of quasi-random mutations both in the practices through which revenue was raised to fund the institutions of the welfare state and in those through which it was distributed. Different levies on incomes, profits, property, capital gains, employment, consumption, imported goods, inheritance, gifts *inter vivos*, and perquisites in kind followed one another in bewildering succession. So did different allowances, scales, exemptions, penalties, and procedural rules by which benefits were allocated to those who could demonstrate their entitlement to them. So, too, did departmental reorganizations, allocations and reallocations of administrative responsibilities, job descriptions, contractual terms, recruitment policies, spending priorities, budgetary controls, location and relocation of offices, ministerially imposed policy reviews, extensions and retractions of the scope and nature of services provided, insourcing and outsourcing, extent and form of answerability to parliamentary scrutiny, and measures for the detection and punishment of fraudulent claims.

Arguments over how to distinguish the undeserving from the deserving were as widespread and intractable as ever. So were arguments over the levels of remuneration and contractual conditions attaching to the providers of the requisite services and benefits. Some policymakers were more, and others less, explicitly aware of the trade-off between one set of practices and another: Kenneth Robinson, Minister of Health under Harold Wilson, recalled how in negotiating with the GPs over the conflict between the prospective alternatives of a salaried service and fees paid per item of service 'we traded the one for the other'.[37] But none of them knew which of the alternative practices, between which their choices were made, would turn out to be the more adaptive in the longer term. Nor did they, or could they, know how the perennial arguments over needs versus deserts would, if they ever could, be settled conclusively.

The selective pressures that the market brought to bear on the institutions of the welfare state were of several kinds. There was always outside competition from practices and roles through which similar goods and services were on offer. But there were also policy initiatives such as those which led to the creation of internal markets within the National Health Service or to a fall in the relative number of houses built by local councils as opposed to private firms. Labour and Conservative governments had, as was to be expected, different priorities and preferences. But policymakers often found that their initiatives led to outcomes that were not merely different from, but directly contradictory to, their intentions. Two examples from opposite ends of the political spectrum on which contemporaries were not slow to comment were Barbara Castle's attempt to phase out pay beds in National Health Service hospitals and Margaret Thatcher's attempt to phase out subsidy of local council housing rents. Not only were pay beds not phased out entirely, but the number of beds in private hospitals, often serviced by the same consultants, rose in response to the rising demand. In housing, as subsidies fell the amounts paid out in benefit to poorer tenants rose, thus increasing their dependence on the state instead of reducing it. As successive governments sought sometimes to increase and sometimes to diminish the control directly exercised by the state, the carriers of commercial practices were always there in the wings ready to supplement or replace what the state was offering, whether in housing, schools, pensions, medicine, or life insurance. Abolition of grammar schools increased the demand for private schooling, the conduct of local councils towards their tenants increased the demand for right-to-buy, private medical insurance became one of the benefits offered by trade unions to their members, and private or voluntary care homes for the elderly subsidized by the state met the rising demand by which local authorities were overwhelmed. Labour ministers could no more drive market practices out of the welfare state than Conservative ministers could trim the proportion of GDP being spent on it by more than a few percentage points.

---

[37] Quoted by Nicholas Timmins, *The Five Giants: A Biography of the Welfare State* (London, 1996), p. 223.

IV

The long upper tail of the Pareto distribution is familiar from studies of the distribution of income and wealth across the range of both capitalist and other economically developed societies, including not least the socialist ones. Time and again, the richest, whatever the sources of their wealth and the means by which they accumulate it, are found to be spectacularly much richer than almost everybody else. That this was true of English society throughout the whole of the period covered in this book cannot be seriously questioned even in the absence of accurate numbers. At the same time, there can be equally little doubt that there was always a significant minority of the population with no, or negative, net assets. But the standard statistical measures of inequality—the Gini coefficient and the Lorenz curve—are well known not to be an adequate guide to the sociological significance of changes between different percentiles. A decline in the share of total wealth in the top percentiles may reflect merely a rearrangement rather than a redistribution of wealth. As a leading authority put it in the 1970s, 'the choice of a single distributional index should clearly not be left entirely to the civil servants—or to the economists'.[38] The very rich, like the very poor, are always there, and however the distance between them is calculated the practices that make them so are as easy to identify as ever.

It is not that free and open markets will automatically generate extreme inequalities of wealth. As I have remarked already in the opening section of this chapter, it is sometimes the imperfections, as economic theory defines them, that afford the opportunities for the accumulation, retention, and reinvestment of exceptionally large stores of wealth in capitalist economies. By the eighteenth century, forcible seizure of property was relevant only to the extent that 'nabobs' brought back to England from abroad fortunes won by means that would not have been open to them at home. But as the national economy grew, and assets other than land both appreciated in value and yielded increasing returns, there were more and more opportunities for wealth to be privately accumulated in more and more ways. Analysis of the probate records has shown the industrial revolution to have enriched the pioneer industrialists less than used to be assumed.[39] But its indirect effects included the accumulation of serious wealth in the financial and service sectors, transport, urban property development, and large-scale retailing, and in enterprises that met growing popular demand across the widening range of consumer goods. Fortunes continued to be made as previously in colonial and international trade. The biographies of the richest reveal, as might be expected, some remarkable mixtures of luck, talent, and application. But the practices that created and preserved their fortunes were reproduced independently of the traits of the

[38] A. B. Atkinson, *The Economics of Inequality* (Oxford, 1975), p. 56.
[39] W. D. Rubinstein, *Men of Property: The Very Wealthy in Britain since the Industrial Revolution* (London, 1981).

individuals who benefited from them, and they included practices whose function was to evade or divert the selective pressures that a free and open market brings to bear.

The ownership of property was never absolute in English law. It was not only that there were culturally acquired inhibitions and socially imposed regulations which constrained the freedom of property-owners to do what they would with their own, but that there were practices encoded in the civil law whose effect was to withdraw stores of wealth, whether in the form of land, houses, investments, or cash and cash equivalents, from the market. But this was in order to preserve wealth, not dissipate it. Among the rich, the practices that did most to preserve and pass on family wealth were those defining the roles of trustees of discretionary family trusts. The accounts of such trusts are inaccessible to academic researchers except by private permission. But although they were made liable to higher rates of tax than hitherto in the late twentieth century, it remained as true as it had been in 1894 that 'there is nothing, perhaps, in the institutions of modern Europe which comes as near to an *imperium in imperio* as the discretionary settlement of a great English fortune'.[40] Taken together with the other means by which the rich were able to maintain their position, including diversification of assets, favourable terms of credit, international connections, and avoidance or evasion of tax aided by skilled professional advice, they were vulnerable (if at all) only to the risk of a levy on capital at punitive levels higher than any government contemplated even in wartime. The fear, moreover, that the very rich would simply take their money elsewhere had already been voiced in the time of the younger Pitt, and was to be repeated by politicians of all parties throughout the twentieth century. In the aftermath of the Second World War, inherited wealth was taxed at rates inconceivable at any time previously. But the rate was subsequently relaxed, the tax was widely avoided by legal means, and no levy on capital was ever imposed.

The practices favourable to the accumulation and preservation of family wealth were not, however, confined to the rich. From the eighteenth century onwards, they were diffused among the middling sort. Testators, legatees, executors, and trustees came together in networks of mutual aid whereby impecunious family members, including unmarried sisters and daughters as well as widows, were able to sustain a middle-class lifestyle after the death of the family head. If there was any single practice that did most to protect the wider kin group it was partible inheritance, which in the verdict of one historian 'ensured the reproduction of an active profit-seeking middle class'.[41] Not only was it a means of spreading risk and making it difficult for an individual heir to withdraw from active business to the detriment of other family members' interests, but also it steadily increased the number of small rentiers of the kind whom Campbell-Bannerman was to

---

[40] Quoted from W. H. Pollock by Richard M. Titmuss, *Income Distribution and Social Change* (London, 1962), p. 99.

[41] R. J. Morris, *Men, Women and Property in England 1780–1878* (Cambridge, 2005), p. 372.

characterize as 'quiet people living on railway dividends'. Railway shares did not become an option for small investors until the rail network began to expand in the 1840s. But a typical portfolio might include consols, loan stocks, insurance company shares, and urban real estate in the form of either plots available for development or houses to be rented out or sold on. Inevitably, as both before and after, some middle-class families were more and others less fortunate in their investments, and some more and others less careful to keep their annual expenditure within the limits of disposable income. But difficult as it is to quantify their effect, there is no reason to doubt the evidence from literary sources that memes both religious and secular were being both vertically and laterally transmitted within middling families which enjoined frugality, thrift, intra-familial financial assistance, the honouring of contracts, and the repayment of debts in full.

It was still, as it had been in the eighteenth century, an economic environment fraught with financial risks of which no middle-class family could be unaware. The contemporary novels, as well as the writings of social and cultural historians, testify to a chronic sense of insecurity which was part of the subjective experience of even the more prosperous who might at any time have to face the consequences of a disabling illness, a premature death, a slump in trade, a defaulting creditor, a sudden drop in dividends, or a bank collapse like that of Overend and Gurney in 1866. The conclusion of the historian of nineteenth-century bankruptcy law that 'Statistics support the Victorians' notion that financial failure was a significant problem for English society',[42] is underwritten by the average £17 million lost annually in the 1870s and 1880s in bankruptcy and composition-type arrangements exclusive of company windings-up and the estimated £28 million lost from all three between 1892 and 1913. A descriptive sociology would need to cover the personal impact of the full range of these, together with the difference in subjective experience from later generations among whom limited liability, secure bank deposits, life insurance, occupational pension schemes, and 'blue-chip' equities would come to be taken for granted. But within the overall role structure, the same sociologically significant dividing line was visible throughout between the roles to which there did, and those to which there did not, attach the prospect of an accumulation of debt-free material assets in the household or family group. When a late twentieth-century Conservative government sought to encourage working-class share ownership in the name of 'property-owning democracy', it was faced with the problem that buying and selling stocks and shares was not something that working-class people did or knew how to do or had ever thought of doing.

Straddling the line was the same intermediate systact of small traders, artisans with their own tools of trade, and independent providers of personal services. But they faced the inescapable trade-off between ease of entry and exposure to competition. A bricklayer could set up on his own with the help of a loan from a builders'

---

[42] V. Markham Lester, *Victorian Insolvency, Bankruptcy, Imprisonment for Debt, and Company Winding-up in Nineteenth-Century England* (Oxford, 1995), p. 299.

merchant, a dressmaker with a sewing machine could mend clothes in her own home, a carrier with a horse and cart, or in due course a petrol-engine vehicle, could meet local need for the short-haul transport of goods from place to place, or a spare bedroom could be fitted out for lodgers. The expansion of fashionable districts of London such as Bayswater and Belgravia created enough opportunities for home laundering for 7 per cent of family heads in Kensal New Town in 1871 to be laundrymen.[43] There were always windows to be washed, drains to be cleared, gardens to be tended, rooms to be decorated, and fittings to be repaired which could be tendered for with a minimum outlay of capital. But the attainable profit margins were under constant pressure from competitors, and an investible surplus unlikely to amount to more than a small deposit in a post office or building society account and perhaps the ownership of the property where a business was carried on.

As society as a whole became more prosperous, contemporary observers of all persuasions wondered whether, and how far, the increasing wealth of the rich would, in what became a standard metaphor, 'trickle down' to the poor. In the eighteenth century, it was taken for granted by Dr Johnson and others that the poor benefited from the expenditure of the rich on personal services and luxury goods. But in the nineteenth, many observers were not only surprised but dismayed by the persistence, as they saw it, of so much poverty in the midst of so much plenty; and in the twentieth, following the 'rediscovery' of poverty by sociologists of the 1960s, it became apparent that the welfare state had done much less than had been widely supposed to shrink the gap between the top and bottom percentiles of the distribution of income and wealth. No measures taken by Attlee's Labour government of 1945–51, let alone its successors under Wilson and Blair, nullified the advantage enjoyed by middle-class relative to working-class families in the accumulation of property. A survey conducted in 1953 found that clerical and sales workers were better off in average net worth than skilled manual workers by nearly a third.[44] A sociologist researching a decade later found that extended middle-class families were performing functions that 'the working-class family cannot through financial ability rather than differences in sentiment'.[45] Commentators on the Right continued, as their predecessors had done, to attribute the failure of working-class families to save more and spend less to personal irresponsibility and lack of self-restraint. But it was a verdict as minimally supported by more than anecdotal evidence as the verdict of those on the Left who continued to maintain that immiseration of an increasingly homogeneous proletariat was intrinsic to the workings of capitalism. Both underestimated, if they did not altogether ignore, the inherent differences between the practices defining working-class and middle-class occupational roles which continued to offer to middle-class families and

---

[43] John Benson, *The Penny Capitalists: A Study of Nineteenth-Century Working-Class Entrepreneurs* (London, 1983), p. 74.

[44] K. H. Straw, 'Consumers' net worth: the 1953 savings survey', *Bulletin of the Oxford University Institute of Statistics* 18 (1956) p. 12.

[45] Colin Bell, *Middle Class Families: Social and Geographical Mobility* (London, 1968), p. 91.

households consistently better opportunities for the acquisition, retention, and onward transmission of both tangible and intangible assets.

It was not until the twentieth century that both researchers and policymakers became actively concerned with the problem of unemployment—a word that came into use only in the late nineteenth century. But it is not one of those which constructs the condition that it is then used to denote. The experience of looking unsuccessfully for paid employment on contracted terms in a diversified labour market was as familiar to artisans, mechanics, and labourers in Defoe's time and to Mayhew's informants in mid-nineteenth-century London as it was to be to the 'men without work' interviewed by the Pilgrim Trust investigators of the 1930s. It was diagnosed in the early nineteenth century as a problem of too many people rather than too few jobs, particularly as rural unemployment rose after the ending of the Napoleonic wars. But whatever the diagnosis, let alone the suggested remedies, lack of demand for labour sufficient to absorb the supply was an uncontested social fact. It was not confined to manual workers. But its incidence was consistently higher among them than among non-manual workers. By the end of the twentieth century, it could be stated by a team of sociologists as a matter of course that 'we know from previous research that unemployment is characteristic-ally a working-class experience'.[46] Unemployment was a topic of particularly intensive study and discussion in the 1930s and then again after it rose to 6.8 per cent in 1977, fell, and then rose again to 14 per cent in 1982. But there was no uncontroversial inference leading from diagnosis to cure, any more than there had ever been. Economists continued to disagree not only about the measurement of unemployment and the quality of the data but also about the relation of structural to cyclical unemployment and the 'natural rate' (if there is one). Full employment was not a sociological impossibility: in Britain, it was reached within a year of the outbreak of the Second World War. There were, moreover, visibly available to rulers of societies of other kinds, who were empowered to put them into effect, practices through which unemployment could be cured, as the examples of German Fascism and Russian Communism both showed. But those solutions depended not on reforming the labour market but on either bypassing or destroy-ing it. Only in wartime, or in short periods of exceptional economic growth in time of peace, could unemployment in Britain remain at a level low enough to take it out of public debate; and whatever the relative importance of its different causes, its impact continued to be inversely correlated with the location in the rank order of economic roles of those who found themselves unexpectedly dependent on what came to be called the 'dole' but was sometimes still referred to in the vernacular as the 'parish'.

The commentators who attributed the poverty of the poor to their lack of prudence and self-restraint were no less ready to attribute to the unemployed an

---

[46] Gordon Marshall, Adam Swift, and Stephen Roberts, *Against the Odds: Social Class and Social Justice in Industrial Societies* (Oxford, 1997), p. 60.

unwillingness rather than an inability to find work. This line of memetic descent is easily traceable from Defoe's attitude to 'stout fellows' who preferred begging to working, through to the nineteenth-century advocates of the workhouse, to the twentieth-century advocates of rules of entitlement to benefit which would prevent those deemed capable of working from receiving relief except on intentionally deterrent terms. The language was very different, but the attitude much the same, and the topic was no less emotive during the twentieth and early twenty-first centuries than it had been during the eighteenth and nineteenth. The supporters of one or another form of the 'genuinely seeking work' test were never without evidence which could be marshalled on their side. Indeed, it would be surprising if there were not a more than negligible number of fraudulent claimants as well as of recipients who preferred living off the benefits available from the state to taking disagreeable jobs at wage rates that would make them only marginally better off. But there were always more who would prefer to be in work than out of it. In the 1980s, a team of sociologists who conducted detailed surveys in six selected areas—two in Scotland and four in England—found not only that a majority of the claimants were actively seeking work but that 'intrinsic work commitment' was highest among the currently unemployed.[47] They did find evidence for a disincentive effect in benefit rules which took away income earned by wives of unemployed men, and there will always be, as there have always been, some who have given up actively seeking work because they believe, whether rightly or wrongly, that there is none for them to find. But nowhere in the academic literature on unemployment in Britain is there evidence that invalidates the conclusion that the majority of the able-bodied of working age, other than rentiers or pensioners or dependants of a paid or propertied household head, would rather be in employment than not, and that in times of high unemployment the chances of finding it are better for workers by brain than workers by hand.

During the twentieth century, the search for a solution to a problem that ought (it was increasingly assumed) to have one became both more imaginative and more diligent. The remedies proposed ranged from subsidized emigration to labour colonies, to across-the-board wage cuts, to public works, to cheap loans, to encouragement of women to remain in unwaged domestic employment in their homes. Some policymakers and commentators were ready, but others were not, to accept that cyclical periods of high unemployment were inescapable and that technological change might do away altogether with occupational roles whose incumbents would not then be able to find another. 'Monetarists' quarrelled with 'Keynesians', 'supply-siders' with 'demand-siders', and Labour politicians and advisers with Conservative ones. But all had to accept that at any one time there would be a percentage of the adult population eligible and capable for work who

---

[47] Duncan Gallie and Catherine Marsh, 'The experience of unemployment', in Duncan Gallie, Catherine Marsh, and Carolyn Vogler, eds., *Social Change and the Experience of Unemployment* (Oxford, 1993), p. 9.

were without it. Their standard of living might be such as would be the envy of the families studied a century earlier by Booth in London and Rowntree in York where the breadwinner, even if in full-time work, was unable to feed, clothe, and house a wife and several young children at what, in Adam Smith's much-quoted phrase, 'the established rules of decency have rendered necessary to the lowest rank of people'. Argument continued over whether poverty should be defined by some supposedly absolute standard of basic need or relative to a rising mean or median of net personal or household income or wealth. But in the well-trodden metaphor of an upward escalator, the people who stand still will fall more and more steps behind those who keep walking, even though they too benefit from the movement of the escalator itself.

The image of a moving staircase is a useful reminder of the trade-off between practices that narrow the distance between the rich and the poor, and practices that slow down the speed at which the stairs are moving and thereby hold back both the standers near the bottom and the striders near the top. But it presents a misleading image of the society's role structure as such, since it fails to allow for the movement of individuals between roles. For that, a more appropriate image is Schumpeter's, who likened classes to hotels whose rooms are always full, but of different people. On any given day, the guests staying at Hotel England are distributed, as they have been for the past three centuries, between the penthouse suites at the top, the three categories of more and less expensive but comfortable rooms with good furnishings and pleasant prospects on the upper floors, the three categories of standard accommodation near the ground floor, and the makeshift quarters in the basement with their shoddy furniture, cheap fittings, and inadequate plumbing. But later, some of the guests will be found to have moved from one room or floor to a different one, and later still to have been carried off to the local cemetery and replaced by children who may then move to either more or less expensive rooms in their turn. The image is obviously not to be pressed too far. But it brings into focus a question of fundamental importance in sociological theory: what is the effect, if any, on the distribution of power between a society's constituent roles of the movement of individuals out of one role into another? Roles, after all, are the same whoever their incumbents, even if different incumbents perform them differently. Butchers, bakers, barristers, brokers, bankers, bureaucrats, bishops, businessmen (and women), bricklayers, bartenders, busmen, bargees, boatbuilders, beauticians, and brothel-keepers *are* those things wherever they come from and whether or not they are following (in another metaphor) in parental footsteps. As I remarked in Chapter 1, ascents from the bottom and falls from the top have been a topic of interest, not to say fascination, to contemporary observers ever since the time of Defoe (and indeed before it). But to a twenty-first-century sociologist concerned to explain how the variation and selection of the practices defining different societies' roles have made their political, ideological, and economic institutions into what they are, the individual biographies of the carriers of those practices are irrelevant. Or are they? It is a question which calls for a chapter to itself.

V

As a single descriptive illustration of what has and hasn't changed in England's capitalist mode of production, I have chosen the experience of a young management trainee in Newcastle-on-Tyne in the 1960s who was sent to observe at first hand a negotiation between the local employers and the foyboatmen on the river. The foyboatmen at the meeting were solidly built middle-aged men with weather-beaten faces and vice-like handshakes. They owned their own boats and gear, but they did not conduct the negotiations themselves. These were entrusted to a briefcased, bespectacled official of the Transport and General Workers Union who had come up from London to argue on their behalf. The employer who chaired the meeting had, as another of the employers remarked in passing to the trainee, one of those accents worth a hundred votes to the Communist Party every time he opened his mouth. But nobody's voice was raised, and nobody even pretended to be getting angry. The employers were neither arrogant nor patronizing and the foyboatmen and their negotiator were neither deferential nor aggressive. Both sides gave a similar impression of speaking to a familiar script and acting out a familiar ritual.

The opening speeches by the two sides were clearly no more than that. Conflicting facts and figures were exchanged in a dialogue of the deaf from which no agreement could possibly emerge. An ostensibly final offer was met with a categorical rejection. The foyboatmen and their union official left the room, came back to it, left it again, and came back to it again. The time by which the meeting was scheduled to finish passed by unremarked. But as it extended further and further into what would have been lunchtime, there began to be detectable a faint sense of urgency and the hint from both sides of a willingness to compromise. Finally, three-quarters of an hour after the notional deadline, the difference between the two opening positions was split exactly down the middle. It was, the trainee reflected, as if he had been shown a playlet designed for instructional purposes as a stereotype verging on caricature of the British system of industrial relations in its evolved maturity (the trainee in question being, as readers will probably have guessed, myself).

5

Why Does Intergenerational Social Mobility Matter?

I

It is for the sociology of sociology to explain why social mobility became a topic of major theoretical concern to, and systematic empirical study by, sociologists only in the second half of the twentieth century. As late as 1999 a British sociologist, at the same time as making the point that the correlation between parental and filial rank is of sociological interest only to the extent that it helps to answer the question 'How does the pattern of mobility affect the way in which societies cohere and function?', described as 'a curious matter' the 'relative neglect of historical social mobility in this country'.[1] That neglect is, however, explicable at least in part by the lack of sources from which there could be extracted the necessary evidence from further back in time than fathers born in the late nineteenth century. Some relevant inferences can be drawn from marriage data as recorded in local registers, and the sociologist just quoted has done so for ten English districts for the period from 1839 to 1941. But they are subject to the limitations that some 10 per cent of men and 14 per cent of women didn't marry at all, that an increasing number of marriages—as many as 40 per cent by 1914—were non-Anglican, and that an unascertainable proportion of the individuals covered may have moved into a different occupational role after marriage. There are also some data to be gleaned from genealogical studies undertaken by families themselves, but however many are found they are a long way from being a random sample of the population. A data set based on the censuses from 1851 to 1901 has been used to link fathers and sons in categories based on the Registrar General's fivefold schema,[2] and rare surnames have been used to follow groups differentiated by wealth, education, occupation, membership of political elites, and average age at death from 1800 to 2013.[3] But these cannot substitute for a continuous set of matrices linking parental and filial location among the entire population according to a consistent criterion of rank.

[1] Andrew Miles, *Social Mobility in Nineteenth- and Early Twentieth-Century England* (Basingstoke, 1999), pp. 5, 2.
[2] Jason Long, 'The surprising social mobility of Victorian Britain', *European Review of Economic History* 17 (2013), pp. 1–23.
[3] Gregory Clark, 'What is the true rate of social mobility? Surnames and social mobility in England, 1800–2012', American Economic Association conference paper, January 2013.

The idea of moving up or down 'in the world' from a point of parental origin to a point of filial destination is, as I have remarked already in Chapter 1, as easy to grasp as the observation of it is familiar. It might therefore seem that once it is possible for a chosen population's parental and filial roles to be ascertained, a sequence of inflow and outflow tables can be constructed on which sociologists of all theoretical persuasions can agree. But even aside from sampling error and the difficulty of checking the information supplied by interviewees, the construction and analysis of mobility tables continue to pose questions to which different sociologists continue to give different answers. The standard indicator of social location in a capitalist liberal democracy is generally agreed to be occupational role, which can be justified both by its correlation with advantages in security, prospects for promotion, and provision for retirement as well as pay, and by its consistency with an ideologically determined prestige ranking as disclosed by opinion surveys and social-psychological experiments. (Differences in the political dimension of power, which in socialist societies rank incumbents of the same occupational roles differently according to the incumbent's relationship to the ruling party, can be largely ignored.) But what is to be done with people who have no occupational role, whether because they are unable to find one or because they have no need for one? Are women (and likewise men) who are not economically independent to be assigned to the rank of a spouse, cohabitee, or household head? How is adequate account to be taken of intra-generational mobility between higher- and lower-ranked roles over the lifetimes of both parents and children? Should 'affluent workers' be ranked above or below the 'genteel poor'? During the last quarter of the twentieth century, the relationship between occupational role and gender gave rise to extensive and sometimes acrimonious debate among sociologists, not least because it inevitably raises the 'central' problem of 'identifying the appropriate unit of class composition'.[4] But that problem is the same for the eighteenth and nineteenth centuries as for the twentieth, and whatever the causes of the gendered division of labour at all systactic levels of English society, the evidence for both its relative diminution and its persistent reproduction is not in dispute.

In sociological theory, there are several ideal types of mobility regime. In an age-set regime, all individuals move up together with their contemporaries from one to the next of a series of junior and senior grades to which there attach fixed obligations and privileges. In a caste regime, all individuals remain from birth in a closed endogamous status group ranked in a ritual hierarchy of contact and avoidance linked to the division of labour. In a meritocratic regime, all higher-ranked roles are filled in accordance with the results of open competition for qualifying credentials. In a perfect mobility regime, the correlation between parental and filial rank is what it would be if it were strictly random. Any society that comes close to any one of these will have to have evolved its own set of institutional

---

[4] Gordon Marshall, Stephen Roberts, Carole Burgoyne, Adam Swift, and David Routh, 'Class, gender, and "the Asymmetry Hypothesis"', *European Sociological Review* 11 (1995), p. 2.

sanctions which impose and perpetuate it. But its constituent roles will be the same whatever is found to be the location of their incumbents' parents at any one time. English society's mobility regime is, as it has been since the time of Defoe, a hybrid. But despite, or perhaps because of, the perennial interest of the topic, much public discussion of it has obscured rather than illuminated not only the rates and distances of movement in social space of successive generations of men and women but also their causes and consequences. Lack of evidence never prevented contemporary commentators from voicing conflicting opinions. By Conservatives, increasing rates of upward mobility could be deplored as both unsettling for the individual and destabilizing for the society. By Liberals, they could be welcomed as replacing the less by the more deserving in the roles most appropriate to their talents. By socialists, they could be dismissed as irrelevant to the transition to a classless society. But few if any of the commentators had a detailed understanding of the demographic, as well as cultural and social, pressures that were making the rate what it was at the time when their conflicting views of it were being expressed.

By 1980, sociologists and historians had available to them the findings of two large-scale national sample surveys. But they were not commensurable. The first was based on interviews conducted in 1949 and used a sevenfold scale of occupational prestige.[5] The second, which covered only men (and was widely criticized in consequence), was based on interviews conducted in 1972 and used a different sevenfold scheme based on occupation and employment status.[6] It was supplemented by data on social mobility collected both in follow-up studies and in independent surveys whose concerns ranged from voting behaviour to household expenditure to opinions about social justice, and its classificatory scheme was subsequently adopted in the *National Statistics Socio-Economic Classification.*[7] But it failed to satisfy critics who continued to question the meaningfulness of the dividing lines and preferred 'a scale of shared experience which may be cross-cut by class issues'.[8] Furthermore, it made no attempt to distinguish the elite in the upper tail of the Pareto distribution of income and wealth. By 2005, there were six competing schemes adopted by different sociologists, each with their different presuppositions and purposes and their consequential advantages and limitations.[9] A large new survey conducted in 2011, which included questions about respondents' resources of social and cultural as well as economic capital, generated another sevenfold scheme claimed to reflect more accurately the nature and extent of the

---

[5] D. V. Glass, ed., *Social Mobility in Britain* (London, 1954), p. 154.

[6] John H. Goldthorpe (in collaboration with Catriona Llewellyn and Clive Payne), *Social Mobility and Class Structure in Modern Britain*[2] (Oxford, 1987).

[7] David Rose and David L. Pevalin, *A Researcher's Guide to the National Statistics Socio-Economic Classification* (London, 2003).

[8] A. Stewart, K. Prandy, and R. M. Blackburn, *Social Stratification and Occupations* (Cambridge, 1980), p. 28.

[9] Manfred Max Bergman and Dominique Joye, 'Comparing social stratification schemes: CAMSIS, CSP-CH, Goldthorpe, ISCO-88, Treiman, and Wright', *Cambridge Studies in Social Research*, vol. 10 (2005), pp. 1–35.

inequalities inherent in the contemporary role structure.[10] Inevitably, however, whatever its merits, it cannot be projected back into the past. It will never be possible to construct, even for the twentieth century, a sequence of tables which would be agreed by all sociologists to reflect precisely the changes in rates and distances of social mobility that there have been in the course of it.

Yet despite all the difficulties raised as the answers to one set of questions give rise to another, the accumulated evidence licenses four generalizations covering the period from the early eighteenth to the early twentieth century which can safely be put forward in the context of the question that gives this chapter its title. First, the elite, while largely drawn from children (usually sons) within or not very far below it, has not been wholly impermeable. Second, the underclass, although containing a statistically significant minority of men and women born into it, has never formed a caste. Third, there has always been widespread intra-generational mobility both up and down in social space. Fourth, the increasing size of the middling sort, while increasing the number of children rising into it from below, has not done away with a persistent difference in the relative chances of working-class children and middle-class children occupying middle-class roles in their adult lives.

At the top of the role structure, the proportion of the population who could plausibly be assigned to the elite, whether the holders of political power or the 'rich and great' more generally, was always so small that the chances of a working-class child entering it could never be other than negligible. But it is agreed among historians to have become increasingly open to entrants born below it. It ceased to be true after the nineteenth century that 'any member of a titled family who entered the House of Commons would very likely find there not only members of his father's family but also men who were related to him on his mother's side'.[11] During the twentieth century, the presence of working-class MPs on the Labour (but not, unsurprisingly, Conservative) benches ceased to be a topic of comment. The role of the 'squire' who had inherited a landed estate from his father and thereby in his own locality been 'a member of the propertied class and hence of the ruling class' became more and more of an anachronism.[12] Children of incumbents of the topmost roles could still be seen inheriting their parents' rank at the end of the twentieth century. But well before the end of the nineteenth, contemporary observers were aware that roles in both local and national government were open to men and (at the local level) some women from parental origins extending down through the middle to the working classes, that honours were no longer bestowed only for political or military services to the Crown, and that the wealth of the rich was coming from other sources than farming rents, mineral rights, government stocks, well-endowed marriages, and passive investment in speculative trading

[10] Mike Savage, Fiona Devine, Niall Cunningham, Mark Taylor, Yaojun Li, Johs Hjellbrekke, Brigette Le Roux, Sam Friedman, and Andrew Miles, 'A new model of social class: findings from the BBC's Great British Class Survey Experiment', *Sociology* 47 (2013), pp. 219–50.

[11] W. L. Guttsman, *The British Political Elite* (London, 1965), p. 217.

[12] G. E. Mingay, *The Gentry: The Rise and Fall of a Ruling Class* (London, 1976), p. 189.

ventures. Senior military and naval officers, higher civil servants, directors of large corporations, accumulators of large personal fortunes, and leaders of the traditionally 'great' professions of divinity, law, and physic were less overwhelmingly likely to be drawn from gentry or aristocratic families. Despite the lack of an agreed definition of the elite and precise calculation of its numbers, there is no evidence that would contradict the opinion of a leading authority who, looking back from the last quarter of the twentieth century, concluded that 'The general movement has been towards greater openness, although the slow pace and unevenness of the development is perhaps the most striking feature'.[13]

The twentieth-century elite was thus composed of a larger proportion of men and women whose fathers had occupied roles further below it in social space than had been envisaged any more by Gladstone than by Walpole. But the chances of a son, let alone daughter, born into (or, depending on the definition used, close to) it remaining in it were still many hundreds of times higher than for a son born into the working class of entering it. Nor could it be otherwise, unless the sons of fathers whose roles were in or close to it were to be debarred from membership of it. Children born into high-ranking families who find themselves both culturally stigmatized and socially excluded, as after the Chinese Revolution for being of 'bad class' origin or as after the French Revolution for being *ci-devants*, may be either forced into lower-ranked roles or driven into exile. But even then, the chance of any one working-class child rising into the elite is still negligible. Reformers could, and increasingly in the twentieth century did, argue that the elite should be more representative of the population as a whole and that therefore (among other things) many more of its members should be women. But to whatever extent this aim might be realized, it did not thereby alter the practices that defined the elite's roles.

The same is true of the underclass. Some sociologists avoid the word altogether because it can be used to imply a caste-like inheritance of poverty, social exclusion, and involvement in activities that contravene the criminal law. But children whose parents are in underclass roles at the time of the children's birth are not, in English society, condemned to remain there, however much the environment in which they have been brought up reduces their relative probability of upward mobility over the subsequent course of their lives. Successive generations of informed observers have found the English underclass to be principally composed of men and women in it only at particular stages of their adult lives: the elderly, the disabled, the parents (particularly widowed, divorced, separated, or unmarried mothers) of several dependent children, and low-skilled workers at high risk of lay-off during economic downturns, together with debtors unable to clear their debts, mendicants, petty thieves, prisoners and newly discharged prisoners, misusers of alcohol or drugs, or immigrants or casuals recruited by employers operating illegally outside the formal economy.

---

[13] Anthony Heath, *Social Mobility* (London, 1981), p. 93.

The most obvious change in the lived experience of the underclass was in the condition of the indigent elderly and the chronically unemployed. No contemporary observer in the second half of the twentieth century could be in doubt that the provision made by then both for those unable to find work and for those past working exceeded on any measure what it had been a century, let alone two centuries, earlier. A mid-Victorian labourer and his wife who survived into their sixties with no savings of their own and a family unable or unwilling to house and feed them had no alternative but the workhouse—a misnomer in their as in many other cases, since it was not a place of work but an infirmary in which they were housed and fed but subjected to a regime over which they had no control. The sociologists who in the 1960s drew a 'poverty line' at 140 per cent of the supplementary benefit level plus an allowance for rent did not need to be reminded of the difference between the living conditions of the 'poor' of 1960 and the 'poor' of 1860 or 1760. But they found that it was still the elderly and the lower-paid breadwinners with several young children among whom the incidence of poverty was highest, and they also pointed to the frequency with which individuals continued to move in and out of poverty as they had defined it. However much the combination of minimal education, overcrowded housing, large families, low incomes, and neglectful parental upbringing was an issue of concern to the makers of social policy, 'a surprisingly large proportion of people reared in conditions of privation and suffering do *not* reproduce that pattern in the next generation'.[14] The effects of intergenerational transmission of multiple deprivation are, in statistical terms, barely significant after three generations. At the bottom of the society, as at the top, the correlation between parental origin and filial destination is a symptom, not a cause, of the distribution of power between roles.

The same is true of the patterns of short-distance intra-generational mobility which are well documented for the second half of the twentieth century. Even where respondents in a national survey have provided accurate information about both their fathers' occupations at the time of the respondent's birth (or at some later age) and their first full-time occupation as well as about their occupation at the time of interview, a reported sequence may conceal other movements over significant social distances between higher- and lower-ranked roles (quite apart from what may be the respondent's work-life experience in subsequent years). There is, however, no doubt that such mobility was widespread in the twentieth century and not unusual before then. There have always been counter-mobile individuals moving back to their location of origin after a period away from it, individuals remarrying up or down later on in their lives, individuals coming into both anticipated and unanticipated inheritances, individuals alternating between periods in manual or unskilled service roles and clerical, administrative, or supervisory ones, individuals trying but failing to set up their own businesses, and individuals achieving a long-held ambition only after many years. There have also been women who leave paid

[14] Michael Rutter and Nicola Madge, *Cycles of Disadvantage* (London, 1976), p. 6.

employment after marrying husbands whose occupations rank above their own. The subjective experience of such mobility may be no less rewarding or frustrating or gratifying or stressful or disconcerting for the individual where the distance is short, or even very short—as, for example, in the catchment area of the 'complex social rules on the margins of the skilled working class and petite bourgeoisie that determined who may be courted by whom' in the late nineteenth and early twentieth centuries.[15] But those experiences too are a symptom, not a cause, of the inter-systactic distribution of power.

The frequency of both intra- and intergenerational mobility between occupational roles can be expected to increase in the environment of an expanding economy, particularly when the relative sizes of higher- and lower-ranked occupational categories within a growing population are changing. But the relative chances of children of middling and of labouring parents entering middling roles in adulthood cannot be assumed to change as a result. The rate of growth of the total population since the first national census in 1811 is accurately known, together with its changing geographical distribution, its birth and death rates, and (less accurately, particularly in relation to women) its occupational composition. But there is no evidence that would license the inference that these changes significantly affected the proportion of middle-class roles not filled by middle-class children. Before that, it is not impossible that there had been more opportunities than there would be later for a son of a working-class father to move into an occupational role for which literacy and numeracy were required: one historian drawing on data from the Lancaster Charity School Register for 1770 to 1816 and from marriage certificates for 1837 to 1839 even suggested that 'in an eighteenth-century commercial society unaffected by the development of the cotton factory industry, the possibility of social mobility for the educated son of a labourer was vastly higher than in 1830'[16]—a conclusion based, however, on comparing a favoured group of children attending a charity school which offered the best education available with a later random sample of labourers' children able merely to sign their names.[17] But by the mid-nineteenth century, the demand most persistently generated by industrialization was for unskilled and semi-skilled labour which was not matched by an equivalent demand for clerical labour, and it was met from the growing number of working-class children, both male and female, supplemented by successive waves of immigrants—particularly the Irish, of whom over half a million were registered in England and Wales in the census of 1871.

Over the course of the nineteenth century there is thought to have been a rise in the proportion of working-class daughters marrying into the middle classes, and to

[15] A. James Hammerton, 'Pooterism or partnership? Marriage and masculine identity in the lower middle class, 1870–1920', *Journal of British Studies* 38 (1999), p. 315.

[16] Michael Sanderson, 'Literacy and social mobility in the Industrial Revolution in England', *Past & Present* 56 (1972), p. 101.

[17] Thomas W. Laqueur, 'Literacy and social mobility in the Industrial Revolution in England', *Past & Present* 64 (1974), p. 97.

that extent more openness in the marriage market than in the world of work.[18] But for as long as some three-quarters of the greatly enlarged population were, whether by occupation or marriage, in the working class, the relative chances of middle-class and working-class children occupying middle-class roles in adult life were inescapably constrained. Even when the expanding middle classes were drawing more and more working-class children into roles located above those of their parents, they were far more likely to remain for life where they were at birth than were middle-class children not to. The ability and determination of middle-class parents to keep their children in the middle class was thoroughly familiar to eighteenth- and nineteenth-century commentators who knew as much as any twentieth-century sociologist about cultural capital, patronage, networking, and presentation of self in an environment of continuous competition for money and status.

This pattern was unmistakable in the detailed evidence that became available for the twentieth century. The perceptive commentator quoted in Chapter 1 who opined in 1828 that 'the middle classes are receiving from the lower in much greater numbers than the latter do from the former' would be unsurprised. There is the obvious difference that in the twentieth century the institutional conduits through which upward mobility was channelled were increasingly the schools which gave selected working-class children the credentials that opened up the prospect of a middle-class career. Not only the clerical and administrative employees required by both the private and the public sectors of the economy but also the higher-salaried managers and higher-feed professionals were increasingly drawn from among the children of working-class parents. But that did not, any more than in 1828, mean that the chances of working-class and middle-class children occupying middle-class roles were being equalized: the study based on rare surnames, for what it may be worth, found no traceable impact on mobility from the arrival of mass education.

Some sociologists of the late twentieth century drew from the data sets by then available the conclusion that there was 'no general tendency for the level of fluidity to either rise or to fall'.[19] But it was questioned by others who argued that meta-analysis of all the available surveys showed that 'aggregate levels of social mobility have increased over time—albeit slightly'.[20] A study based on the British Household Panel Survey for 1991 and General Household Survey for 2005 concluded, contrary to claims that relative mobility was (if anything) declining, that 'for both men and women, the evidence suggests some increasing social fluidity over the period covered even though the extent of the increase is rather small'.[21] But neither

---

[18] Miles, *Social Mobility*, p. 186.

[19] John H. Goldthorpe and Michelle Jackson, 'Intergenerational mobility in contemporary Britain: political careers and empirical findings', *British Journal of Sociology* 68 (2007), p. 541.

[20] Paul Lambert, Kenneth Prandy, and Wendy Bottero, 'By slow degrees: two centuries of social reproduction and mobility in Britain', *Sociological Research Online* 12 (2007), p. 3.

[21] Yaujun Li and Fiona Devine, 'Is social mobility really declining? Intergenerational class mobility in the 1990s and the 2000s', *Sociological Research Online* 16 (2011), p. 15.

those who saw an increase nor those who saw a decrease in fluidity argued that it was, by whatever their chosen criterion, a 'large' one. Nowhere has the search for statistically significant trends yielded evidence for anything that could be claimed to approach a modal change of mobility regime.

It was not as if seventeenth-century English society had been socially immobile. On the contrary, before the commercialization, urbanization, and incipient industrialization of the eighteenth century, 'social mobility was a constant feature' of the 'world we have lost'.[22] But that world's role structure was too unlike that of Hanoverian England for sociologically meaningful comparisons to be drawn between eighteenth- and seventeenth-century mobility rates. In seventeenth-century England, the social space between an elite of aristocratic and gentry families at the top and an underclass dependent on parish relief at the bottom had been filled by an overwhelmingly rural population whose members' incomes in cash or kind, social prestige, and local political influence depended almost entirely on access to land, whether they were larger or smaller yeomen, tenants of different acreages holding under a variety of leases, cottagers doing seasonal wage work or exploiting common rights, craftsmen raising livestock or keeping poultry or growing their own fruit and vegetables, servants-in-husbandry hoping sooner or later to establish households of their own, or widowed survivors of marriages lasting a median of no more than a decade.

By the mid-eighteenth century, however, even though more than three-quarters of the total population were residentially rural rather than urban, they were by no means all rural by sector of employment.[23] For a farm labourer's son or daughter who remained on the land, the prospects of upward social mobility were nugatory. But as the movement of the population off the land accelerated, the 'world we have lost' became increasingly like the world as it had evolved into being by the time that men and women born in or after the late nineteenth century were being included in inflow and outflow mobility tables based on representative samples of the population. The roles and the power attaching to them were recognizably similar, whatever the different terms denoting them. In an eighteenth-century provincial town like Colchester, where one household in five was part of a 'middling sort' defined in terms of 'occupation, rateable value, participation in genteel culture, household structure, and office-holding',[24] the children born into such a household were protected, just as their nineteenth-century and twentieth-century counterparts would continue to be, from downward social mobility by 'strategies involving education, marriage, or capital to start a business'.[25] In this role structure, the

---

[22] Peter Laslett, *The World We Have Lost* (London, 1965), p. 157.

[23] E. A. Wrigley, *People, Cities, and Wealth: The Transformation of Traditional Society* (London, 1987), ch. 7.

[24] Shani D'Cruze, 'The middling sort in 18th-century Colchester: independence, social relations and the community broker', in Jonathan Barry and Christopher Brooks, eds., *The Middling Sort of People: Culture, Society and Politics in England, 1550–1800* (London, 1994), p. 199.

[25] Jonathan Barry, 'Introduction', in Barry and Brooks, *The Middling Sort of People*, p. 1.

number of middle-class vacancies for working-class children to fill depended much more on the total number of middle-class roles than on the failure of middle-class children to occupy them. For all the differences in the nature and conditions of both manual and non-manual employment, it is difficult not to see the pattern of significant absolute but low relative intergenerational mobility as having been already in place two centuries earlier.

II

Sceptical readers may object that since there is no possibility of finding evidence from which rates of either intra- or intergenerational social mobility could be accurately and consistently calculated even for the entire twentieth century, let alone the nineteenth and eighteenth, there can be no warrant for projecting the mobility regime of the twentieth century back into the past. But that is to ignore the inferences that can be drawn from exercises in simple arithmetic which demonstrate the degree to which the relative mobility rates cannot but have been influenced by first, the relative sizes of the middling sort and labouring people, and second, the capacity of middling parents to look after their own. Such an exercise is not an attempt to estimate the actual figures with which a census-taker would have filled in the cells of a sequence of inflow and outflow tables, but simply a set of rudimentary calculations which will serve to underwrite the argument that for the children of working-class parents the probability of remaining within the working class during adulthood is unlikely to have changed to a more than limited degree from the proto-industrial society of the mid-eighteenth and early nineteenth century, through the mature-industrial society of the mid- to late nineteenth century, to the late-industrial society of the twentieth and post-industrial society of the early twenty-first. As with the modes of coercion, persuasion, and production themselves, the changes were within the mobility regime, not of it.

Suppose, accordingly, a starting point of a hypothetical proto-industrial society with an adult population of a million within which women without non-domestic roles of their own are classified with their husbands or household heads. Then suppose that 150,000 are classified above, and 850,000 below, a line which separates landowners, farmers, business proprietors, administrators, clergymen, doctors, lawyers, financiers, rentiers, shopkeepers, merchants, salesmen, contractors, army and navy officers, schoolteachers, authors, artists, actors, technicians, clerks, bookkeepers, small masters, and practitioners of assorted non-manual skills, from craftsmen, factory hands and foremen, farmhands, tramping artisans, mechanics, builders, carters, journeymen, casual and migrant labourers, sole (or man-and-wife) street traders, 'petty craftsmen pretending to trades merely ostensible',[26]

---

[26] Quoted from William Godshall, *A General Plan of Parochial Police* (1787), p. 5, by T. S. Ashton, *An Economic History of England: The Eighteenth Century* (London, 1955), p. 21 n.1.

domestic servants, common soldiers and seamen, mineworkers, dockworkers, home-based outworkers, prostitutes (as opposed to 'courtesans' above the line), petty thieves, beggars, manual workers of any and all grades of skill, and dependants on poor relief. Suppose further that in a given year all the members of that population have supplied the census-taker with accurate information about both their own or their household head's current occupational role and that of their fathers in the year of their (the respondents') birth. That will not, of course, show the distribution of the fathers' roles as it was in any one previous year. But in a period of incipient urbanization, commercialization, and industrialization, it is plausible to expect that the proportion of fathers above the dividing line would be found to be smaller than that of their children—say, 12½ per cent as against 15 per cent. The marginal totals are then in place for the construction of a 2×2 mobility table in standard form in which the critical number is the one for higher-ranked children of higher-ranked fathers in the top left-hand cell. Suppose now that as many as one in five children born above the line have been unable or unwilling to find or to create or to marry into a role that would keep them there. The adult population in any given year will then consist of 120,000 higher-ranked children of higher-ranked fathers, 5,000 lower-ranked children of higher-ranked fathers, 30,000 higher-ranked children of lower-ranked fathers, and 845,000 lower-ranked children of lower-ranked fathers.

In this notional population, the higher category is a long way from being a caste, since 20 per cent of those in it were born below it. But the chances of a child born in the lower category being found in the higher one are only just over 3½ per cent. It is, no doubt, arguable that the assumptions that yield this percentage are too restrictive. Perhaps at this stage of the hypothetical society's evolution the higher category totals more than 15 per cent of the adult population, even though the majority of the lower category are agricultural labourers and their wives. It may also be that children of fathers in the higher category have been emigrating in order to better their prospects elsewhere, and that children of fathers in the lower category have been able not only to move into vacant roles within it or to marry up into it, but also to bring new-made roles with them into it by offering new-found skills and services to a market willing to pay for them. Suppose accordingly that the higher-ranked category comprises 20 per cent of the adult population and that 20 per cent of those found in it are, as before, the children of fathers born in the lower-ranked category. The lower-ranked fathers (many of whom will be the fathers of several of the same people) now add up to 820,000. Although one in nine of this set of children of higher-ranking fathers is downwardly mobile, the chance of upward mobility for a child born into the lower-ranked category is still under 5 per cent. If the population of two actual societies with the same mode of production were found to be like this at a similar evolutionary stage, it would invite the comment that a child born below the dividing line would have a perceptibly better chance of rising above it in the one than in the other. But where the percentages are as small as these, the difference is insignificant in relation to the likelihood (or unlikelihood) of anything approaching a modal change of mobility regime.

Once urbanization and industrialization gathered pace and the total population expanded at a rate that took it over 20 million by the census of 1871 and over 30 million by the turn of the century, 2×2 mobility tables calculated for those years would reflect, whatever the exact figures, a widening range of occupational roles, a shrinking number of independent proprietors, a steadily declining agricultural workforce, and a by then substantial number of children of immigrant-born working-class fathers. Between one decade and another, there might appear noticeably different marginal totals depending on the state of the national economy: in the twentieth century, children born into the lower category had for historically obvious reasons significantly less chance of rising out of it in the two decades before than in the two decades after the Second World War. But only a very implausible manipulation of the hypothetical figures for the final quarter of the nineteenth century would show anything other than a self-reproducing working class out of which the probability of a child rising into the middling sort (or above) was very many times smaller than the probability of a child born above the line remaining there (or moving higher).

In any event, whatever the mobility rates that might have been calculated for the nineteenth century, it is hard to see how a plausible argument could be constructed to the effect that by comparison with the mid-eighteenth century the chances of working-class children moving into the middle class would be found to have risen. Even if the rate of downward mobility from the middle class increased during the period when Marx and Engels saw the petty bourgeoisie being 'hurled', as they put it in the *Communist Manifesto*, into the proletariat, that will not have improved the chances of upward mobility for children of working-class parents. It was not going to generate the kind of exchange mobility in which a vacancy unfilled by a downwardly mobile middle-class child is filled from below if the proportion of middle-class roles in question was shrinking. As the mid-Victorian economy grew, the expansion of the armies of manual workers in the mines, factories, mills, forges, engineering works, shipyards, railways, and building sites on whose labour it depended did not generate a proportionate increase in the number of clerical, technical, administrative, and sales workers needed to support them. In the year that Marx published the first volume of *Capital*, the chance of a labouring family's child rising into the middling sort could, hypothetically, have been as little as half what it had been a hundred years earlier. But even if so, the change was inconsequential in relation to the overall role structure.

By the end of the twentieth century, the working class was not only different in its occupational composition but also relatively smaller, so that one major constraint on the chances of a child born into the working class rising out of it was therefore relaxed to that extent. But that did not, by itself, affect the advantages enjoyed by middle-class children in competing for middle-class roles. The cultural environment of a middle-class home was agreed among sociologists of all persuasions both to encourage children brought up in it to acquire linguistic and self-presentational skills, for which employers were more likely to be looking (and were less likely to find among applicants of working-class upbringing), and also to provide associational contacts through which information could be acquired that would be helpful in guiding children through the school system: a small-scale study of doctors and teachers carried out in Manchester in 1996–97 clearly (and unsurprisingly) brought out the value of information coming not just from 'objective facts and figures' but from 'like-minded friends and acquaintances'.[27] Formal schooling, which some reformers had looked to as the principal institutional means by which an increasing proportion of working-class children would be enabled to rise into the middle class, turned out not to make as much difference as the reformers had hoped. Not only did middle-class children continue to be over-represented at the higher levels where credentials for middle-class occupational roles could be obtained, but even where education was held constant middle-class children were found to have better prospects of entering middle-class roles than their working-class counterparts. This might not preclude intra-generational mobility in later life. Calculations of relative mobility chances based on first occupational role take no account of possible opportunities to obtain a formal credential as an adult or to move up at a later stage into a role to which a qualification obtained earlier might have some relevance. But the expansion in the number of middle-class occupational roles available to be filled, although it created significantly increased opportunities of upward mobility for working-class women as well as men, did not of itself do anything to decrease the advantages enjoyed by children brought up in middle-class families in competing for them.

Successive studies throughout the twentieth century also confirmed a continuing difference between middle-class and working-class families in attitudes to education and the prospects of a middle-class occupational role associated with it. Between the two world wars, what one contemporary commentator called the 'upthrust of new strata of the population' into the secondary schools did not prevent frequent refusals of free places by working-class children whose parents wanted, as the children themselves did, to see them in paid work sooner rather than later.[28] By the 1950s, it could be claimed that 'there has undoubtedly been a post-war revolution in parents' attitudes to their children's education, especially at the bottom of the social scale'.[29] But there persisted a relative lack of personal ambition among working-class children and aspiration among their parents on their behalf for educational qualifications by comparison with the middle-class families where it was a matter of course. Several different (but not incompatible) explanations were

---

[27] Fiona Devine, *Class Practices: How Parents Help their Children Get Good Jobs* (Cambridge, 2004), p. 169.

[28] G. A. N. Lowndes, *The Silent Social Revolution: An Account of the Expansion of Public Education in England and Wales, 1895–1935* (London, 1937), p. 128.

[29] Jean Floud, A. H. Halsey, and F. M. Martin, *Social Class and Educational Opportunity* (London, 1957), p. 147.

on offer. Some sociologists saw it as a rational perception of the unlikelihood of success, others as a reluctance to move away from the milieu and lifestyle of family and friends, and others as a repudiation of the dominant criteria of social prestige—why would a prospective craftsman apprenticed to a skilled trade want to become a 'shiny-arsed pen-pusher', particularly when the pen-pusher was, unless and until promoted, no better paid? Working-class children going on to higher education faced what many found an uncomfortable choice between 'standing out' and 'fitting in'.[30] Reactions like these came as no surprise to the sociologists reporting them. More remarkable, if anything, is that when an inquiry was carried out in the 1960s into the careers of boys educated at Winchester who had been born between 1900 and 1922, there should be even a solitary one found, as was the case, in a manual occupational role.[31] Nor is there any research that points to the conclusion that parents upwardly mobile from the working class into managerial, professional, or proprietorial roles are any more likely than those born in the middle class to encourage their children to leave school early for lifetime working-class jobs rather than stay on and pursue middle-class careers. A study carried out for the Ministry of Education in 1957 found that only 8 per cent of fathers who had stayed on at school beyond the minimum age allowed their children to leave as soon as free to do so.[32]

To look back, therefore, from the early twenty-first century to the early eighteenth is to see a less open society, but not one with a radically different pattern of absolute and relative intergenerational mobility rates. There remains the possibility that there was a causal relationship such that the mobility regime either accelerated or retarded change in the society's role structure. Perhaps there were memes of some kind in the heads of the upwardly—or, for that matter, downwardly—mobile which had an effect on behaviour which favoured the reproduction of some mutant practices over others. Or perhaps intergenerational mobility influenced the behaviour of the *im*mobile in some way which affected the inter-systactic distribution of power. But these are questions of a different kind from those addressed in this chapter so far.

III

Some sociologists, of whom Durkheim was one, have assumed that the upwardly mobile will become not merely conformist but reactionary. Examples are not difficult to find, in England as elsewhere, of men and women who on rising from their location at birth, or at some early stage in their adult lives, forswear an initial hostility to their society's existing institutions and become outspoken defenders of

---

[30] Diane Reay, Gill Crozier, and John Clayton, 'Fitting in or standing out: working-class students in UK higher education', *British Educational Research Journal* 32 (2010), pp. 1–18.

[31] T. S. H. Bishop, *Winchester and the Public School Elite* (London, 1967), p. 61.

[32] *15–18: A Report of the Central Advisory Council for Education (England)*, vol. 1 (1962), p. 9.

the status quo. It is plausible at any evolutionary stage to expect that individuals who move into occupational roles ranked higher than those of their fathers will 'share a common commitment to the "career" in which their endpoint, rather than their starting-point, helps to define a class identity'.[33] There is no evidence (so far as I have been able to discover) relating to English society that contradicts the expectation that destination has a stronger influence than origin and that the influence increases with length of time in the higher role. But upward mobility can affect different individuals in different ways. In twentieth-century England, 'the experience of mobility could itself prove conducive to radicalism through the exposure to different conceptions of status and social worth',[34] and this could be detected among, for example, 'scholarship girls' of working-class origin.[35] Moreover, the experience needs to be viewed from within the individual's wider environment of family, friends, and associates. The men in the national survey of 1972 and follow-up study of 1974, when questioned about the 'class' of their friends and in-laws, disclosed a range of cross-cutting associational affiliations within which the upwardly mobile had by no means cut themselves off from their parental origins, and questions about how they had voted in the General Election of 1970 disclosed a pattern in which they could be seen to have been influenced by pressures coming in opposite directions from the environments of their locations of origin and destination. Not all the upwardly mobile need be unequivocally committed to either the cultural norms or the social practices of the environment into which they move. But that does not make them carriers of memes by which the fitness of those norms and practices will be undermined.

Nor is there any evidence that the downwardly mobile are carriers of memes that will affect the practices defining the roles into which they fall. In a small-scale study carried out in London in 1970, the downwardly mobile were found likely to have experienced relatively short-distance slippage from families 'only nominally part of the middle class' whose lifestyles and relations with family and friends were not sharply differentiated from the upper-working class.[36] The 1972 national survey included very few men downwardly mobile from the middle class to the unskilled working class, and sons of middle-class origin who had failed to obtain any educational qualifications were found more likely than their working-class equivalents to secure a subsequent qualification for entry by way of technical training or apprenticeship into an upper-working-class occupational role. There is no sign of the formation among the downwardly mobile of a group or category of resentful déclassés ready to take collective action which might change existing institutional

[33] Mike Savage, *Class Analysis and Social Transformation* (Buckingham, 2000), p. 84.

[34] Kevin Morgan, 'Socialists and "mobility" in twentieth-century Britain: images and experiences in the life histories of British Communists', *Social History* 36 (2011), p. 167.

[35] Janet Howarth, 'Classes and cultures in England after 1951: the case of working-class women', in Clare V. Griffiths, James J. Nott, and William Whyle, eds., *Classes, Cultures and Politics: Essays on British History for Ross McKibbin* (Oxford, 2011), p. 89.

[36] C. J. Richardson, *Contemporary Social Mobility* (London, 1972), p. 270.

practices in a way that would enhance their prospects of counter-mobility back into their systact of origin.

On this topic, two alternative hypotheses have been put forward from time to time. On the first, the movement out of the relevant category of the underprivileged of a small number of its ablest and most ambitious members functions as a safety valve which deprives it of potential leaders who would otherwise be active in mobilizing organized opposition to the existing institutions of their society. On the second, the inability of the majority of the underprivileged to move upwards as they see a successful minority doing generates a sense of relative deprivation which finds expression in active opposition to the existing regime.

The first hypothesis implies that among the underprivileged there is only a limited number of able and ambitious individuals who have the requisite capacity to be leaders of effective movements of protest. But in England, as in many other societies, working-class rebels have not lacked leaders, whether the spokesmen and organizers of the corresponding societies, or the pseudonymous 'Captain Swing', or the prominent Chartists (both 'moral-force' and 'physical-force'), or the authentically militant syndicalists, to say nothing of the atypical members of the bourgeoisie ready to act, in the phrase of Robert Michels, as 'fencing-masters of the proletariat'. In a regime where absolute mobility is rising but relative mobility remains low, there will be enough both of the mobile who retain allegiance to the radicalism of their youth and of the immobile who are unreconciled to the collective disabilities of their class to make it highly implausible to attribute the non-revolutionary character of the working class to the loss to it of those born into it who move out of it into middle-class roles.

The second hypothesis, on the other hand, faces the immediate objection that in the English case social mobility was nowhere on the agenda of either Chartism or Syndicalism. Nowhere in the speeches and writings in which the Chartists articulated their demands is there a complaint that the existing regime is denying the children of working-class parents their rightful opportunities of moving into middle-class roles. In the case of the Syndicalists, the demand for 'workers' control' could be said to imply the replacement of existing incumbents of managerial roles by men of presumptively working-class origin. But the grievance that prompted the demand was not the lack of opportunity for such men to be upwardly mobile. If an existing manager was of working-class origin, that would make no difference to his being threatened, as in the example quoted in Chapter 2, with being 'turned out' and a representative of the shop floor put in his place. Far from a higher rate of intergenerational mobility being a Syndicalist objective, an ambition to rise out of the working class, to the rank and file who suspected their union negotiators of being too ready to collude with the employers, implied disloyalty to the common cause. There was only one group or category of workers among whom the widespread working-class discontent of the years preceding the First World War was related to a perceived reduction in opportunities for promotion. Some skilled craftsmen, of whom an increasing number were being radicalized by their loss of prestige as well as of earnings, were aggrieved by a division of labour 'which tended to throw up new management hierarchies, with their own recruitment schemes, blocking the upward mobility of the ambitious artisan'.[37] But whatever sense of relative deprivation this generated, it did not find expression in behaviour which checked the diffusion and reproduction of the practices that defined the new managerial roles.

The concept of relative deprivation, which was first coined by the authors of a study of attitudes to promotion opportunities in the different branches of the American army during the Second World War, is sometimes invoked in support of a generalization to the effect that increased opportunities for promotion, far from acting as a safety valve, exacerbate the resentment of those left behind. In a seemingly paradoxical finding which generated widespread discussion among both American and British sociologists, discontent with promotion prospects turned out to be highest in the air force, where they were highest, but lowest in the military police, where they were lowest.[38] This, it can be argued, is symptomatic of a general tendency for dissatisfaction with an existing regime to be heightened precisely because the relatively deprived have been made aware of the possibility of a hitherto uncontemplated change which would be to their advantage. Tocqueville, in discussing the antecedents of the French Revolution, famously observed that popular discontent ran highest in those parts of France where there had been most improvement, and the proposition that revolutionary movements are fuelled by rising expectations is sometimes cited as a truism: it has, for example, been said of the Chartist strategy that 'in Tocquevillian fashion' it 'depended on the climate of raised expectations fostered by the existing of a reforming, interventionist Whig administration'.[39] But the members of the US Army Air Corps who felt relatively deprived of promotion weren't social revolutionaries any more than were the members of the military police who were resigned to remaining where they were.

The choice of comparative reference group is bound to be a significant influence on individual satisfaction or dissatisfaction with the distribution of power within an existing role structure, whether at the level of the society as a whole or of one or more institutions within it. But in a national sample survey of the population of England and Wales conducted in 1962 for the purpose of ascertaining popular attitudes to social inequality, it was found that most people chose comparative reference groups close to their own location,[40] from which it could plausibly be inferred that they were not much, if at all, preoccupied with their opportunities (or their lack of them) for significant upward mobility from their location of parental origin. That study has not been replicated since. But whatever dissatisfactions are

---

[37] G. R. Searle, *A New England? Peace and War 1886–1918* (Oxford, 2004), p. 270.

[38] Samuel A. Stouffer et al., *The American Soldier*, vol. 1: *Adjustment During Army Life* (Princeton, 1949), pp. 250–3.

[39] Miles Taylor, *The Decline of British Radicalism, 1857–1860* (Oxford, 1995), p. 101.

[40] W. G. Runciman, *Relative Deprivation and Social Justice: A Study of Attitudes to Social Inequality in Twentieth-Century Britain* (London, 1966), part 3.

voiced to opinion pollsters by respondents to sample surveys about the workings of their society's political, ideological, or economic institutions, and however strongly they may be motivated by a desire to better their own and their families' condition, the rate of intergenerational mobility was not obviously an issue of pressing concern to the twentieth-century working-class electorate any more than it had been to the Chartists petitioning for the vote. The same mobility regime continued to operate through a similar combination of methods of recruitment, and the rates of mobility within it to be determined by the same demographic, cultural, and social pressures. It had no independent effect on the practices defining the roles constitutive of English society's modes of coercion, persuasion, or production, whatever the personal frustrations to which it might give rise. It may well be that 'If class membership becomes more fluid, then cultural differences between social classes tend to diminish.'[41] But that does not mean that it brings about a change in the distribution of political, ideological, or economic power between the society's constituent roles.

IV

The answer to the question that gives this chapter its title is, therefore, that in the English case, rates of intergenerational social mobility matter to sociologists and policymakers not so much because of any significant effect on the evolution of the role structure within which the mobility takes place as because of their normative concerns. The principal authors of the national surveys of 1949 and 1972 were both explicit about this. Glass averred that he intended to 'put forward personal views which are explicitly "loaded" in that they have a value bias',[42] and Goldthorpe that 'we must declare an interest of a positive kind in mobility, in so far as it is associated with greater openness: that is to say, with a tendency towards greater equality of chances of careers, for individuals of all social origins, to positions differently located within the social division of labour'.[43] Sociologists' motives and values no more determine the accuracy of their reports and the validity of their explanations than the motives and values of policymakers determine the success or failure of the mutations of practices of which they are the initiators. But sociologists may nonetheless hope that their findings will influence the decisions of policymakers who can be persuaded to agree with them that the existing mobility regime is inefficient and unjust. Undeserving men and women are occupying higher-ranked roles than they should, as more deserving children of lower-ranked parents are excluded from those roles, inheritance of privilege continues unchecked, and talent goes unnecessarily to waste.

---

[41] David J. Smith, 'Defining the underclass', in David J. Smith, ed., *Understanding the Underclass* (London, 1992), p. 5.
[42] Glass, *Social Mobility*, p. 22.   [43] Goldthorpe, *Social Mobility and Class Structure*, p. 27.

The 'waste-of-talent' argument was not exclusive to commentators on the Left. On the Right too it was a matter of increasing concern from the late nineteenth century onwards that England lacked the forward-looking elite, innovative managerial class, and highly skilled workforce that would enhance the productivity and growth of its economy and sustain its military and naval strength. The long-standing disputes among historians about why England's economic performance was no better then and thereafter than it was, and how it could (or perhaps couldn't) have been improved, are for them to settle as best they can. But sociologists concerned to demonstrate how rates of upward mobility might be increased must specify the mutant practices whose diffusion and reproduction would either narrow the social distance between roles to the point that vertical mobility loses its meaning, or prevent parents in higher-ranked roles from passing their advantages down to their children. There needs to attach to the roles of educators, inspectors, assessors, and administrators the power to nullify the influence of inheritance and patronage, and direct, or at least encourage, the largest possible proportion of children of lower-ranked parents into as many higher-ranked occupational roles as are there to be filled.

The resulting mobility regime would approach the ideal type of meritocracy to the extent that the methods of recruitment imposed under it succeeded in displacing less with better credentialed incumbents of higher-ranked roles. The educators and administrators imposing them then act like the selectors of national sporting teams in their search for athletic talent. But politicians of the early twenty-first century advocating meritocracy sometimes forgot that the word was coined in 1958 by the sociologist Michael Young to depict a dystopian fantasy.[44] Earlier in the twentieth century, the trade-offs inseparable from meritocratic selection were brought into view in increasingly vehement debates over 'IQ'—that is, a presumptively innate general intelligence, to the possession of which examinees' parentage and upbringing were (it was hoped) irrelevant. Welcomed at first by reformers who saw in them a means of identifying children from underprivileged backgrounds whose capacity to occupy and perform higher-ranked roles was going unrecognized, IQ tests came to be denounced as testing for abilities defined in ways that favoured middle-class children, and stigmatizing children who scored less well as fit only for jobs calling for inferior education and training. Hence the (to Michael Young) unpleasing prospect of the emergence of an increasingly caste-like higher-ranked systact in which parents in influential, prestigious, and remunerative roles are increasingly better able to pass their advantages down to their children at the expense of the relative probability of upward mobility for the children of the rest.

To many commentators, it had always been less the composition of the middling sort than of the elite which was the object of disapprobation. By the end of the nineteenth century, there were commentators from all bands of the spectrum of public opinion concerned that too many of the topmost roles were occupied by

---

[44] Michael Young, *The Rise of the Meritocracy 1870–2033* (London, 1958).

Kipling's 'flannelled fools at the wicket' whose parental origin, boyhood upbringing, education (or what passed for it), and inherited cast of mind did not fit them to
perform such roles as they should. The idea that ruling elites will sooner or later be
displaced by a counter-elite of a different composition has a long history in
sociological theory. It goes back through Pareto's 'circulation of elites', which he
envisaged as a cyclical replacement of power-holders of one kind ('lions') by power-
holders of another ('foxes'), to the cyclical theory of Ibn Khaldun in which ascetic
warrior elites who seize power in Islamic societies become increasingly decadent
themselves and thereby provoke a successful uprising against them by another set of
ascetic warriors who become equally decadent in their turn. But the critical
sociological distinction is between the replacement of one set of incumbents of
elite roles by successors who leave the practices defining their roles unchanged, and
the replacement of the existing elite by successors who impose a modal change in
the society's existing political, ideological, and economic institutions. In an autocratic society, there can be a high turnover among rulers and their acolytes by
expulsion, demotion, or assassination without the mode of coercion itself being
disturbed; in a hierocratic society, there can be a high turnover among intellectual
and spiritual leaders without the mode of persuasion being modified in any way;
and in a plutocratic society, there can be a high turnover among the topmost
wealth-holders within an unaltered mode of production.

   England's rulers always had examples to hand of societies of other kinds where
the ruling elite was reconstituted by the demotion of one set of incumbents and the
promotion of another. In the eighteenth century, the readiest example was England
itself in the seventeenth century. In the nineteenth, it was France. In the twentieth,
it was first Russia and then Germany. In none of them, however, was it the ascent
into an existing elite of 'new men' that brought about revolutionary change. Only
after, not before, the punctuation of the pre-existing institutional equilibrium and
the abdication or expulsion of the ruling elite were the roles through which political
power was exercised filled by recruits of lower social origin. In the English case, the
entry of such men, and later women, into higher-ranking political roles was the
consequence, not the cause, of institutional changes which had taken place over
many years. However improbable it would have seemed in the eighteenth century
to members of either House of Parliament that they might one day be joined by
colleagues both male and female whose fathers had worked with their hands, it
made no difference to the practices defining the roles into which they moved.

   For as long as this was so, the rate of upward mobility into the elite could have no
more than a demonstration effect. A society in which it becomes possible for a
labourer's son from the dockside to become Foreign Secretary, a woman from a
working-class family to become a supreme court judge, or the son of an impover-
ished immigrant to become the head of one of the largest business corporations in
the country may well motivate an increasing number of aspirants to emulate them.
But the social distance across which the mobility takes place need not be affected
at all. The effect of higher rates of long-distance upward mobility was on the

psychology of prospective incumbents of higher-ranking roles from lower-ranking parental origins who were thereby encouraged to behave in ways that would enhance their individual probabilities of reaching them. It is another example of the part played in cultural selection by frequency-dependence and indirect bias. Once the first working-class trade union leaders were being elected to Parliament, more thought of following them; once women saw some of themselves entering the professions of medicine and law or becoming university professors, more aspired to do so too; the more sons of working-class fathers were aware of people like themselves rising from rags to riches, the more encouragement it gave them to think of making the attempt. But their successes came about not because they changed the rules of the game, but because they played to win within them.

It is, accordingly, relevant to the description and evaluation rather than the reportage and explanation of the evolution of English society that the answer to the question 'Does intergenerational mobility matter?' is that it obviously matters to those whose experience it. A descriptive sociology which sought to convey to its readers what 'moving up in the world' was like for *them* would need to include representative life stories from across the whole period from Defoe's time to the present day. Some familiar themes would no doubt reappear: the inspiring school-teacher, the ambitious parent, the astute patron, the opportune marriage, the critical bank loan, the serendipitous invention, the fortunate adoption by a political clique or sectarian coterie, and the skilful exploitation of a network of favours given and received. But the individual stories of rise and fall have to be set within the contemporary set of memes and practices that defined the cultural and social environment that determined the nature and significance of success or failure. That is what makes Smiles's *Self-Help* such a cardinal document (as it is often described) of the Victorian age. His exemplary lives are all of men whose personal experience of surmounting the obstacles in their path was as different from that of their predecessors in the eighteenth-century Johnsonian world of toil, envy, want, the patron, and the jail, as from that of their twentieth-century successors in the world of mass literacy and mass communication. The historians and biographers who set themselves to convey to their readers what it was like for their chosen subjects to rise or fall as they did from their location at birth have to understand enough of their subjects' experience in their subjects' own terms to be able to bring out the aspects of it that are unique to their particular cultural and social environ-ments. But however authentically they succeed in doing so, it will add nothing to the explanation of the variation and selection of the practices that made the role structure within which they rose or fell into what it was.

V

If a single example is to be chosen of the flavour, so to speak, of the experience of upward social mobility within English society as the age of Samuel Smiles was giving way to 'an age apparently prepared to boast that it belonged to the "common man"',[45] there is a ready candidate in the often-quoted reminiscence of J. R. Clynes, one-time militant of both the Independent Labour Party and the National Union of Gas Workers and General Labourers, about his reception as a member of the first Labour government by King George V at Buckingham Palace in 1924. In his *Memoirs*, published in 1937, Clynes echoed the impression shared with MacDonald and his colleagues of the King's 'genial, kindly, considerate personality'. But he also 'could not help marveling at the strange turn of Fortune's wheel, which had brought MacDonald the starvelling clerk, Thomas the engine-driver, Henderson the foundry labourer and Clynes the mill-hand to this pinnacle'.

Readers' reactions will no doubt vary in accordance with their political predilections. If to Conservatives it exemplifies the wisdom of a constitutional monarch ready to accept an elected government representing the interests of Labour in confident reliance on its members' patriotism and respect for tradition, and to Liberals a paradigm case of merit receiving its due, to socialists it exemplifies every failing that drove Engels to despair about the lack of revolutionary consciousness among English workers and their leaders. But to Clynes himself, the audience with the King was vividly symbolic of the social distance across which he had risen from a starting point so far below the elite of the society into which he had been born. It was not, perhaps, as remarkable a career as that of John Burns, who in 1905 had become the first artisan to reach cabinet rank eighteen years after serving a term of imprisonment for his involvement in the events of 'Bloody Sunday'. Nor was Clynes's the kind of career that tempts biographers into metaphors such as 'meteoric rise' or 'catapulted to fame'. It was a career in which hard work, determination, and a refusal to be diverted from the aim in view received their reward when for the first time an authentically working-class parliamentary party came (albeit as a minority government) to power. But that outcome can hardly have been in Clynes's mind when he started out as a union organizer in an Oldham mill.

It is worth drawing attention also to Clynes's reference to 'Fortune's wheel'. The symbol of the rotating wheel, on which some are rising at the same time that others are falling, dates back in the European cultural tradition to the thirteenth century or earlier, and its use in the twentieth century can be dismissed as little more than a cliché. But the idea that individual life-chances are governed by a mechanism in perpetual motion, over which individuals themselves have no control, has not lost its potency. It carries the implication, just as it did in the later Middle Ages when social mobility was a focus of increasing normative as well as sociological interest, that even in a society where power and privilege are highly unequally distributed at birth, unforeseeable contingencies will topple at least a few of the mighty from their seats and raise at least a few of the humble and meek. The disjunction between the underlying evolutionary process by which institutional change is being driven, and the subjective experience of the individuals whose lives are affected by it, is as stark

---

[45] S. Maccoby, *English Radicalism: The End?* (London, 1961), p. 207.

on this as on any of the topics covered in Chapters 2 to 4. People are not only disposed to attribute to luck many outcomes that are anything but random, but to refuse to recognize as random many outcomes that are. The speeches, letters, and autobiographies of politicians less modest and candid than Clynes are full of examples where they attribute to bad luck more of their failures, and to good luck fewer of their successes, than the evidence warrants. But in relation to social mobility, there is a sense in which they are right. We are all, as individual men and women, born at systactic locations we cannot alter (except by telling lies) into a structure where the social distance between role and role is not of our choosing and the range of opportunities to rise or fall is not of our making. If the Wheel of Fortune that landed Clynes the mill-hand into the role where he might even, at one point, have been invited to form a government is a cliché, it has become one because the metaphor is still so descriptively apt.

Conclusion

I

I said in the Introduction that a central theme in the chapters to follow would be the disjunction between contemporaries' awareness of the magnitude of the cultural changes through which they were living and their unawareness of the nature and strength of the forces of social selection which were continuing to reproduce much the same distribution of power between their society's constituent roles. But it is not as if the imperviousness of England's institutions to radical change was hidden from their view. On the contrary, contemporary as well as subsequent commentators from both ends of the spectrum of political opinion were as conscious of it as each other. The difference between them was, and is, in how to account for it. Seen from the Right, it is the strength of English institutions that they have consistently allowed for the representation of conflicting interests through a parliamentary assembly and delegation of power to local authorities while containing the risk of instability through judicious toleration of alternative opinions and lifestyles and prudent oversight of a market in commodities and labour. Seen from the Left, the entire apparatus of government has been the instrument of a self-serving ruling class determined to retain its control of the means of coercion and persuasion as well as production by whatever devices and stratagems have been required. No unexpected discovery of evidence hitherto concealed or re-examination of evidence already to hand is going to bring the two sides together. But they are at one in recognizing how little has changed in the basic form and function of England's political, ideological, and economic institutions despite all the changes that have taken place within them and in the culture within which they have evolved.

Saying so, however, must not be construed as an invitation to the reader to agree that *plus ça change, plus c'est la même chose*. That familiar dictum owes its impact to the insinuation that the claims of rulers and policymakers to have abolished an outdated set of institutions and replaced it with a better one are regularly belied by the ongoing reproduction under other names of practices supposedly consigned to the past. No doubt an anthology could be compiled of quotations from rulers and policymakers or their propagandists claiming more for the effects of their innovations than can be justified by the difference actually made. But in the English case, a reformed electoral system did give more influence over domestic policies to the hitherto disenfranchised; a reformed educational system did narrow the gap in social prestige between the more and the less literate and credentialed; and a reformed system of what came to be called 'industrial relations' did strengthen the bargaining power of Defoe's 'mere labouring people'. To what extent these are to be judged good things is, as always, a separate matter. But from no perspective can the difference be dismissed as illusory, however far it fell short of the fears of the Right or hopes of the Left.

Agreement across the spectrum of opinion extends also to the interdependence of the political, ideological, and economic practices that define English society's roles. Wherever the emphasis is placed by sociologists or historians of different persuasions, there is an evident selective affinity between democratic, liberal, and capitalist practices that enhance the reproductive fitness of one another. This has nothing to do with a supposedly distinctive national character. Had the institutional equilibrium been punctuated and novel practices emerged that defined modally different roles, there would always have been English men and women there to occupy and perform them. But punctuation was consistently impeded by the mutual support of a mode of coercion resting on parliamentary sovereignty and the rule of law, a mode of persuasion resting on open dissemination of ideas and choice of lifestyles, and a mode of production resting on private property and market exchange.

The practices, whether political, ideological, or economic, that reinforced each other's probability of reproduction did so in various ways, many of which the preceding chapters have touched on. But the selective affinity between them was strengthened throughout by a long cultural tradition whose constituent memes were reproduced with a high degree of fidelity down successive generations. At any one time, there can be documented an often bewildering range of attitudes and beliefs extending from millenarian visions of a social order in which all distinctions of rank would be swept away to diehard defences of a transcendentally legitimated hierarchy of roles from the monarchy downwards. But between the extremes, and underneath all the changes in manners, mores, beliefs, attitudes, and tastes, a self-replicating memetic core can be identified and traced. Common to all the forms it took at different times and in different contexts was an idea of 'freedom'—freedom from monarchical despotism, freedom from arbitrary detention, freedom of movement from place to place, freedom of both secular and religious opinion, freedom of speech, freedom of assembly, freedom of contract, and not least 'free trade'.

Long before 'freedom to dine at the Ritz' became an ironic catchphrase, it was obvious to rulers and ruled alike that 'freedom' could be disingenuously deployed in defence of vested interests and that it meant very different things to the rich than to the poor. Legal historians have elucidated in detail the logic of judicial decisions by which, for example, in the nineteenth century compensation for injury suffered by workmen at work was refused in the name of an employee's freedom to decline employment at a dangerous workplace. But those who appealed to 'freedom', however disingenuous their pleas and self-interested their motives, were drawing on an inherited conception of what was held to be distinctively English liberty and an often explicit contrast with societies despotically ruled through large conscript armies, compliant judges or magistrates, servile functionaries, spies, censors, and priests. However much of the rhetoric in which it was propounded can be discounted as noise, it did visibly and on many occasions affect the behaviour of both rulers and ruled.

To a merchant seaman kidnapped by the press gang, a peaceful protestor cut down by the yeomanry, a respectable workman imprisoned for organizing a withdrawal of labour, a striker starved into acceptance of lower wages, a pamphleteer facing an official campaign of suppression of the unstamped press, or a humorous parodist imprisoned for seditious or blasphemous libel, the rhetoric of the rights of the freeborn Englishman offered no help at all. But even during the eighteenth and early nineteenth centuries, there occasionally emerges from the prosecutions of both the actually and the allegedly insubordinate a whiff, so to speak, of embarrassment. The belief that the laws of England guaranteed certain rights, including due process, to all of its citizens is agreed, even by a historian as disapproving of the rulers as E. P. Thompson, to have been shared at all levels of English society and to have been acted out both in the arguments deployed against the rulers by the ruled and in the methods by which the ruled sought redress for their grievances.

This did not mean that during and immediately after the years when the French Revolution made the rulers most fearful of domestic insurrection they had any inhibitions about bringing the coercive sanctions of military force and capital punishment, as well as imprisonment or transportation, to bear on rioters, mutineers, and machine-breakers. The gentry's dislike of a standing army was quickly dissolved when magistrates feared for their own persons if they tried too hard to enforce order on their own. No historian disputes that once the military had been called in, unarmed fellow-citizens could be killed with little or no compunction. But, for example, in 1765 the judiciary denied the legality of the general warrants deployed against anyone involved in the publication of the notorious No. 45 of Wilkes's *North Briton*; in 1775, none of the seamen who went on what became a bloody and violent strike in Liverpool were sentenced to death (and those convicted were offered the option of joining the navy); the naval mutineers of 1797 were not punished as severely as they could have been (and their demands were conceded); the Combination Act of 1799 was repealed in 1825; and the Tolpuddle Martyrs were pardoned once Melbourne was no longer Home Secretary. Recall also from Chapter 2 Camden's denial of the government's right to order a search of domestic premises. It makes no difference if the authorities' restraint was motivated more by self-interest than benevolence. Whether they are to be admired or condemned is up to you. But, as one historian has put it, 'Though it was important for the ruling order that a show of force be sufficiently impressive there was also a need for it not to be so brutal as to outrage the beholders and damage the mystique of justice . . . Britain's rulers, national and local, spent much time weighing this delicate balance;

and the fact that they sometimes got it wrong is less significant than the fact that they often, from their own point of view, got it right.'[1]

Invocations of the tradition of English liberty were often based on versions of its history that could only stand up to scrutiny with difficulty, if at all. But myths, even one as tenuous as that of the 'Norman Yoke', can affect the behaviour of people who carry them in their heads, no less, and sometimes more, than can dispassionately told stories of well-attested historical events. Not all the rhetoric, however inflated, tendentious, or hypocritical, can be discounted as noise. The familiar difficulty facing historians of popular discontent is that they have no way of getting at the memes inside the heads of men and women who have left no documentary record from which it could be inferred what they were: the occasional autobiographical reminiscences of literate working-class men (and some women) are self-evidently atypical. How much difference would it have made to the nature and incidence of working-class protest in the era of the French Revolution if Tom Paine's *Rights of Man* had never been published? Conversely, how deeply felt were the patriotic sentiments acted out by the revellers in the East End of London on Mafeking Night in 1900? Attendance at a public meeting or participation in a demonstration is not a reliable indicator of commitment to a cause which will find expression in collective action. Circulation of books, tracts, or pamphlets is no surer a predictor of actual behaviour where the message is insurrectionary than where it is an injunction to accept the status quo. Even in the era of professionally designed sample surveys of public opinion, the answers given to questionnaires administered by doorstep interviewers, however good a guide they may be to the interviewees' behaviour in their roles as purchasers of consumer goods or voters in a forthcoming election, are no guide to how they might or might not behave in an environment where the ruling elite is divided against itself and its monopoly of the means of coercion has been broken. Historians of ideas have traced in detail the intellectual genealogies of the political theorists whose doctrines dominated discussion and debate among those of the population who read or knew of them. But the 'King and Country' mobs of the late eighteenth century were no more acting out the doctrines of Burke than the TUC, in its 'widespread, immediate, and thorough-going' opposition to the Industrial Relations Act of 1971,[2] was acting out those of Marx.

The problem of explaining when, why, and how the underprivileged have taken (or failed to take) collective action in furtherance of a common aim has been dominated in the historical as well as the sociological literature by protracted debate over class consciousness. That the incumbents of subordinate roles are aware of their subordination is not in doubt. But what difference, if any, does it make to the

---

[1] Alan Fox, *History and Heritage: The Social Origins of the British Industrial Relations System* (London, 1985), p. 75.
[2] Brian Weekes, Michael Mellish, Linda Dickens, and John Lloyd, *Industrial Relations and the Limits of Law: The Effects of the Industrial Relations Act, 1971* (Oxford, 1975), p. 224.

practices defining their roles? In Marxist sociology, the propertyless workers who come to see themselves as collectively deprived of their rightful share of the wealth generated by their labour will—one day—be the carriers of the practices destined to replace bourgeois with proletarian rule. But that prediction has been so far invalidated by the actual trajectory of social evolution as to lend credence to the critics of Marxism who interpret it not as an explanatory sociology but as an eschatological myth. The class-conscious manual worker was not a wholly fabricated socialist construction any more than the self-improving artisan was a fabricated Liberal construction or the loyal employee of a paternalist family firm a Conservative one. But by the beginning of the twenty-first century, the search for a revolutionary proletariat had come to be as unrewarding to left-wing academics lamenting the 'false consciousness' of the workers as to right-wing employers and members of the security services seeing 'reds under the bed' in every strike called in breach of negotiated procedures or outbreak of violence on a picket line. Whatever the extent and degree of working-class distrust of the agencies of the state, hostility to employers and managers, indifference to, if not contempt for, middle-class lifestyles, resentment of condescension from superiors in social prestige, and disapproval (often accompanied by ridicule) of the idle rich, none of these posed a threat to the existing structure of roles.

It is intrinsic to the mechanism of cultural selection that memes, unlike genes, are transmitted from mind to mind by blended, not particulate, inheritance: the relationships of descent among the units or bundles of information affecting behaviour are represented 'not as a branching tree but a braided stream, with different channels flowing into one another and then splitting again'.[3] The English libertarian tradition was just such a stream in which divergences and confluences can be followed down successive generations as they are more and less widely reproduced and diffused in different idioms at different systactic levels. Its two principal channels carried separate but related messages whose working-class formulation can be approximately rendered in the vernacular as 'don't let them push you around' and 'do your own thing if you can'. Both extended down from the skilled through the semi-skilled and unskilled to where, as it is put by the historian of Campbell Bunk, Islington between the two world wars, 'it was the lumpen blend of egalitarianism and individualism which forged the pass key' to 'a legitimation for casual theft (and some other crimes) as a natural ally to casual labour or irregular economic enterprise'.[4] Resentment of the authority of the employer and a wish to make a living through some form, however precarious, of self-employment would be as immediately recognizable to Defoe as would the practices by which employers sought to impose the disciplines necessary to maintain the enterprises, whether

---

[3] Steven Shennan, *Genes, Memes and Human History: Darwinian Archaeology and Cultural Evolution* (London, 2002), p. 84.

[4] Jerry White, *The Worst Street in North London: Campbell Bunk, Islington, between the Wars* (London, 1986), p. 128.

privately or publicly owned, under their managerial control. Neither overrode the differences of interest and outlook between different fractions of the working class(es). As historians of the labour movement have not failed to point out, they coexisted with not only inter-union rivalry, prejudice against women, and rejection of outsiders, but also lack of fellow-feeling for the unemployed among those in work. They never precluded an awareness of a shared relationship to the mode of production and the disabilities and constraints associated with it. But there is general agreement among sociologists (and others), whatever their political persuasions, that awareness of occupying a role at an inferior location in social space cannot be assumed to be the evolutionary precursor of class consciousness of a prospectively revolutionary kind.

Part of the explanation lies in the adaptiveness of the practices defining the roles of the officials of the friendly societies, trade unions, and in due course constituency Labour parties whose bureaucratic rules and procedures were replicated down successive generations of incumbents. But part of it lies in the adaptiveness of the 'customary practices' which 'provided a critical source of self-defence in a highly unequal society'.[5] 'Customary' practices are generators of collective behaviour patterns of the kind which lie on the sociological boundary between associations and institutions. It was 'out of natural sociability and customary practices' that in the eighteenth century there 'emerged a habit of cooperation around common interests which could easily become the basis of "combination" to impose conditions of work and rates of pay, whether or not it gave rise to formal organization'.[6] The workers going slow or working to rule or coming out in 'wildcat' strikes, like the rioters protesting about the price of bread or breaking machines or tearing down tollgates, are joining together for an immediate common purpose which they pursue through culturally acquired strategies in accordance with culturally acquired norms. But the memes of which these are composed are being acted out within the existing structure of roles. It is sometimes said of such behaviour that it is inherently conservative in that it implies an appeal to traditional standards of fair dealing or good custom in the relations between governments and people, or social superiors and inferiors, or employers and employees. But it may just as well involve a departure from precedent as a return to it. What the forms that it takes have in common is that, as with all the lobbies, pressure groups, and voluntary organizations encountered in earlier chapters, the political, ideological, and economic institutions of the society are taken as given.

Of all the customary practices that could be cited in illustration, one of the fittest is petitioning. The 200 Jarrow marchers who arrived in London in 1936 to petition Parliament for work in an area where unemployment was particularly severe were the sociological descendants of Abel Couldwell, the solitary 'Blanketeer', who (perhaps—the sources are questionable) reached London from Manchester to

---

[5] R. W. Malcolmson, *Life and Labour in England 1700 to 1780* (London, 1981), p. 106.
[6] Alastair J. Reid, *United We Stand: A History of Britain's Trade Unions* (London, 2004), p. 10.

present the unemployed Lancashire weavers' petition to the Prince Regent in 1817.[7] The authorities' response to the Blanketeers was barely more restrained than the Peterloo massacre of which it was the forerunner. But the organizers' avowed determination to avoid 'riot or disturbance' is all the more striking a counterpoint to the authorities' determination to treat them as if threatening public order. Petitioning was—unsurprisingly—more a customary practice of the middle than of the working classes, whether by trade associations or chambers of commerce or like-minded signatories seeking the repeal of the corn laws, the abolition of slavery, the limitation of children's hours of labour, or the outlawing of sport on Sundays. But as the Chartist petitions of 1839 and 1842 and National Un-employed Workers Movement's petition of 1932 alike were to demonstrate, it was by no means confined to them. Like the law courts, Parliament was seen as accessible to the concerns and grievances of the 'people', however much both judges and parliamentarians might favour the interests of the well-connected, the presti-gious, and the rich. Petitioning was adaptive both because of its selective affinity with the cultural tradition of freedom to engage in it and because the more people did engage in it, the more others were likely to do the same.

For the eighteenth century, a well-known quasi-experimental test is provided by the career of Wilkes, which has intrigued the historians of the period as much as it provoked his contemporaries to either fulsome admiration or scandalized disap-proval. The 'spirit of plebeian libertarianism' in which the freeholders of Middlesex returned him to the House of Commons in 1768 after he came back from outlawry in France,[8] and the tone of the petitions organized by his 'friends' in alliance with self-interested opponents of the ministry, were at the same time outspokenly defiant of the government and tacitly accepting of the institutional status quo. The cry of 'Wilkes and Liberty!' was in no sense revolutionary. The rhetoric was of resistance to the exercise of arbitrary power and deference to the myth of an enduring struggle for individual freedom extending back from the events of 1688 to Magna Carta. The riots that broke out in Wilkes's name had as little to do with modal change in the structure of English society's constituent roles and the distribution of power between them as would the Gordon Riots in 1780.

Despite the impossibility of getting inside the heads of the anonymous men and women who have left no record of their attitudes and beliefs, there is much indirect evidence showing that complacency about the superiority of England's institutions over those of other societies extended well beyond the elite and middling sort. The salient comparison was for much of the time with France, not only because of its geographical proximity and the long history of Anglo-French warfare but also because of its Catholicism (and therewith its support for the Jacobite cause). Patriotic and anti-papal memes blended in a combination whose reproduction

---

[7] Margrit Schule Beerbuhl, 'The march of the Blanketeers', in Matthias Reiss and Matt Perry, eds., *Unemployment and Protest: New Perspectives on Two Centuries of Contention* (Oxford, 2001), p. 63.

[8] Paul Langford, *A Polite and Commercial People: England 1727–1783* (Oxford, 1989), p. 377.

and diffusion extended, either orally or in print, to self-consciously loyal Protestants at all systactic levels: 'However poor or unimportant or ill-educated they might be, they still had direct access to the word of God in a way (they believed) that Roman Catholics did not, and for this reason, if for no other, Protestants, even the poorest of them, were free men.'[9] The story might have been different if the wars against France had been lost rather than won, just as it might have been in the twentieth century when the enemy was not France but Germany. It might also have been different if the children in the late Victorian primary schools had not seen so much of the world in their atlases coloured in red and been encouraged as explicitly as they were to see this as proof of Anglo-Saxon superiority. A German socialist who was in England at the time of the first Labour government was struck by the workers' 'naive and rapturous pride' in the Empire which stretched 'far beyond the party organization and the Socialistic electorate'.[10] It was a pride that depended in part on an unawareness that 'behind the façade of imperial pageantry was a continuous sequence of crises, improvisations and local wars which time and again failed to produce lasting solutions to the problems which had given rise to them'.[11] But no historian, whether approving or disapproving, has questioned that the majority of the British people shared something of that pride and the sense of national solidarity that went with it.

In hindsight—and even without it—the ironies are multiple. The presumptive rights of the freeborn Englishman extended neither to the Catholic peasantry of Ireland nor to the darker-skinned populations of the Indian subcontinent and colonial territories of Africa or the Caribbean. The freedom of local communities from central control allowed legislation passed by Parliament to be flouted or ignored. Freedom of contract left the parties with the least bargaining power at the mercy of those with the most. Free trade, whatever it might do to lower the cost of food, exposed workers in vulnerable domestic industries to the ravages of foreign competition. A free press was dominated by the proprietors who could apply the most financial resources to expanding their readerships. It is for philosophers rather than sociologists to debate how far the ideals of liberty and equality are logically compatible. But sociologically, the effects of popular commitment to the idea of liberty on the evolution of a society's political, ideological, and economic practices and roles can be as supportive of existing institutions in some environments as they can be subversive of them in others. Halévy, in the conclusion of his magisterial survey of the condition of English society in 1815, had no doubt that 'England is a free country', and that 'this meant, at bottom, that England is a country of voluntary acceptance, of an organization freely initiated and freely accepted'.[12]

---

[9] Linda Colley, *Britons: Forging the Nation 1707–1837* (London, 1992), p. 42.

[10] Egon Wertheimer, *Portrait of the Labour Party*[2] (London, 1930), p. xii.

[11] W. G. Runciman, 'Empire as a topic in comparative sociology', in Peter Fibiger Bang and C. A. Bayly, eds., *Tributary Empires in Global History* (Basingstoke, 2011), p. 102.

[12] Elie Halévy, *A History of the English People in the Nineteenth Century*, vol. 1: *England in 1815* (London, 1924), pp. 588, 591 (first published in French in 1911).

But he did not suggest that it was other than highly unequal in the distribution of political, ideological, and economic power between its constituent roles or that it was not, as Disraeli famously said to Hyndman, a 'very difficult country to move'. And so it remained.

II

Although it is a central tenet of neo-Darwinian theory that the evolutionary trajectory of societies of any and all kinds is, like that of both cultures and species, inherently open-ended, there are nevertheless some hypothetical futures that can be ruled out of account. The notion that at any time in the past three centuries England could somehow have evolved into a society of free and equal citizens in which conflicts of interest have been abolished and the state withered away is as fantastical as the notion that it could have evolved into a tripartite society of soldiers and sailors who fight, clerics who teach and preach, and cultivators and artisans who make the goods and till the soil. That doesn't mean that such visions have no cultural influence. But they are no more realistic than would be in evolutionary biology the idea that terrestrial species might all grow wings, or in evolutionary psychology the idea that in all human cultures the spoken word might be replaced by sign language. Comparative sociology is concerned with trajectories that societies could have followed but didn't, not with trajectories that they never would or could.

When—but only when—the Hanoverian succession was assured, monarchical absolutism became as diminishingly likely as military dictatorship. An English king or queen who in the mid-eighteenth century sought to rule through a standing army officered by a service nobility, a subservient judiciary, and a corps of royal officials chosen by and answerable to him or her would have had no more chance of success than a victorious general who on return from a foreign war sought to overturn the monarchy and establish a Cromwellian dictatorship. But by the time of the rebellion of the American colonies and the outbreak of the French Revolution, the possibility that the 'United Kingdom' might become ungovernably *dis*united did begin to raise the question of what alternative form of rule might under some not impossible combination of circumstances replace the existing one. As it turned out, it was the collapse of the power of the notionally absolute monarchy of France that presented to contemporary observers the prospect of modal change of a kind as alarming to some as it was appealing to others. If, as I have implied, Pitt and his ministers overreacted to the threat of being overthrown by violence from below, it was not, as I have at the same time conceded, irrational on their part to decide on the precautionary measures that they did. But from the perspective of evolutionary sociology, it makes no difference whether it was irrational or not. To look, with the benefit of hindsight, at the practices rather than the people is to see that the differences between the role structures of the two societies were such that the probability of an English revolution on the model of the French was negligible.

For all the intractable differences between rival interpreters of the French Revolution, they are agreed that it would not have come about as it did without what one of its most authoritative historians called '*un concours vraiment extraordinaire et imprévisible de causes immédiates*'.[13] That does not rule out the possibility that some different combination of equally unforeseeable *causes immédiates* could not have provoked an English insurrection which would have led to the transfer of control of the means of coercion to a Jacobin Assembly, the exile (if not execution) of the King, and the dispossession of the landed aristocracy and gentry. But all observers could see that George III did not have the same powers, and did not provoke the same resentments, as Louis XVI; the convening of a national assembly did not arise in a society with a sovereign parliament; there was no English peasantry holding under feudal tenure and suffering from as disastrous a sequence of bad harvests; there were no tax-farmers on whose loans back to it of its own money a state which was effectively bankrupt depended; the army's ability to restore order in the capital if called on to do so was not in doubt; and there was no organized fraction of the elite seeking to overturn the existing modes of coercion, persuasion, or production and replace them with another. To be sure, the cultural ramifications of the French Revolution on the lived experience of the British people extended well beyond those of them directly involved in the wars with France which resulted from it. It is reflected not only in a voluminous output of speeches, letters, pamphlets, and tracts but also in both contemporary and subsequent works of fiction. Many practising politicians as well as political theorists defined their positions, at least in part, in relation to its origin, course, and outcome. But it had no effect on the distribution of power within English society between political, ideological, or economic roles other than to retard, as it seems plausible to suppose, the extension of the parliamentary franchise. If Lord Liverpool, during his long tenure as prime minister, 'constantly fretted lest hunger or national bankruptcy or a licentious press should spark off a French-style revolution',[14] that says more about his psychological temperament than his sociological acumen.

In the twentieth century, when first Russia and then Germany presented contemporary observers with examples of revolutionary transition to modally different regimes, there were again some who were as attracted to communist or fascist practices and the roles defined by them as others were alarmed by them. But to look at the practices rather than the people is to see how improbable it was that the institutional equilibrium of English society would be punctuated to similar effect. Even if there had been a home-grown Lenin (whatever that implies), the role of the tsar was even further from that of a constitutional monarch than Louis XVI's had been; there was no defeated and demoralized British army wanting only to stop

---

[13] Georges Lefebvre, 'La Révolution française et les paysans', in *Études sur la Révolution Française* (Paris, 1954), p. 247, quoted by W. G. Runciman, 'Unnecessary revolution: the case of France', *Archives Européennes de Sociologie* 24 (1983), p. 295.

[14] Boyd Hilton, 'The political arts of Lord Liverpool', *Transactions of the Royal Historical Society*, 5th series, 38 (1988), p. 148.

fighting and go home; there was no land-hungry peasantry with its own tradition of social levelling and communal self-government; Russia lacked the cultural conventions as well as the social practices of a parliamentary assembly whose legitimacy was accepted by both those in and those outside of it; and no British government was without sufficient control of the means of coercion to prevent a seizure of power by a *coup d'état* on the Bolshevik model. Similarly, no home-grown Hitler (whatever that implies) could, if elected as Hitler was, have then created a one-party regime in which the means of coercion were passed to paramilitary auxiliaries, the means of persuasion controlled by Nazi propagandists imposing an ideology of stigmatization, exclusion, and in due course genocide, and the means of production left in the hands of acquiescent private employers whose workers' obedience was underwritten by the apparatus of a totalitarian state.

There were, however, other less improbable modes into which twentieth-century English society might have evolved under selective pressures discernible within its political, ideological, and economic institutions. The lack of an empirically precise and theoretically well-grounded taxonomy is equally unfortunate when questions in the form of 'how come?' are supplemented by questions in the form of 'what if?'. But provided that the practices and roles subsumed under whatever heading is chosen are sufficiently clearly specified, the definitional arguments that the term may provoke can be ignored for the purpose of estimating the likelihood that if certain hypothetical conditions had been met an evolution out of one into another mode of coercion, persuasion, and production might have occurred and been agreed by observers of all persuasions to have done so. The two headings which, for all the definitional arguments inseparable from their use, best lend themselves to this exercise are first 'socialism' and second 'authoritarianism'.

By 'socialism' is emphatically not meant the 'really existing socialism' of the Soviet Union and its satellite societies in Eastern Europe. But nor is meant the 'ethical socialism' of the visionaries who looked forward to a world in which shared commitment to a universal norm of cooperative interpersonal conduct would transcend any form of inter-systactic competition for power. The critical transition would be to a mode of production in which market practices are subordinated to those carried by agents of the state empowered to reallocate distributable resources in accordance with the priorities of a government mandated to impose a centrally planned economy. All major industries are then nationalized, land cannot be bought and sold but only leased from the state, and there are no private banks or insurance companies. Private property is not abolished entirely—people can own their own homes as well as personal chattels, and there can be a legitimate as well as a 'black' market in consumer goods and personal services. Nor are rival political parties necessarily debarred from fielding candidates for election to the single house of parliament. But any that does is required to adhere to the terms of a socialist constitution. The monarchy is presumably abolished. Both the civil and the criminal courts are controlled and staffed by a Ministry of Justice: there are no more barristers or Inns of Court. Both the schools and the universities are controlled and staffed by a Ministry of Education. Both benefits and services free at the point of delivery are allocated by a Ministry of Welfare and funded out of general taxation including a steeply graduated income tax and tax on inherited wealth. The means of persuasion are owned by the state, although writers, broadcasters, playwrights, and film-makers may be left uncensored except where there is a violation of the criminal law. Internal order is the responsibility of the Ministry of Justice which imposes it through a centrally controlled police. Employees are enrolled in trade unions or professional associations which present their claims to a Ministry of Labour which monitors rewards and determines conditions of work. The ideology in accordance with which the population is ranked in social prestige is meritocratic but at the same time favourable to positive discrimination.

Counterfactual speculation has a bad name both among historians, who see it as tempting but futile, and among philosophers, who see it as postulating things that don't 'really' exist. But suppose, if only for a moment, that a Labour government had gone to the country in 1950 on a manifesto along the lines of the preceding paragraph. The obvious response is that such a manifesto would have played so far into Churchill's hands as to guarantee the Conservatives' return to power. But that leads back to the familiar question addressed in Chapter 2: what is it about the proposal of practices claimed to advance the interests of the underprivileged majority which fails to cause more of that majority to vote for the party that claims to speak for them? The opinion polls of the time suggest that the Conservatives would have won an election held in 1940 had the country not then been at war with Germany. It took the unforeseeable events of 1940 to 1945 to create an environment in which 'Labour won because it was identified with Beveridge and because it was the beneficiary of a widespread but imprecise hostility to the old order'.[15] Analysis of the result of the 1945 election is complicated by the number of votes cast for parties other than Labour and the Conservatives and the inability of the Liberals to field candidates in all constituencies: the authors of the first of the Nuffield College studies of successive general elections concluded that if Liberal candidates had stood in 200 more constituencies, 'We can safely assume that the number would have been sufficient to produce an anti-Socialist result in the reckoning of all the votes cast at the election'.[16] Furthermore, they at the same time count all Labour votes as votes for 'Socialism', which under even a very broad definition they were not. In the event, although the circumstances of 1945 were uniquely favourable to the Labour Party as it had by then become, in 1951 it failed to dissuade over 6 million working-class electors from voting Conservative. Unless the evidence cited in previous chapters for working-class as well as middle-class hostility to, and suspicion of, the agencies of the state is significantly exaggerated, the likelihood of an evolution into a socialist mode was minimal.

[15] Ross McKibbin, *Parties and People: England 1914–1951* (Oxford, 2010), p. 138.
[16] R. B. McCallum and Alison Readman, *The British General Election of 1945* (Oxford, 1947), p. 253.

A hypothetical evolution into an 'authoritarian' mode is (I suggest) equally so. The word has as many competing definitions as 'socialism' does, and the study of societies deemed to fall under one or another of them is a major subdiscipline within comparative sociology,[17] whose agenda extends from Franco's Spain and Salazar's Portugal to a multitude of societies in Latin America and postcolonial Africa and Japanese society between the Meiji Restoration and the end of the Second World War. This list may suggest that an authoritarian future for twentieth-century Britain could be as confidently ruled out as an evolution into German-style fascism or Russian-style communism. But when an eminent public servant and industrialist is on record as saying in the summer of 1970 that 'we are moving towards an authoritarian regime, presumably of the Right',[18] the possibility should perhaps not be immediately dismissed out of hand. The source, admittedly, is Cecil Harmsworth King, who as owner of the *Daily Mirror* had made what was agreed to be a futile, not to say farcical, attempt in 1968 to bring down the Wilson government and replace it with a government of national unity. But is it any more wholly inconceivable that a Conservative Party with an impregnable parliamentary majority might have used it to install a recognizably authoritarian regime than a Labour Party might have done to install a recognizably socialist one?

The critical transition would be the transfer of political power to the roles of a self-appointing, unregulated, unified military-cum-technocratic-cum-business elite which might seek to legitimate its position by plebiscite but would outlaw any would-be alternative party of government committed to reversing the transition. The ideology which it would use the means of persuasion to promote would be not only nationalistic but xenophobic, and in all three dimensions of power its control would be exercised principally through patronage dispensed in accordance with loyalty to the regime. Trade unions would be incorporated within the institutions of the state as government-regulated syndicates but their members would be denied the right to strike. There could well be imposed a period of compulsory military training for all young adult males. Voluntary associations would likewise be incorporated if their objectives were consistent with the priorities of the state and proscribed if they were not. Within the elite, there would be a high degree of 'role-substitution'—that is, multiple career patterns allowing movement across institutional boundaries facilitated by common educational background such as could be observed in, for example, Portugal under Salazar.[19] There would be no independent judiciary, no institutional means of challenging the decisions of government, and no statutory body empowered to scrutinize the performance of the police, let alone the security services. The media would be strictly censored, and the curricula taught in the schools required to conform with the hegemonic nationalist

---

[17] E.g. Milan W. Svolik, *The Politics of Authoritarian Rule* (Cambridge, 2012).

[18] *The Cecil King Diary 1970–1974* (London, 1975), p. 25.

[19] Herminio Martins, 'Portugal', in Margaret Scotford Archer and Salvador Giner, eds., *Contemporary Europe: Class, Status and Power* (London, 1971), p. 71.

ideology. Immigrants would be admitted as guest-workers on a temporary basis but denied the prospect of citizenship.

The implausibility (as I expect readers to find it) of this notional scenario is due first of all to the cultural tradition of individual liberty of which anti-militarism was a long-standing part. But it is due also to the institutional impediments in the way of the imposed diffusion of the practices of military or quasi-military discipline. A transition to a bureaucracy on the Prussian as opposed to the Fabian model may appear less implausible when viewed alongside the practices through which the British Empire had been governed: precarious as their rule may have been, the handful of military and civilian agents of the Crown who controlled for as long as they did such numerous populations and extensive territories might be argued to be a demonstration of the fitness of an authoritarian combination of the practices of coercion and patronage. But the domestic environment was no more favourable to their diffusion and reproduction in the twentieth-century world of mass parties, universal literacy, and organized labour than it had been in the eighteenth-century world of rival aristocratic factions, intransigent local gentry, and rioting plebeians. Ireland was a very different matter throughout, as were Scotland and Wales to the extent that they were subjected to a form of internal colonialism of which the pacification of the Highlands after 1745 was the most exemplary manifestation. But practices adaptive at the periphery were demonstrably maladaptive at the centre except when war, or the threat of war, legitimated them as a necessary but explicitly temporary expedient.

The advocates of authoritarian regimes like to claim that they override the destructive political, ideological, and economic antagonisms by which the unity and efficiency of the nation are being undermined. 'Authoritarian' is not the word that is necessarily used: 'authoritarianism' is a twentieth-century American neologism, and its *Oxford English Dictionary* citation from the *British Weekly* in 1927 is in an ecclesiastical rather than a political context. It was the rhetoric of 'National Efficiency' which in the aftermath of the Boer War was deployed to promote the vision of a government and people dedicated to the common purpose of making the country better fitted to outcompete its rivals (particularly Germany). To many who shared that objective it was as much a matter of persuading the incumbents of existing roles to perform them more in accordance with what the critics saw as the national interest as of radically altering the institutions within which they performed them. Only on the wilder fringes of memetic variation was it seriously believed that 'It is not an exaggeration to say that the whole fabric of British life and inspiration is being steadily undermined by the effect of the alien presence, his propaganda, and the evil practices which he has brought with him to this country.'[20] But implicit in the idea of national unity was the suspension both of party-political

---

[20] [Colonel] A. H. Lane, *The Alien Menace*[2] (London, 1929), p. 10, quoted by G. C. Webber, *The Ideology of the British Right 1918–1939* (London, 1986), p. 56.

electioneering and of zero-sum (again, a term not yet coined) contests between employers and workers.

In the early years of the twentieth century, 'the quest for "National Efficiency" cut completely across the conventional distinctions between "left" and "right", "liberals" and "conservatives", and even "socialists" and "capitalists"'.[21] The idea of a permanent political coalition legitimated by plebiscite was attractive not only to civil and military servants of the Crown who regarded themselves as above party but also to some practising politicians. But for such a coalition to impose an authoritarian mode of production on the national economy would involve not only curtailment of the freedom of employees to withdraw their labour but also abolition of any restriction on the freedom of employers, whether public or private, to hire and fire and lay down terms and conditions of employment as the rulers' definition of the national interest might require. An authoritarian Britain is no more of a sociological impossibility than is a socialist Britain. But if the nearest approach to a quasi-experiment is the National Efficiency movement, its failure and the reasons for its failure suggest that the probability is minimal.

To look back, therefore, as an exercise in reverse engineering, at the evolution of English society over the past three centuries is to see a set of political, ideological, and economic institutions which might as well have been deliberately designed to constrain the variation and selection of the practices defining their constituent roles within those institutions rather than enhancing the probability of their dissolution and replacement, whatever the intentions, expectations, hopes, or fears of the individual agents involved. There is nothing new in the proposition that social institutions are the product of human action but not of human design. It was as familiar in those very words to Adam Ferguson at the time of the eighteenth-century Scottish Enlightenment as to any twenty-first-century sociologist. But the idea that the coherence and functioning of the different societies in the historical and ethnographic record could be the outcome of a non-teleological, non-providential, non-predictable process of heritable variation and competitive selection of information affecting behaviour was not only unthought of but unthinkable to sociology's founders.

That is not to deny that much in the writings of Weber, Durkheim, and Marx that set the agenda for twentieth-century sociology is consistent with neo-Darwinian theory. Weber did not need to be told that the practices of a parliamentary democracy favour the continuation of periodic institutionalized competition for votes. Durkheim did not need to be told that a society's hegemonic ideology is mirrored in the practices and roles of its familial and educational institutions. Marx did not need to be told that market practices are strengthened by legal institutions which underwrite contracts entered into by formally free contracting parties. But notwithstanding Marx's professed admiration for *The*

---

[21] G. R. Searle, *The Quest for National Efficiency: A Study in British Politics and Political Thought, 1899–1914* (Oxford, 1971), p. 2.

Origin of Species, none of them saw modal change in the evolution of human societies as driven by an underlying process of variation and selection on the Darwinian model.

Explanations framed in these terms are as vulnerable as any to invalidation by evidence which they are unable to accommodate. The reported observations whose causal antecedents are being sought may themselves be flawed; in the absence of any seriously close approximation to a natural experiment, it may not be possible to test against each other rival hypotheses that fit the reported observations equally well; and the critical mutations whose success brings about institutional change may be overdetermined by environmental pressures whose relative force it is not possible to assess. But however elusive the answers to the 'how come?' questions may be, it is always by the variation and selection of the practices defining its political, ideological, and economic roles that the society's evolutionary trajectory is determined. The perennial competition for political, ideological, and economic power is driven by information coded in the practices defining the roles of the individual incumbents whose collective behaviour gives comparative and historical sociology its agenda, however little the individuals themselves understand what is going on.

III

There will always be some policymakers—and some sociologists—whose predictions of the future condition of their society are less wide of the mark than others. Some of their guesses are shrewder, or at any rate luckier, than others. But guesses are all they can be. This is particularly, not to say painfully, obvious where relations with other societies are involved. The outcomes of England's eighteenth-, nineteenth-, and twentieth-century wars were as impossible to foresee as their outbreaks, and even in hindsight few historians agree among themselves about what caused them. But the situation is not so very different in domestic matters. It is not difficult to compile a list of topics on which prediction is categorically impossible. Nobody in the time of Defoe could conceivably have foreseen the impact on England's mode of production of the technology which powered the industrial revolution, since in order to do so they, or their scientifically minded contemporaries, would have to have had the relevant 'techno-memes' in their heads already.[22] Demographic prediction was impossible not only because of medical and contraceptive techniques still unknown, but also because there was no way of calculating the aggregate effect of individual decisions yet to be taken about childbearing by millions of men and women who might in any case not know what motivated them. In the mode of persuasion, nobody could foresee the consequences of the competition that the Established Church and its rivals would face from arguments

---

[22] Rikard Stankiewicz, 'The concept of design space', in John Ziman, ed., *Technological Innovation as an Evolutionary Process* (Cambridge, 2003), p. 52.

not yet formulated and scientific and scholarly advances not yet made. Nor could anyone, however astute and well-informed, foresee what parties or factions under what names and with what programmes would be competing for political power within even a single generation.

It was, therefore, inevitable that much of the legislation enacted by Parliament would turn out, in hindsight, to be little more than clutter, and much of the rhetoric surrounding its passing little more than noise. If some measures, such as those intended to protect nineteenth-century chimney sweeps and mineworkers, were almost entirely ineffective, others, such as the uncovenanted benefit introduced after the First World War, led to a lasting change in existing practices and roles. There were always some commentators who became entitled to look back in later years in a spirit of 'Told you so!', not least in relation to the exaggerated hopes and fears that attended the proposals most strenuously debated in one or other or both of the Houses of Parliament. But neither the policymakers nor the men and women whose lives would be most affected by their decisions had any possible means of telling why it would be that the changes they were to experience would turn out to be within, but not of, modes of coercion, persuasion, and production which remained so much the same for so long.

That is not, on the other hand, to suggest that the policymakers, whoever they were and whatever their motives, were mistaken in seeing themselves as having regularly to choose between alternative strategies whose success or failure could have as much of an unanticipated effect on the lives of themselves and their fellow-citizens as might an exogenous punctuation of the institutional equilibrium. Just as the people who feel themselves to be experiencing 'revolutionary' change *are*, if their descriptions are authentic, doing so, so are the policymakers who feel themselves to be confronting successive 'crises' which force them to make choices (including the choice to do nothing) on which, apart from their other consequences, their own careers and reputations will depend. It is not in question that, for example, the South Sea Bubble of 1720 confronted the rulers of the day with a crisis, as did likewise the banking and stock market crash of 1825 and the so-called 'bankers' ramp' of 1931. But the practices defining the roles constitutive of the capitalist mode of production continued in each case to be reproduced much as previously. 'That *South Sea* Deluge' or 'Days of our *South Sea* Madness', as Defoe called it,[23] brought financial disaster to many imprudent investors. But there is much evidence suggesting that at the level of the economy as a whole, 'its effects were relatively modest and that other apparently powerful evidence of disruption was often politically inspired'.[24] In this, moreover, it was the precursor of many such episodes in the late twentieth and early twenty-first centuries, when, after the circulation of information (or misinformation) in print or by word of mouth had

---

[23] Defoe, *Tour*, vol. 1, pp. 91, 300.
[24] Julian Hoppit, 'The myth of the South Sea Bubble', *Transactions of the Royal Historical Society*, 6th series, 12 (2002), p. 155.

been accelerated by television as well as radio, 'Each new media-manufactured crisis saw ministers and shadow ministers scuttling from television studio to television studio to offer reassurance or to ratchet up the crisis with more accusations.'[25] This scenario would come as no surprise to Walpole, whose subjection to continuous personal abuse during his tenure of political power included the persistent allegation that during the South Sea Bubble he had, for the sake of his own career, shielded from blame those on whom it should rightly have fallen.

There can always be constructed a narrative in which the protagonists are the rulers and their acolytes whose decisions at moments of crisis are to be judged wise or foolish according to whether their effects accorded or not with the plans and purposes in their heads when they took them. But like all decisions taken by the incumbents of influential roles, they are quasi-random inputs into a process of variation and selection of practices whose institutional outcome the decision-makers' motives and states of mind do nothing to explain. Crises may be of short duration and centre on a single event, such as the Abdication Crisis of 1936, or of long duration and involve a series of disparate events, such as the Crisis of Liberalism (or 'Strange Death of Liberal England'[26]) of the period before the First World War. But their sociological significance is in the light they shed on the relative strength of the selective institutional pressures acting on the society's role structure and the concomitant influence of meme-practice co-evolution. Historians will never reach agreement on what would have happened if the 'real crisis', which 'eventually' occurred on 28 June 1914,[27] had not then led to the British government's decision to declare war on Germany. The possibility of a 'revolutionary' breakdown of order was being taken seriously by more contemporary commentators than merely the firebrands of the Left and alarmists of the Right. But the disjunction between contemporaries' perceptions and the fitness of the practices determining the distribution of power was as wide as usual. When, after the war was over, the government again faced the prospect of civil war in Ireland and a renewed outbreak of large-scale industrial militancy at home, its strategy in response was acted out within the same domestic political, ideological, and economic institutions none of which came near to breakdown.

In one particular area of social policy briefly touched on in Chapter 2, a series of what were perceived as crises were resolved in ways that provide an exemplary illustration of meme-practice co-evolution in operation: the punishment of 'crime'. Although crime is of course a cultural construct, there are in all societies forms of behaviour sufficiently unacceptable to the controllers of the means of coercion to attract punishment in one or another form, and in the ethnographic and historical record there is documented a formidable range both of crimes and of punishments.

---

[25] David Marquand, *Britain Since 1918: The Strange Career of British Democracy* (London, 2008), p. 403.

[26] George Dangerfield, *The Strange Death of Liberal England 1910–1914* (New York, 1935).

[27] G. R. Searle, *A New England? Peace and War 1886–1914* (Oxford, 2004).

England has its own distinctive place within that range (as Scotland has likewise), and its judges, juries, magistrates, rules of evidence, standards of proof, and statutory penalties have often been contrasted with those of other European as well as American and more distant (and supposedly 'primitive') societies. But its penal policies evolved alongside its categorization of offences in a sequence of interacting cultural and social variation and selection whose outcome was explicable only in hindsight.

What has been called the 'penal crisis of the 1890s' was one of a series of dilemmas facing successive governments of the day,[28] whose members could not but be aware of the concerns both of the general public as potential victims of crime and of the officials to whose roles there attached responsibility for the administration of the current penal system. Not infrequently, legislation was passed in response to moral panics in which heightened fear of crime caused a counteractive initiative of some kind to be seen as a political necessity. One such was the Murder Act of 1752. Another was the Garrotters' Act of 1863. In 1869, when a Habitual Criminals Bill imposing on the accused the burden of proving their innocence was debated in the Commons, the Home Secretary's care to deny 'the existence of panic, or of cause for panic' could be interpreted without undue cynicism as disavowal of the kind that gives the game away.[29] But severity of punishment, in contrast to probability of prevention or detection, was not convincingly correlated with a decrease in the incidence of behaviour not only culturally defined but also socially sanctioned as 'criminal'. From the eighteenth century onwards, policymakers sought to reconcile, or alternatively to prioritize, the three objectives of retribution, deterrence, and reform. But reconciliation and prioritization were equally difficult to achieve. The story of English penal policy is both complex and contested: where some historians have seen a steady trend in the direction of humanitarian reform, others have seen a steady trend in the extension of the state's control over categories of the population hitherto outside its reach. But from the perspective of evolutionary sociology, the story is one of competing practices whose diffusion and reproduction reflected selective cultural pressures which the policymakers could no more anticipate than they could control.

A constant theme in public discussion and debate was (and is) the self-replicating rhetoric of philanthropic humanitarianism on one side and hard-headed anti-sentimentalism on the other. Much of it was noise (including some characteristically thunderous denunciation of sentimentalism by Carlyle). But some memetic mutations did impact on the critical practices. In the early nineteenth century, the same alliance between Evangelicals and Utilitarians which delegitimated practices of patronage previously taken for granted, also delegitimated penal practices taken

---

[28] Martin J. Wiener, *Reconstructing the Criminal: Culture, Law, and Policy in England, 1830–1914* (Cambridge, 1990), p. 337.

[29] W. L. Burn, *The Age of Equipoise: A Study of the Mid-Victorian Generation* (London, 1964), p. 193.

for granted in the eighteenth century which now came to be seen as capricious, ineffectual, degrading, and abusive. In their place were imposed practices driven by an injunction to the effect that the treatment meted out to offenders should be uniform, the length of their incarceration predictable, and the prison regime so designed as to compel them to accept responsibility for their crimes. But by the end of the nineteenth century, the eighteenth-century trade-off between probability of conviction and severity of punishment had evolved into a trade-off between deterrence and rehabilitation.

The relative strength of the selective pressures brought to bear in the new environment is impossible to measure with any accuracy. Humanitarian attitudes blended with would-be scientific beliefs about the causes of behaviour defined as criminal for which the criminals themselves could not be held responsible and from which they could be neither diverted nor converted by either Evangelical or Utilitarian doctrines and methods. Long sentences, solitary or 'silent' confinement, hard labour, refusal of remission, rigorous prison discipline, and deliberate infliction of suffering came to be regarded in the twentieth century as both cruel and ineffective in much the same way as the eighteenth-century system had come to be regarded in the nineteenth. The late nineteenth-century crisis was resolved by the cultural diffusion and reproduction among the policymakers of repudiation of practices which had earlier been regarded as both individually and socially beneficial. The timing and extent of the changes that resulted were, as might be expected, dependent in part on the actions of individual incumbents of the roles to which there attached the power to formulate and administer the new set of rules by which the prisons of the twentieth century would be governed. But there can be seen at work the same two mechanisms of frequency-dependence and indirect bias by which cultural evolution is so often driven and which so often make the orthodoxy of today into the heresy of tomorrow.

To look back, accordingly, from the early twenty-first century to the time of Defoe is to see a change in attitudes and beliefs in relation to criminals which, as I suggested in Chapter 1, might surprise him little less than the change in attitudes and beliefs in relation to women and children. But he would, at the same time, be unsurprised to see those apprehended and charged with a serious offence still being tried before a judge and jury and, if convicted, being sent to prison. He would remark that the 'gaolers' of his day had become 'prison officers', that the 'chaplains' working in prisons were supplemented by members of a 'probation service', that conditions in prisons were overseen by a government-appointed 'inspectorate', and that a Criminal Division of a Court of Appeal was empowered to overturn convictions deemed either 'unsatisfactory' or 'unsafe'. But he would also remark that reconciliation of the objectives of punishment, deterrence, and rehabilitation was as elusive as ever, and that one section of public opinion (supported by the so-called tabloid newspapers) regarded conditions in prison as too lenient, while another (supported by voluntary associations such as the Howard League and the Prison Reform Trust) regarded them as too harsh. He would appreciate the perennial problem of recidivism and perennial distinction between the hardened criminal or habitual offender and the rest. He would, when retracing the steps of his tour, see that although some prisons had been converted to other uses, prisons were as much a feature of the local landscapes where they were sited as they were when he singled out for mention a newly built 'Jayl' in Northampton.[30] Whatever his personal opinions about crime and the causes of crime, he would surely conclude that although beliefs about, and attitudes to, the criminal were very different, the practices of conviction, incarceration, and release were much the same.

IV

T. S. Kuhn, in *The Structure of Scientific Revolutions*, says of paradigm-shifts that 'the transfer of allegiance from paradigm to paradigm is a conversion experience that cannot be forced'.[31] 'Conversion' is perhaps too strong: it is not a matter of faith and apostasy so much as of seeing familiar things in a different way and thereby coming to explain them differently. But the 'hold-outs', as Kuhn called them, are not going to change their minds for as long as they can interpret the paradigm in which they were brought up in such a way that it can continue to be fitted to the evidence confronting them in their chosen field of inquiry. Twenty-first-century sociologists are not required to see collective human behaviour patterns as the acting out of heritably variable and competitively selected information transmitted by three different mechanisms at three different levels unless and until they thereby come to acknowledge, or themselves arrive at, explanations of cultural and social change (or its absence) which have hitherto eluded them. The future of sociology is just as unpredictable as the future of the societies that are its subject matter. But it is not to be wondered at that there should still be as many hold-outs as there are.

It would for that, and not only that, reason be naïve to believe that the advances made in recent decades, in the application of what has somewhat extravagantly been called by an American philosopher Darwin's 'single best idea that anyone has ever had' to the study of human behaviour,[32] are about to bring together, through a unifying process of 'consilience',[33] all the academic disciplines directed to studying how human beings conduct themselves towards each other in their diverse cultural and social environments. The latest findings from the frontiers of behavioural-scientific research are reported in an increasingly wide range of more and more specialized journals, and they give rise to as many disagreements as agreements both across and within subdisciplinary boundaries. Evolutionary psychologists may have

---

[30] Defoe, *Tour*, vol. 2, p. 485.

[31] Thomas S. Kuhn, *The Structure of Scientific Revolutions* (Chicago, 1962), p. 150.

[32] Daniel C. Dennett, *Darwin's Dangerous Idea: Evolution and the Meanings of Life* (London, 1995), p. 21.

[33] Edward O. Wilson, *Consilience: The Unity of Knowledge* (London, 1998).

conclusively disposed of the model of the human mind as a 'blank slate' on which different cultures inscribe their instructions,[34] but an evolutionary sociologist who looks to them for guidance will find a plethora of unsettled arguments about how much or little behavioural variation can be accounted for by mechanisms of adaptive thinking traceable to the ancestral environment of the Pleistocene. The gulf that separates the readers of a journal such as *Behavioural and Brain Sciences* from the readers of one such as the *English Historical Review* is only a little, if at all, less wide and deep than was that between their intellectual precursors in the era when Darwin was writing *The Descent of Man*.

Evolutionary sociologists are, moreover, denied the possibility of conducting controlled experiments that is open to evolutionary psychologists to at least some small degree.[35] No amount of technical ingenuity in research design can alter the fact that the quasi- or natural experiments on offer from within the archaeological, ethnographic, and historical record are too few and far between to furnish evolutionary sociologists with the comparisons and contrasts which they need. It can, admittedly, be claimed that 'the difficulties historians face in establishing cause-and-effect relationships in the history of human societies are broadly similar to the difficulties facing astronomers, climatologists, archaeologists, evolutionary biologists, geologists, and paleontologists'.[36] But historical and comparative sociologists may well find that remark more discouraging than heartening. Does it not merely go to show that by comparison with evolutionary biology, evolutionary sociology is in its infancy (and evolutionary psychology barely into its adolescence)?

The most, therefore, that a book such as this one can hope to achieve is to identify and trace some of the selective pressures that have favoured the mutant practices responsible for the form and function of one chosen society's institutions over one chosen period of time. But to whatever limited extent it can succeed in doing so, it makes a contribution not only to the explanation of what did (or didn't) change in that society's role structure but also to the understanding of the social-evolutionary process as such. The concentration on practices rather than the people whose roles are defined by them, and the insistence on the categorical distinction between cultural and social selection, are not just restatements of familiar truths in a different idiom or retellings of a familiar story with a different emphasis. I am in no doubt that the conclusions advanced in the previous chapters are vulnerable to criticism on grounds both of historical detail and of sociological inference. But there is more to be learnt from tentative answers to the right questions than from confident answers to the wrong ones.

---

[34] Steven Pinker, *The Blank Slate: The Modern Denial of Human Nature* (London, 2002).

[35] Leda Cosmides and John Tooby, 'Cognitive adaptations for social exchange', in Jerome H. Barkow, Leda Cosmides, and John Tooby, eds., *The Adapted Mind: Evolutionary Psychology and the Generation of Culture* (Oxford, 1992), pp. 181–4.

[36] Jared Diamond, *Guns, Germs and Steel: The Fates of Human Societies* (London, 1997), p. 524.

Index of Names

Index of Subjects